About Island Press

Island Press is the only nonprofit organization in the United States whose principal purpose is the publication of books on environmental issues and natural resource management. We provide solutions-oriented information to professionals, public officials, business and community leaders, and concerned citizens who are shaping responses to environmental problems.

In 1994, Island Press celebrates its tenth anniversary as the leading provider of timely and practical books that take a multidisciplinary approach to critical environmental concerns. Our growing list of titles reflects our commitment to bringing the best of an expanding body of literature to the environmental community throughout North America and the world.

Support for Island Press is provided by The Geraldine R. Dodge Foundation, The Energy Foundation, The Ford Foundation, The George Gund Foundation, William and Flora Hewlett Foundation, The James Irvine Foundation, The John D. and Catherine T. MacArthur Foundation, The Andrew W. Mellon Foundation, The Joyce Mertz-Gilmore Foundation, The New-Land Foundation, The Pew Charitable Trusts, The Rockefeller Brothers Fund, The Tides Foundation, Turner Foundation, Inc., The Rockefeller Philanthropic Collaborative, Inc., and individual donors.

CHANGING THE BOUNDARIES

CHANGING THE BOUNDARIES

Women-Centered Perspectives on Population and the Environment

Janice Jiggins

ISLAND PRESS

Washington, D.C. □ Covelo, California

This publication was made possible through the generous support of the Pew Global Stewardship Initiative, with additional funding provided by Turner Foundation, Inc., and The Rockefeller Philanthropic Collaborative, Inc.

Copyright © 1994 by ISLAND PRESS

ISLAND PRESS is a trademark of The Center for Resource Economics.

Jiggins, Janice.
    Changing the boundaries: women-centered perspectives on population and the environment/Janice Jiggins.
        p.   cm.
    Includes bibliographical references (p.   ) and index.
    ISBN 1-55963-259-3 (cloth: acid-free paper). — ISBN 1-55963-260-7 (paper: acid-free paper)
    1. Women in development.   2. Women in development—Environmental aspects.
    3. Population policy   I. Title.
    HQ1240.J54   1994
    305.42—dc20
                                                                    94-21949
                                                                    CIP

Printed on recycled, acid-free paper ✺ ∞

Manufactured in the United States of America
10   9   8   7   6   5   4   3   2   1

Contents

PART III.

The Education of Women and Girls: The Best Bet 103

PART IV.

An Exploration of Reproductive Health 147

PART V.
Women, Agriculture, and Natural Resources 195

Foreword

Justifiable alarm over increasing degradation of global environments is fueling current debates on population growth, development, and environment. Women, long the targets of population control efforts, and now of some environmental campaigns, have been largely excluded from these discussions. For instance, women were virtually absent from the formal deliberations at the United Nations world conferences on population in 1974 at Bucharest and in 1984 at Mexico City. In the decade of the nineties, women will no longer be ignored or silent. Now they are center stage as nations prepare for the 1994 third decennial United Nations Conference on Population and Development to be held in Cairo. By redefining the relationships between population, environment, and development, women may contribute markedly to achieving a new world consensus on an action agenda.

In this masterful analysis establishing the essential need for policies and programs based on women's experiences, knowledge, and leadership, Janice Jiggins leads us to the wellspring of women's redefinitions. Women live, work, and care for their families and communities in a rich context of relationships to people, their physical world, and other living things. Women's development is the essential condition of sustainability, for only women's full participation will lead to new ways of solving problems—ways that do not forfeit the future of children; ways that respect the earth and the diversity of life; ways that foster collective thought and action, thus strengthening communities.

Emphasizing the unsustainability of our present world, Jiggins points out that world military expenditures of more than $800 billion a year far exceed all others. Military activities also account for great amounts of pollution and destruction of local environments. In Jiggins view, patriarchal approaches lead to misallocation of resources and investment, creating an unbalanced world:

> It is a world that counts weapons of destruction as economically productive and women's domestic work as economically valueless. It is a world governed by the public decisions of men who choose to solve problems by force. It is a world in which women and children form the majority of the poor, the displaced, and the hungry. Such a world is not sustainable. (page 41)

For women, a sustainable world is one in which societies address issues of excessive consumption, expenditures for destruction, and inequities based on class, race, gender, or ethnicity. A definition of sustainability that encompasses principles of social and economic justice can contribute to a more productive dialogue among nations as they discuss population and development issues.

For over 20 years, through the United Nations, developed countries of the world have urged consensus on action to stabilize population. Since the first decennial World Conference on Population held in Bucharest in 1974, conflicts over emphasis have flared between developing and developed countries. At Bucharest, the least affluent nations were more concerned with economic assistance than with population control, while the richer nations emphasized the preeminence of population programs. In 1984, at the second conference in Mexico City, the donor countries, led by the United States, reversed positions, declaring the effects of population as neutral to development. They then markedly curtailed their economic assistance to international family planning programs. Women and advocates for choice suffered a particularly heavy defeat in Mexico City when the United States embraced a policy restricting international aid to countries that maintained abortion rights. Worldwide, that cruel restriction has caused deaths of women estimated to be into the tens of thousands each year. Ironically, by the time of the United States' withdrawal of funds for international family planning programs, a majority of countries accepted and provided family planning services. As a result, most nations with far reaching programs had experienced marked improvements in women's and children's health and survival.

Women were not standing by passively during the 12 years of the United States government's restrictive policies. On the contrary, the ingenuity of women at grassroots community organizations was the main factor enabling the continuation of services to women. Many of the leaders of nongovernmental community-based organizations are now seasoned participants of decades of struggles. Skilled in organizing, they are now turning to influencing policies and programs.

At the Earth Summit Conference on Environment and Development held in Rio in 1992, conflicts between the haves and have nots precluded major agreements on the environment. Although many agreed on the concept of sustainable development, that is, development in harmony with resources, they also questioned, "sustainable for whom?" In Rio, developing countries underlined the excessive consumption patterns of the industrialized world as a major source of environmental degradation and therefore as unsustainable.

Women are redefining the issues central to a world agenda that fosters sustainable development and safeguards the environment and human rights while it enables nations and peoples to develop humane population policies. The fundamental question of gender equality and equity underlies much of the debate as women struggle to secure their right to their own bodies, to regulation of their fertility, and to make decisions on their livelihood.

Women's progress is not uniformly applauded. There are many countries that are vehement in opposing notions of equality, and in which culture, religion, and laws hamper the full participation of women. Still, women continue to organize at grassroots levels, in villages, towns, cities, and the halls of international conferences, gaining a voice and increasing influence. From her extensive experience in the field as an expert on development, Jiggins provides us with a rich collection of successful projects that foster women's economic development, health, and empowerment. They serve as examples of effective organizing. Women-centered approaches have changed the values, design, and operation of programs. In some cases, women were successful in changing local and national policies toward increased gender equity as well.

From these and other experiences, women are forging broader agendas. These include (1) a definition of reproductive and sexual health that affirms the rights of individuals and couples to obtain health services as well as to make decisions concerning their fertility; (2) the right to education; (3) the right to maternal and child health; and (4) increased access to economic resources.

We are poised at the threshold of a new stage in women's struggles for their rights. In April 1994 at the United Nations second Preparatory Committee meeting (for the 1994 Cairo Conference), the United States announced new policies. Timothy E. Wirth (former Senator from Colorado and a staunch advocate for the environment) received unprecedented applause from members of nongovernmental organizations and official delegates when he announced that President Clinton was "deeply committed to moving population to the forefront of America's international priorities." The President, he assured the audience, "understands the cost of excessive population growth to the health of women, to the natural environment and to our hopes for alleviating poverty. We must recognize that advancing women's rights and health and promoting family planning are mutually reinforcing objectives. Even more fundamentally, all barriers which deprive women of equal opportunity must be removed." When he spoke in strong support of abortion rights, women rose, enthusiastically applauding his words.

Women may very well choose to de-emphasize the population issues and further emphasize the economic and social equity issues as they prepare for Cairo and the next decade. However it plays out on that world stage, one thing is clear—the women are crafting a holistic agenda for all of humanity, and they will not be stopped by those who wish to maintain the status quo of grossly unequal power between the sexes. The timing of this publication could not be better. Its valuable insights and information will inform our discussions for many years to come.

Helen Rodriguez-Trias, M.D., FAAP

In November 1992 Dr. Rodriguez-Trias became president of the American Public Health Association for a one-year term that ended in October 1993. She will remain on the Executive Committee and Executive Board as immediate past president through October 1994. Dr. Rodriguez-Trias is currently based in California, where she publishes and lectures extensively on women's and children's health and health care issues. Over the past 20 years she has served as a consultant to numerous foundations and government agencies aiming to provide primary care and services to prevent and treat HIV infection in women and children.

Preface

The idea for this book grew out of a sense of frustration. I work in a number of rather different fields, primarily in agriculture and women's reproductive health, with occasional forays into education. Moving from task to task, I was struck by the weak transfer of experience, theories, and evidence across the disciplines about the nature of population–environment interactions.

My agricultural colleagues routinely claimed they could not make a meaningful contribution to ensuring there was sufficient food in the world if populations continued to grow unchecked. Their remarks did not seem to fit with the truly dramatic declines in birth rates and fertility that most of the world was experiencing, a cause for hope rather than despair.

At the same time, agriculturalists too readily, it seemed to me, accepted without reflection the numbers generated by other disciplines. A recent example illustrates the more general case. At the 17th International Grasslands Congress held at Massey University, New Zealand, in February 1993, one of the keynote speakers stressed the need for births to be restricted to 2.1 children per woman in order to stabilize the world's population and thus save the world's grasslands from the effects of overpopulation. Such numbers are by definition correct, but they are partial. (One might ask, for example, how men's responsibility for fertility outcomes might be expressed with comparable statistical exactitude.) Policies driven by demographic data, applied uncritically without reference to the poverty that makes it rational for people to choose larger families, tend to lead to interventions that are totalitarian and inequitable in effect and, because of the backlash they provoke, ultimately counterproductive.

Meanwhile, my colleagues in reproductive health were growing increasingly disturbed at the apparent willingness among influential members of the population-control establishment to subordinate the world's women once again to contraceptive-led fertility control policies. Notwithstanding the earlier evidence from India, Bangladesh, and China of the abuses to which such an approach could give rise, the urgency of the environmental message seemed to be giving new impetus to old follies.

For their part, environmentalists, with little exposure to the developmental experience of the past half century, seemed all too eager to save large mammals and rain forests and too little concerned about people's role in managing natural and agricultural resources sustainably for their own survival. Further, the message that high population density is necessarily incompatible with sound management of natural resources ignored the evidence that rising population density is sometimes a precondition for effective environmental management and increased agricultural productivity.

The widespread belief that rapid population increase and large population size is detrimental to economic growth and to a more egalitarian sharing of national income also seemed curious. Much of Asia has been notably successful over the past half-century in accommodating an increasing population, while achieving sharply falling fertility, rising incomes, and greater income equality.

The apparently casual treatment of women in much of the population-environment debate was also cause for frustration. Are women really subordinate persons, their fertility to be subjected to control policies they have had little role in formulating? Is it really possible to continue to increase the productivity of farming if women's roles in agriculture are not supported with appropriate inputs, services, and training? Can natural resources be managed well if women, the primary users and managers of much of the world's water, land, and forests, have no property rights or lose those they have customarily enjoyed in the name of modernization? Can voluntary changes in behavior be brought about in time and on a scale that makes a difference, if governments continue to neglect the education of girls?

By bringing together experience, information, and perspectives from different fields, I argue for a more sensitive and humane dialogue among policymakers and practitioners. The uncritical sloganizing that characterizes much of the population control–environmental debate must be challenged if counterproductive policies are to be avoided. Crisis-driven advocacy of urgent environmental action and population control is both exaggerated and misdirected. My engagement with different aspects of the developmental experience in contrasting parts of the world has convinced me that no one holds a monopoly on the truth, least of all in areas of human behavior in which values play a large role.

The scientific study of the environment and the rigor of demographic analysis must be complemented by the insights of the social sciences into the contextual, contingent, and diverse ways in which people and societies shape their futures and adapt to circumstance. Bringing together contrasting expertise involves learning some part of one another's disciplinary language, a willingness to make underlying assumptions transparent, a sensitivity to the historical and political dimensions of the debate, a more reflective handling of the data, and above all, a respect for one another's humanity.

I am convinced that, given appropriate methods, citizens of any country can express a meaningful understanding of population control–environmental interactions. Further, their involvement is an essential element in devising appropriate solutions to both local and larger-scale problems. Analytic maps of causal relations, diagrams and matrices correlating complex spatial and temporal information generated by ordinary men, women, and children are providing timely, cost-effective, reliable data for watershed-based planning and design in environmental management and for community-based family planning services and health (including reproductive health).

Participants in the neighborhood meetings organized under the Green Plan hearings in Ontario generate in the course of an evening their own analytic maps of local environmental problems and options for action. Farmers and other members of rural communities in Australia use participatory methods to reach agreement on what to try out, and where and when, to combat widespread soil erosion and salting and to put back into the landscape some of the native vegetation that earlier farm clearances stripped out. Illiterate women in southern India work with scientists at the International Center for Research in the Semi-Arid Tropics at Hyderabad to develop more pest-resistant varieties of sorghum. Others are working with health workers to improve the quality of care at family planning clinics and to train clinic personnel to be more responsive to clients' needs.

Even participatory methods, however, do not ensure that women, and women's distinct experience of life, are necessarily involved adequately, or at all, in defining the nature of the problem and what might be done about it. Practical and attitudinal barriers mean that women do not as a matter of course sit at the tables where decisions are made. Their voice often is ignored in the debate. This book is one expression of women's views of population control and environmental policy. It is not the only vision, it is not one that all women share, but it captures an important dimension of the debate. It is certain that global environmental and population-related problems cannot be managed in a sensitive, nonauthoritarian fashion unless and until women are more centrally involved.

Acknowledgments

With generous support from The Rockefeller Brothers' Fund and the International Women's Health Coalition, New York, I spent 1990–1991 exploring the various disciplinary perspectives and data regarding population control, the environment, and related concerns. Visiting fellowships and scholarships at the Department of Human Ecology at Cornell University, the Department of Forestry and Resource Management at the University of California at Berkeley, the Department of Rural Extension Studies at the University of Guelph, and the Department of Agricultural Extension at Stuttgart University, Hohenheim, provided access to stimulating colleagues and sharp-minded students, whose numerous contributions are gratefully acknowledged, and to valuable library resources.

The Graduate School of Geography at Clark University, numerous population control and environmental lobby groups based in and around Washington D.C., the Department of Human Nutrition at Pennsylvania State University, the international program at the University of Iowa, The Center for Indigenous Knowledge in Agriculture and Rural Development (CIKARD) at Iowa State, and the agricultural university at Vila Real in Northern Portugal also provided much food for thought.

A visit to India as a guest of the Indian Center for Agricultural Research to speak at a conference on minimizing risk in dryland agriculture, followed by intensive discussions with environmental and natural scientists and visits to a number of areas of special environmental interest, complemented my previous involvement in India with rural women's education. Moving on around the world, I participated in an extended field study of Land Care groups, regional climate modeling, and farmer involvement in the development of agricultural technology in Australia. I was a guest of the Department of Agriculture and the University in Western Australia, the University of Western Sydney, Hawkesbury, and the Queensland Department of Primary Industries.

I cannot end without special reference to the caring yet critical support of my colleagues and friends at the International Women's Health Coalition and, through the coalition, the women and men around the world who are so courageously fighting to protect the reproductive health of women and their families. I also gratefully acknowledge colleagues at BRAC in Bangladesh, who have been kind enough to invite me to review their experience from time to time, and the remarkable pioneers who have set up and championed the Education for Women's Equality program in India.

My thanks also are due to my many agricultural colleagues, especially those who strive to ensure that women farmers and gender analysis are taken seriously by international and national researchers, extensionists, and agricultural policymakers. I would like to mention in particular those with whom I have worked in developing "Africulture," a simulation game designed as a learning tool for exploring African farming systems, fertility choices, and rural-urban linkages, and *Tools for the Field*, a methodology handbook for those interested in applying gender analysis to agriculture development. In addition, I have benefitted considerably from interaction with the members of the Association of Farming Systems Research and Extension and from the many participants in international training courses, workshops, and seminars who have applied gentle pressure to make me sensitive to context.

I would also like to thank Island Press, in particular Deborah Estes, Nancy Olsen, and Heather Boyer, and Karen Bierstedt of Editorial and Production Services, California. Their commitment and professional support have been invaluable throughout the preparation of this book.

It is customary to thank one's partner. As I write this, the leaves are falling in our half-hectare of agroforestry garden. We experience almost daily the problem of achieving a satisfactory gender division of labor in the orchard and vegetable plot, in the home, and in our professional lives. I can only say that without Niels's patience, intellectual support, and willingness to take over chores without demur, this book would not have been finished.

Women and Sustainable Development

1

Why Women's
Perspectives Matter

Questioning the Crisis

The idea that urgent global environmental action and population control are needed is both exaggerated and misdirected. Although serious and growing problems exist, policy and action will not accomplish their goals unless they are accompanied by an understanding of the relationship between the laws of nature and the patterns of human behavior that drive global change.

The outcome of human behavior is sensitive to the ways that the interactions among people are organized. Although history, to a certain extent, locks people into particular forms of organization, institutions are not immutable. One of the key principles underlying the organization of human interaction is that of gender. The form of relations between the sexes changes over time and varies from place to place, but there is no society, class, age group, or household that is not structured by the different and distinctive experiences of men and women in their relationships to each other and to the material world.

The nuances of gender relations are the key to understanding impacts on the environment and fertility. Gender relations influence fundamental interactions in the network of collective behavior that links events at the intimate, domestic, or local (micro) levels and at larger scales such as at the nation, region, or global (macro) levels. That is, gender analysis can help explain how individual decisions and behaviors in the local, domestic, and intimate spheres result in the collective behavior of human beings that drives environmental change. A purposeful effort to change the relations between the sexes, in order more fully to honor the values of women and to draw on women's knowledge and skills in nurturing and protecting life, is one of the keys to changing the outcome of collective behavior.

Crisis-driven arguments for policies to bring about global change are sustained by extrapolation of present trends. Human behavior is adaptive, however, evolving organically as people respond to circumstances and learn their way into the future. People are responding, and will continue to respond, to changing circumstances. The question is not if but how, and how fast, people will adapt their behavior in response to the evidence of accumulating pressure on resources.

More specifically, the question of gender relations addresses how men and women experience poverty and environmental degradation and what their different responses are. If policies treat men and women alike, or meld women's interests with those of men, the desired results cannot be achieved. Measures taken to relieve household poverty may not necessarily improve the condition of women, nor is it obvious that what benefits the environment automatically benefits women, or conversely, that what benefits women necessarily benefits the environment.

Further, the faster or more radically that social, economic, and physical conditions change, the more hazardous it becomes to assume that the relationships underlying present trends will continue. Past behaviors cannot be extrapolated to conditions that do not have historical or present analogues. Beyond the near term, the future cannot be predicted.

Nonetheless, we can comprehend and explore observed trends and determine the general principles that govern the relationship between natural law and human behavior. The principles of gender relations provide powerful guidelines for the interventions that will encourage sustainable development.

Investing in Women

This book explores gender relations with respect to three interventions that are widely understood to promote the goals of gender equity, population stabilization, and environmental sustainability. These are educating women, providing access to reproductive health services (including maternal and child health services), and providing women secure access to agricultural resources, such as land, and to production inputs, such as credit and training.

According to data from the World Bank, if the education of girls and women had been raised 30 years ago to the level that boys and men then enjoyed, fertility levels today would be nearing the target of global population stabilization. Further, household welfare among the poorest would be higher and local management of natural resources less problematic.

An analysis of national survey data gathered from 300,000 women in 44 countries between 1985 and 1992 shows that about a third of married women in developing countries are now using modern contraception.[1] The needs of many people in developing countries still are not being met, however, including those of men and women who do not currently have access to services, adolescents of both sexes, unmarried women, women and men who are dissatisfied with their present method of birth control or are using it incorrectly, women faced with an unwanted pregnancy, and those who have a reproductive health problem. If all such people had access to services, fertility levels would approximate lower level population targets.

As in most parts of the world, in Africa women carry out a major part of all farm work and are responsible for most of the domestic food production. A recent study conducted in four countries in Africa by the World Bank shows that a 15 percent increase in food production could be achieved, without new resources, if women only had better access to land, production inputs, such as credit, fertilizer, and improved seeds, and markets.[2]

The three interventions do not sound particularly challenging or controversial. The evidence of their efficacy has been available for some time. There are two main reasons, however, why what is known has not been acted on, has been acted on with insufficient vigor, or has been acted on with disappointing results. One is the reluctance of male-dominated establishments around the world, at all levels, to make investment in women a priority. This is changing, as men come to realize that it is in everyone's interest to put women at the center of the developmental and environmental agenda. The second reason is more problematic. It is not sufficient simply to educate women, provide contraception, and give women land. The way in which these things are done and the complementary adjustments that are necessary to make them effective are important.

The imperative that links the three interventions is the need to remove the constraints on the ability of women to make decisions and to act on those decisions. Far from threatening the social good, strengthening the power of women to choose and act is congruent with the social good and an essential condition for the achievement of environmental and population goals.

Although women are perceived as the means by which the goals of development, population control, and environmental sustainability can be achieved, the views of women themselves may not coincide with those of planners and policymakers. It is in the detail of how the policies and programs are constituted and implemented that the benefits or costs to women become clear. The detail must be sensitive to the context that colors existing relations between men and women. Assumptions about how women might react are often wrong. In parts of Africa, for instance, women may choose to use modern contraception to space their children rather than to reduce the total number of children they have. In India there has been a long-term decline in the proportion of females in the population in relation to males; the decline has occurred largely as the result of systemic discrimination against females. Yet in these areas even educated women may choose, or be forced by family pressures, to use family planning services to bear sons rather than daughters.

Assumptions about what is in the interests of women also can be wrong. Women in Zimbabwe, for example, often grow drought-sensitive maize even in drought-prone areas, with adverse effects on land management. The reason is that grinding mills are available for the large-seeded maize but not for the more drought-resistant but small-seeded millets and sorghums that still must be processed by women by hand. Moreover, men are expected to carry the costs of such a crisis as crop failure by purchasing food in the cash economy and sending it back home to support their families, thus reducing the incentive for women to maintain sorghum production. This example illustrates that what is desirable in terms of rural household food security and land and water management may not be the best or even a viable option for women bounded by the prevailing division of labor by gender.

Safeguarding Women's Rights

Women need to be at the forefront of the global agenda to ensure that developmental, environmental, and population policies are sensitive to gender relations and to women's own interests. They need to be there especially because many of the current proposals profoundly threaten the basic human rights of women. For example, although it is true that the goal of population stabilization could be reached by restricting births to 2.1 children per woman, policies that start from such cold arithmetic tend to lead to coercive control of female fertility. Population and environmental policies that target the reproductive functions of women have in the past threatened women's personal freedom and choice.

Pressure to direct the reproductive choices of women has been exerted through a spectrum of incentives and sanctions that include financial and fiscal measures and material rewards such as the promise of securing title to land. Governments have applied pressure in favor of increasing birth rates, as in the early revolutionary years of the Ayatollah Khomeini's Iran, or in Romania under Nicolae Ceausescu. Pressure also has been brought to bear to channel women's sexuality and fertility into behaviors approved by the Roman Catholic church, as in contemporary Poland. Most notably, China's stringent population control policies have given rise to a marked imbalance in the ratio of boys to girls. It is thought that this imbalance is due mainly to a combination of the underregistration of girls at birth, selective abortion, and the registration of the neonatal death of girl babies as stillbirths, but infanticide also occurs.[3] Many Chinese demographers estimate that possibly a fifth of female births now go unrecorded.

In situations in which women's access to resources for survival are already limited, the pressure to control childbearing may remove the one livelihood strategy available to women. Policies that seek to improve land management by assigning title to a private owner typically give title to men, thereby depriving women farmers of access to land or pushing them onto land that is marginal for cultivation. These examples argue for deeper reflection on the choices to be made and who is making them.

Some might wish to sweep aside the human rights argument in the name of global necessity, but to do so undermines the very conditions for large scale, rapid transformation in human behavior. Attempts at enforced, involuntary change breed reactions, as in China, that undermine the achievement of policy goals. Conversely, voluntary transformation requires, as a condition of change, widespread participation in determining the nature of the problem and what needs to be done about it. Women as well as men must be involved in decision-making.

Further, women bring to the debate a unique voice. For many women, their experience of life and the way they relate to people and the natural environment bring a different vision of the relationship between physical and human resources. Women's vision includes nurturance rather than control, the management of networks of relationships rather than hierarchical dominance, and a concern for future generations as a guiding principle for today's decisions.

In brief, the crisis needs to be redefined. By working with the human capacity to adapt to circumstance in ways that strengthen the capacity of women to make decisions, take action, and contribute to the debate, we can meet the challenges of controlling population growth and sustaining the environment humanely as well as effectively.

Honoring Women's Values

For humankind to have a future, the deep economic and social inequities that divide people must be healed. Although women from different backgrounds each have their own sense of the priorities that are relevant in their context, many find common ground in the values and principles that shape women's experience of life in society, the workplace, and the family. The heart of the current human dilemma, many women argue, lies in an imbalanced reliance on masculine values and experience and on the power of patriarchy, that is, the social and economic arrangements by which men dominate women.

From Dualistic to Holistic

Women are materially connected to food, water, and energy, biologically connected to reproduction, and socially connected to family and community in ways that men are not. Their distinctive experience gives rise to a strong sense of the interconnectedness of life. Characteristically, women experience life without a marked distinction between what needs to be done for material survival, for bearing and raising children, and the maintenance of the family and household. This experience is what gives rise to an instinctive appreciation of wholeness, of life as a system in which everything is connected to everything else.

Theorists in the women's movement reject the assumed dualism of a separate self and other on which the rationalization, specialization, and quantification of industrial economies ultimately rest. They argue that the violence, dominance, and hierarchy that accompany dualism represent only part of the human potential. Respect for diversity, nurturance, and a potential for oneness mediated by reciprocity are also part of the human capacity. In the views of many women, the worldwide human dilemma cannot be resolved until these feminine qualities and potentials are valued more strongly, shared more widely, and expressed more clearly in the solutions to the global challenge.

From Masculine to Feminine Spirituality

Women and sympathetic male colleagues also are rediscovering or reaffirming the distinctive feminine experience of spirituality in their effort to develop the moral and spiritual basis for a common future. For the most part, feminine spirituality has been lost or subordinated in the dominant religious ideologies of today. The supremacy of the masculine has become deeply enshrined in structures of power and spiritual leadership.

Three threads are intertwined in the essence of the feminine experience. One thread has to do with the need for women to generate at the personal level the courage and energy to engage in action and to channel that energy creatively and constructively. As one activist confessed, "It is very difficult to stand on the front lines with only outrage to sustain us."[4] The personal quest is affirmed and nourished through honoring historical female spiritual leaders, through assertion of the role of women and the experience of feminine spirituality within established religions, and through the rediscovery of feminine attributes in the religious pantheon.

Another thread follows the biological and social transitions of women's experience of life as a series of biological and social thresholds that are moments of personal, social, and spiritual transformation. These transformations, for example at the onset of menstruation, marriage, and menopause, are typically transitory, conditional, and vulnerable experiences. The idea of rapid changes in state, which is central to ecological theory, is inherent in the feminine condition and, feminist theorists argue, confers on women a preparedness to deal with the abrupt transformations in global resources that environmentalists predict. Neither the timing nor the occurrence of change can be wholly determined or controlled. Because women are biologically vulnerable, for example, to sexually transmitted infection, infertility, and unwanted pregnancy, and socioeconomically vulnerable to the death of a spouse, divorce, and being forced to raise children on their own, the unforeseen and unforeseeable at any moment can open up another pathway, across other thresholds.

Women's experience of natural and social forces thus is fundamentally contingent and embedded in larger systems of interaction and complexity.

The third thread seeks to enable women to enhance and build on the knowledge they derive from experience. When knowledge derived from experience is devalued compared with knowledge derived from scientific endeavor, the understanding that everyone and every community must possess in order to survive is demeaned. To say this is not to dismiss the essential contribution science has to make to sustainable development, but neither the formulation of the nature of the problem, nor the search for the solution, can rest solely on scientific knowledge. It is only by shared learning from experience that rapid, voluntary transformation of society can occur.

The idea of sanctuary is central to the validation of knowledge gained from experience. Defined, in the women's movement, as a safe place where women together can discover their sense of themselves as women and explore the potential of the feminine, the sanctuary is a place where shared learning can take place and the collective strength of women acting together is forged. It is within the sanctuary that women develop the organizational power to act on what they know.

From Hierarchical Power to Activist Energy

In a male-dominated world, masculine norms and definitions are taken as the standard. In the absence of strong female leadership, patterns of male preference reassert themselves in policy, bureaucracy, and implementation. As J. Mujuru, one time Minister of Community Development, Cooperatives and Women's Affairs, Zimbabwe, points out with respect to women farmers, "we women will have to take the struggle into our own hands. We have to organize ourselves so that we become very powerful and effective movements that know our rights and methods of getting them. We have to stand by each other and have powerful lobby centers if need be. We should organize ourselves so that we get out of the lowly status of being considered peasant farmers."[5]

Whereas the commitment of men to increasing women's welfare and opportunities can be the means to supply some of the tools women need to empower themselves, it cannot in itself empower women. Women seek the spiritual bases of their own power to act to change standards and preferences. They do not seek to assert the feminine over the masculine, or the power of women over men. They see clearly, however, that human activity can no longer be sustained on the basis of the present bias and imbalance.

The worldwide women's movement is by now sufficiently large to be taken seriously as a constituency in the domestic politics of an increasing number of countries. It is opening up political discourse to new protagonists and expanding the meaning of democratization. It is also informing and strengthening developmental policy and environmental activism worldwide.

More than 14,000 women attended the unofficial meetings at the Nairobi conference to mark the end of the International Decade for Women in 1985; the international meetings of the Association of Women In Development regularly bring together more than a thousand women from 40 countries; a series of meetings in Miami gathered more than 1200 women leaders, activists, and environmentalists from more than 70 countries to develop women's contribution to the 1992 Rio Conference; the DAWN network numbers more than 4500 Third World feminists. Most of the people attending meetings such as these are themselves members or leaders of networks and grassroots movements that are spread even more widely.

The women's movement brings a number of characteristic strengths to the debate about global change. First, as in male-led movements, charismatic leadership is important, but women leaders less often stay for a lifetime at the head of the organizations they inspired. As they move through the transitions in their own life cycle, they move on to be active in the movement in another role. As a consequence, women's organizations tend to maintain a high capacity for creativity and self-renewal and a high potential for expansion by the generation of new centers of energy and action.

The second strength of the women's movement is that women are creating management styles and organizational structures that are efficient yet loose enough for democracy and diversity to be a reality. It is more than coincidental that women have evolved ways of channelling communication and action within the framework of networks, caucuses, campaigns, and coalitions, rather than through large bureaucracies and rigid organizational structures. Women's organizations have had to do a great deal with very little in order to survive, by drawing on each other's goodwill, willingness to share, and ability to do more than one thing at a time, just as in family life.

Two broader consequences of the women's movement are important to global environmental and population policy. One is that an increasing number of women have learned how to act in concert at the lowest point at which the physical and socioeconomic dimensions of human existence interact, for example, in developing clean water resources that benefit the community as a whole, or developing tree nurseries and tree planting campaigns that, as in Kenya, have nationwide impact. The other is that women have learned how to set goals and define the nature of problems by managing the multiple relationships needed to build a basis for action across whole landscapes and domains of human behavior. The remarkable consensus expressed, for example, in the forward-looking strategies endorsed at Nairobi in 1985 was achieved by encouraging everyone's voice to shape the principles and values underlying specific strategies.

Humanizing the Politics

As population and environmental issues become caught up in preexisting debates about development and international trade relationships, the vision of women is needed. Current international and domestic relationships are divisive and unequal, often profoundly so. Given these divisions, the common interest cannot be assumed. What people see as important and desirable, what they identify as priorities, depends in large part on where they are. A starkly unequal material and social reality inevitably creates disparate agendas. Women environmental activists in Malaysia, for example, join hands with the worldwide environmental movement in their desire to protect the Malaysian rain forest but reject the right of already industrialized countries to limit the developmental policies of the Malaysian government in the name of a global policy that does not reflect Malaysia's need for economic growth.

Poor people everywhere have more urgent concerns, such as clean water, sanitation, housing, and secure livelihoods, than the conservation of the large mammals that attract so much attention among Western environmentalists. For poor countries, the need to generate wealth is a more immediate concern than the chemical pollution affecting the air, soils, and waterways of the richer countries. Even such global issues as climate change, although a universal phenomenon in its consequences, are specific in their antecedents. It is such specificity that creates political tension in the allocation of responsibility and resources.

The North-South Dimension

Discussion of development, the environment, and population control has split along a north-south divide. These are broad identities of interest, not geographic divisions, with the North encompassing the industrialized countries whose economies are linked in the Organization of Economic Cooperation and Development (OECD) and the South the world's developing economies. The former communist states of eastern and central Europe and the former Soviet Union make up a further entity without a clear label.

Handy as the terms North and South are in signaling negotiating positions and common interests, they also obscure important differences that are, in some respects, of greater importance. Small island economies have little in common with large continental economies in terms of their potential and structure. Oil exporters and oil importers have opposing interests in regard to energy pricing. The world's most wasteful energy consumers, Canada and Australia, sit in the same OECD club as Japan, one of the world's most efficient energy users.

Nonetheless, the rhetoric of the north-south divide echoes through the debate on sustainable development. The population control and environmental establishment in the North often has spoken in the name of the common interest while locating both the problem and the solution in the South. For instance, because some two-thirds of the world's people live in developing countries, the high, though declining, fertility of poor women in populous countries in the South has been identified by such organizations as the Population Crisis Committee as the most important aspect of the population problem.

High fertility in the populous South is seen.as a problem in terms of governmental capacity to provide schools and clinics and to create jobs, the availability of water and cultivable land, and pollution emissions as consumption and industrial activity increases. When the problem is described in these terms, the obvious solution appears to be to control the fertility of poor women in populous but poor countries.

Politicians and researchers in the South respond, however, that it is mainly the consumption and production patterns of the North that generated the pollution that drives global climate change, as well as the hazardous wastes that are exported in increasing amounts to countries in the South. From this perspective, the obvious solution is for the North to change its pattern of consumption and production and to compensate the South for any adverse impacts that the South so far has had little part in bringing about.

Similar differences of view arise in discussion of the protection of the world's animal and plant genetic resources. As it happens, most of the major areas of genetic diversity lie in the countries of the South. Historically, it is the commercial interests based in the North that have derived the most commercial advantage from exploitation of these resources. However, the Biodiversity Convention signed at the 1992 United Nations Conference on the Environment and Development (UNCED) held in Rio de Janeiro enshrines the principle that genetic resources belong to the country in which they are found and thereby shifts the potential balance of advantage and concern toward the survival needs of the South.

Although women are not free of these differences in geographic and developmental perspective, many of them see an overarching commonality, too. The more than 1200 women from around the world who attended the Women's World Congress for a Healthy Planet held in Miami before the United Nations Conference on the Environment and Development recognized that the debate could not fruitfully be continued along divisive north-south lines. If population and environmental agencies based in the North are concerned about the fate of plant and animal species, the state of the natural environment, and the contribution of the South to global pollution, they must take on the developmental needs of the South. Specifically, they must address the needs of poor women.

Women in their daily lives are the ones who manage and nurture the relationships that bring biological and socioeconomic phenomena together within the basic units of family and community life. If too great a demand is placed on women's time, energy, and health, then neither the goal of population control nor that of environmental sustainability can be achieved. The development of women is not an option; it is the essential condition of sustainability.

The Biocentric-Anthropocentric Dimension

The biocentric vision values the conservation of biodiversity as a good in itself. Biocentrists argue that humans must be excluded from vulnerable areas and their exploitation of animal and plant species brought under control. Because people are seen as the problem, a reduction in the number of people in the world is seen as part of the solution. The World Wildlife Fund and Conservation Foundation, for example, stated recently: "The rapid growth of the Earth's human population underlies diverse environmental threats, from deforestation and the loss of biodiversity to pervasive pollution and global warming."[6]

In contrast, the anthropocentric vision values the conservation of biodiversity only because it matters to human beings, whether as an aesthetic or ethical good or in utilitarian terms. It is people who determine and interpret the apparent trends in the state of biological and physical phenomena. No referent is independent of people's capacity to observe and measure these trends, and ultimately no outcome is consequential except in terms of people.

These two opposing visions have tended to set environmental agencies funded or based in the North against the developmental needs of poor people in the South. Again, from the perspective of women, this is a false and unhelpful dichotomy, as the case of agricultural biodiversity illustrates.

The conservation of biodiversity in agriculture raises unique challenges. Agricultural biodiversity is a dynamic phenomenon, manipulated for human ends. The conservation of agricultural biodiversity can be accomplished by removing germ plasm (seeds, other planting material, and animal semen) from its environment and storing it in special collections (*ex situ* conservation). It also can be accomplished by helping farmers and farming communities to conserve their own seeds, planting materials, and animals within their own farming systems and local environments (*in situ* conservation). These two approaches in combination offer a spectrum of opportunity.

Gender relations are an essential part of the way in which genetic materials are conserved at the farm, community, and landscape levels. For example, in south and southeast Asian rice farming systems there are three main aspects of seed quality[7]: maintaining genetic and physical purity, testing seed for germination and vigor, and keeping seed free from seed-borne diseases and pests. As a self-pollinated crop, rice maintains its genetic purity relatively easily, and the seed can be stored *in situ* for up to 12 months without loss of vigor or viability. Nonetheless, specific and conscious management choices must be made.

Women on average perform more than 50 percent of the rice harvesting and share decisions with men about when to harvest. Through observation and physical examination, men and women select rice for seed to secure optimal maturity and dryness. After harvest, however, it is women who are largely responsible for separating pure seed from other seeds and inert material, through winnowing, picking over for off-types, and floating techniques.

Women often are responsible for testing seed for germination and vigor before the next growing season. In some instances, for example, they grow seeds in flat pots filled with earth from the main rice fields in order to test seedling emergence and growth. Or they might promote seedling emergence in the field by soaking planting seed in a mild salt solution and then drying it, or break dormancy by using dry or moist heating techniques. In addition, women frequently are responsible for keeping planting seeds free from seed-borne diseases and pests.

The precise distribution among men and women of the knowledge and responsibility for these three aspects of seed quality varies from place to place and cannot be determined *a priori*. The challenge is for scientists to accept men and women farmers as germ plasm consultants and research curators and to develop field methodologies and management strategies that support farmers in these roles. What is at stake is not "women's welfare" but the social and economic viability of households and the future of the environment.

The case of agricultural biodiversity suggests that North, South, biocentric, and anthropocentric perspectives can be reconciled if policies are informed by and respectful of local realities.

The Male-Female Dimension

In the end, the seemingly global issues of population control policies and the conservation of biodiversity come down to individual human decisions and behaviors that are structured by the gender relations of power.

Population control policies target women as bearers of children as if they were solely responsible for their own fertility, yet in reality women may have little say in fertility decisions. To bring about change we must use more subtle approaches that include men and communities as a whole, beyond the mere provision of contraceptives to women. Initiatives need to be developed to change the sexual and fertility behavior of men. We must also offer more explicit commitment to strengthening women's status and autonomy.

The management of land and natural resources is similarly affected by the gender relations of power. Economists expect that land and natural resources will be managed more sustainably and productively where a single owner holds secure title. However, the modernization of land title everywhere has favored men, collapsing complex rights of access, use, and management into single ownership by male heads of household. The access of women farmers to land typically has become less secure, with their rights of cultivation more transitory, while women who rely on gathering fuel, fodder, and foodstuffs, or on grazing animals on common property, are losing the entitlement that secured their livelihood. Moreover, the provision of secure title to land to women farmers in their own name is not in itself necessarily the solution either. As long as women do not also have access to the male-dominated and male-oriented services and markets that support farming, their production will remain below its potential. For example, where incentive pricing is used as a policy instrument to stimulate production, its effects are blunted if women food farmers have low access to male extension workers and, hence, to subsidized inputs such as fertilizers and no access to formal markets because sales are tied to cooperative membership and only men are registered as members.

Many of the changes that are needed are practical adjustments that are not particularly costly. A great deal is now known about what needs to be changed and how to make these adjustments in particular settings.[8] Men cannot themselves empower women; they only can develop an enabling structure and resources that allow women to take this step themselves. If men are not willing to do this, then either the goals of sustainable development will not be achieved or male-female relations will become increasingly dysfunctional.

Contrary to the expectation of many men, women's increased sense of power typically does not lead to female dominance or to female hierarchies of power over men. It leads to an increased social capacity to determine common goals at the level of the family, the community, and the nation. It is profoundly democratic, enhancing the civil capacity to act in ways that satisfy societal goals. The call by women for an end to all forms of discrimination against women is not self-interested special pleading. The end of such discrimination is an essential condition for sustainable development.

The Moral Boundary

Finally, women's humanizing vision is needed to guard the moral boundary in what is becoming a deeply misanthropic discourse. The suggestion that unmarried teenage mothers accept Norplant, a long-acting hormonal contraceptive implant, as a condition for public assistance and criticism of United Nations agencies for "premature" investment in child survival are just two symptoms of an unfeeling advocacy.

Another symptom is the presentation of the debate in terms of irreconcilable either-or policy choices, based on a psychological split between the self and the other, the very antithesis of the holistic visioning of the women's movement. Highly visible lobbyists display an apparent readiness to force on others conditions that they would find unacceptable if applied to themselves.

For example, industrial countries seek to dump hazardous wastes in poor countries, presenting such dumping as an opportunity for economic development, rational in light of the low health costs and low land values to be found in the "underpopulated" areas of the South. Many people challenge the notion that poor people's lives are worth less than those of the better-off. Many people also challenge the notion that health care costs in conditions of poverty are low. In survival terms, the opportunity costs of women's health care roles are high. Time spent in caring for the sick is time not spent on environmental management and productive farming.

An additional moral commitment, which women especially bring to the debate, is their concern for future generations. As participants in the Women's World Conference on the Environment noted, one of the main reasons women cite for their involvement in environmental activism is their concern for the well-being of future generations. Male respondents tend to rank this reason much lower in their list of concerns. The daily investment—emotional, physical, and material—that women make to create and maintain a safe domestic environment for their children fosters an involvement that fathers typically experience differently, and many men, separated for long periods from their families, never at all.

The notion that the present generation is responsible for not compromising the survival of future generations is, of course, not the special property of women. As women at the Miami meeting said, however, they are outraged at the idea that their fertility must be controlled as the price of future generations' survival. Population policymakers need to understand why women find statements such as the following by P. R. Erlich and A. H. Erlich in their 1990 book *The Population Explosion* so deeply objectionable: "One must always keep in mind that the price of personal freedom in making childbearing decisions may be the destruction of the world in which your children and grandchildren live."[9]

Solutions to the population control and environmental challenges that compromise other people's choices in the name of global necessity lead to dehumanizing policies at a time when recognition of our common humanity is needed more than ever.

Understanding Collective Behavior

One of the seductive features of a debate framed in terms of simple policy prescriptions such as population control is the apparent power of interventions such as the provision of family planning services to bring about large-scale change. The apparent independence of women may be greatest where environmental degradation is most severe if men are forced to leave their families to seek a livelihood elsewhere. The freedom of such women to manage a declining resource base might (or might not) then translate into greater propensity to use modern contraception for controlling fertility. If it does not, it may be because women value the additional labor that children provide. If it does, a lessening of population pressure on the land does not necessarily in turn translate into less pressure on the environment. Women in these circumstances often lack the labor and energy to restore the productivity of their surroundings and have no option but to continue environmentally damaging exploitation of resources.

Such relationships and their consequences are not the inevitable outcome of a given history and context. Societies are neither closed, nor in equilibrium, nor locked into their destiny. Each situation contains multiple potential patterns. The actual pattern that emerges is the outcome of innumerable organic interactions, as people adapt, learn, compete, and make choices. Sustainability is thus a *potential*, the emergent property of collective behavior that is more than the sum of its parts.

The Ways People Adapt and Learn

The processes of learning and adaptation depend in part on the feedback people receive from their social, economic, and physical environment as they try to do something. Everyone engages in trial and error, guided by his or her upbringing and education. Formal research, experimentation, and testing, that is, systematic observation, theory-forming, and experimentation as a scientific activity, are needed to produce generic knowledge, but they are not always needed for problem solving. The challenge of sustainable development increasingly presents itself as a problem-solving activity.

In conditions of high variability, uncertainty, and complex interactions, however, experience based on trial and error, as well as scientific inquiry, becomes less sure a guide, both for individual people and for governments. It becomes harder to sort out cause and effect. Judgment of the appropriate moment to respond becomes more imprecise. The danger increases of reinforcing negative effects rather than dampening them. The social costs of getting it wrong increase, while damage to the natural resource base accumulates.

Models of how complex, dynamic systems work can help support decision-making. Everyone carries in his or her head an implicit model of how the world works and uses this as a guide to dealing with it. Planners and researchers build explicit models to analyze and explore theoretical and empirical expectations of how the world works. Models that do not fit changing circumstances fail; that is, they no longer help people to take effective action for survival. Many models of how economies work, for example, are no longer effective guides to decision-making in the context of increasing pollution. Many of the models about how families work and the proper role of women are no longer effective guides to family survival.

Nonetheless, models can help people understand better what might happen if current trends continue. They can help people to play with alternative scenarios, by changing the relationships and assumptions and numbers built into the model. They can help forecast what might happen if different technologies, price relationships, or forms of human organization were to evolve. The more swiftly conditions change, however, the less reliable is the support of models in decision-making.

The processes of learning and adaptation depend also on what people consider important to observe and measure in their social, economic, and physical environment. One's knowledge about the world is formed out of what one considers to be significant and desirable to know.

Goals are derived from what people consider appropriate, effective, and feasible things to do. Visions and dreams also play a part in the setting of goals. Backcasting, or working back from visions and dreams to what needs to be done today in order to realize tomorrow's dream, is another way in which people adapt and learn.

These processes of adaptation and learning are common to everyone and form the basis of human communication about the world as we experience it. This is not the same, however, as saying that people share a common experience of the world. They do not. They therefore define the world's problems differently.

The key to changing behavior on a large scale, voluntarily and yet relatively quickly, is to help people to learn their way into the future as effectively as possible. More timely and visible feedback is one of the keys. Providing opportunity for people to communicate their different experiences, and thereby to build a new collective rationale for doing things differently, is another. The United Nations Conference on the Environment and Development was the first global attempt at shared learning in a forum that linked environmental, developmental, and population issues. It is not surprising that difficulties and misunderstandings arose. However, we must not let future global meetings pass by without women's voices being heard equally to those of men.

The Misguided Assumptions of Population Policy

Population policies rely heavily for their justification on extrapolation of numbers. According to United Nations Population Fund 1990 data, by the end of the century an additional billion or so people will increase the world's population to 6.2 billion, an increase roughly equivalent to the combined present populations of Latin America and Africa. The World Bank's current high forecast is that world population might stabilize at around 14 billion by the year 2085. Such numbers lend themselves to scaremongering. For example, Robin Cole, Chairman of the Condor Conservation Trust, speaking to the 1992 British Association for the Advancement of Science meeting, said, "We are going to suffer a major food crisis in the not very distant future with appalling human suffering and devastation of the environment unless we do something about population growth now."[10]

Statements such as these are unprovable at the present time. To be fair, demographers have long recognized that population dynamics are properties of complex systems of direct and mediating relationships. One of the most popular attempts to find patterns in these relationships was first formulated by Frank Notestein in 1945. Using data from Western Europe, he elaborated a theory of demographic transition. The theory postulated that, with economic development, societies moved through three stages, in which high death rates and high birth rates gave way to a period of declining death rates and continuing high birth rates, to reach an end stage of low death rates and low birth rates.

Developmental experts subsequently appeared to find confirmation of the theory in the rapid passage after the Second World War of many Asian countries through the second period of demographic transition and their entry into the third. More recently, the transition appears to have stalled in Asia, Africa, and parts of the Arab-speaking world. In fact, the transition is not predictable on the basis of demographic data. The theory cannot explain anything that deviates from overall long-term trends; the theory can explain only the demographic causes of the transition, after the fact.

Deviations from long-term trends are quite common and wholly unpredictable. The baby boom in Western Europe after the Second World War was no less unexpected than the sharp decline in fertility over the past two decades, by nearly two-thirds, in the 14 largest developing countries, including India and China. The declines are not associated in any satisfactorily predictable or regular way with general patterns of economic growth or reduction in poverty, or with culture or types of social organization, wage levels, degree of industrialization or the distribution of landholdings, or with religious belief or national policies. In specific cases, any of these singly or in combination might contribute to falling or rising population growth, as historical analysis has shown.

Moreover, in specific cases, decline in fertility historically predates the widespread use of modern contraceptives—as did the steady decline in birth rates in nineteenth century France. It can occur in the face of pronatalist government policies and, as in the case of Italy, in the face of religious discouragement of the use of contraception. It has come about in countries with extremes of poverty and wealth and in more egalitarian societies, in poor countries with relatively high standards of welfare and in countries with relatively low standards of welfare.

Many different methods have been used to understand these differences and to explain the causal pathways at both the household and national levels. Although some models fit the data better than others, no grand conclusions can be drawn. The only sensible conclusion is that human behavior is distanced in many ways from biological constraints and reproductive forces. Trend is not destiny.

Organizing Purposeful Change

In 1991, a group of 70 U.S.-based population and environmental organizations signed a joint statement that begins: "There is no issue of greater concern to the world's future than the rapid rise in human population. Together, the increase in human population and resource consumption are basic causes of environmental degradation and human suffering."[11] It is difficult to see in this statement, or in the pronouncements of the world's multilateral developmental agencies, any deep appreciation of the dynamics of population growth and the interaction between people and their environment.

Further, it is taken as axiomatic that more people means more degradation. Yet local studies show that, while this might be the outcome, increased population densities or high rates of growth also can lead to more sustainable environmental management, less waste, more efficient use of resources, and higher productivity of natural resources. In some settings, more people are needed for positive change in resource management and income growth.[12] It is the context that determines the outcome. Does this mean that gender equity and developmental, environmental, and population problems are separate problems, requiring separate solutions, each carefully tailored to the context? Or are the separate problems susceptible to a common solution?

The World Bank's View

In its 1992 World Development Report, the World Bank expressed the view that it is possible and desirable to approach gender equity, development, the environment, and population growth with an integrated set of policies. The report argued that complementary interventions with multiple objectives are synergistic, that is, their interactive result is greater than the sum of each individual contribution.

The Bank proposed that strong opportunities for accelerated economic growth and environmental sustainability go hand in hand through a set of win-win interventions, principally removal of subsidies, modernization of land rights, accelerated provision of clean water, expanded provision of family planning services, expanded provision of credit to farmers, the education of girls, and the participation of farmers, communities, indigenous people, and women.

This package might seem attractive, refreshing, and uncontroversial. Yet it is based on uncritical acceptance of a particular view of the world. For instance, as mentioned previously, modern land titling can diminish rather than enhance the access of women farmers to land, thereby promoting rather than reducing further land degradation. Even where women achieve greater security of land use, this may have only feeble consequences unless other measures are taken to remove constraints on women's access to production services and to reduce their existing burden of work. Nor can it be assumed that, where childbearing is the main avenue to status, social security, and economic resources, women will use modern contraception to limit their family's size rather than to space their children. In other words, synergy cannot emerge unless policies are informed by a deeper sensitivity to gender relations in specific contexts.

Further, although the Bank has signed on to the idea of empowering women, it maintains the expectations of patriarchal society, based on the unrewarded work of women and on control of women's sexuality, fertility, and mobility. However, in conditions that offer preferable alternatives, women might choose not to contribute unremunerated time, for example, to weeding or watering trees planted and owned by men or to controlling erosion, if they have no long-term rights to the land. They might, as in parts of Africa where social relations have been most damaged by the colonial and postcolonial experience, increasingly choose not to marry. They are then free to use childbearing as a strategy for gaining access to resources without incurring the obligation to submit to male control.

Again, the removal of subsidies might appear economically rational in terms of balancing the national exchequer and as a stimulant to growth, but it can have devastating effects at the household level, thrusting the burden of care and economizing back onto women to the point that basic family welfare is compromised. Mothers in such circumstances can be the first to keep their daughters out of school, simply because there is no way to cope without their help in the home.

In brief, the Bank's view is based on three incorrect assumptions. First, it assumes that the specifics of gender relations are not significant to the outcome of policies. Yet numerous political science studies show that the effects of policy are highly sensitive to the starting conditions. Second, it assumes that the household or the family is an undifferentiated unity, seeking a common interest. Again, the wealth of the evidence is against this view.[13] Women as well as men make individual and joint return on investment calculations in the allocation of their time, labor, and energy. Policies   .

and interventions that are not sensitive to these differences cannot achieve their stated purpose. Third, the Bank assumes that the empowerment of women, if achieved, has no consequences for the way that human behavior is organized, problems are defined, and policies are designed. Yet the inclusion of women as partners in the dialogue always has consequences for the outcome.

The United Nations Population Fund's View

The United Nations Population Fund (UNFPA) is the lead agency in the United Nations family for population policy, maternal and child health, and family planning services. In a hard-hitting report, *Investing in Women: the Focus of the '90s*, Nafis Sadik, the Executive Director of the Fund, places women at the heart of development. Investments in women, including services such as health and education, it is argued, are important in their own right and also as signals that women are vital and valuable members of society. Complementary initiatives to enhance the status of women are also crucial. The investment priority is family planning, however, according to the report, because "it represents the freedom from which other freedoms flow."

The remainder of the report uses powerful statistics and case material to justify and expand these statements. Nonetheless, the UNFPA places women at the heart of development largely in an instrumental fashion. The focus is on women as wives and mothers, leaving large areas of women's reproductive health, sexuality, and fertility management untouched. The imperative clearly is to get contraceptives and maternal and child health care to as many women as possible in order to secure population and environmental objectives. According to the report, "the population crisis is a matter for action now, not next century. By then it will be too late."

Both the Bank and the UNFPA give some emphasis to the need to bring women into the mainstream of development, that is, to design assistance that is sensitive to women's needs across the board, rather than targeting assistance in special women's projects. Yet there is little recognition that bringing women into the mainstream, seriously considered, means changing the nature of the mainstream. It is precisely because gender is a relational phenomenon that gender-sensitive development necessitates changing the standard.

Both the World Bank and the UNFPA also give attention to women's self-determination. Here again, there is no accompanying recognition that women might not choose as priorities the activities that currently constitute the mainstream. If one part of an interactive relationship changes, then by definition, the whole changes, too. Nor is there sufficient recognition that the wider availability of contraceptive technology may become the means by which women are deprived of the freedom and the right to determine and manage their own sexuality and fertility.

What Women Want

There is little doubt that women in general want expanded access to contraception but not necessarily to serve the goals of the World Bank or the UNFPA, nor on their terms. The agenda of women goes beyond a limited contraceptive service or even a family planning perspective. They want to be able to conceive when they desire and to carry wanted pregnancies to term. They want to bear and raise healthy children. They want to manage their sexuality and fertility safely and remain free of the disease, disability, pain, fear, and death associated with reproduction and fertility.

An increasing number of women are willing to accept the risks of using contraceptives and of ending an unwanted pregnancy in the case of contraceptive failure because they cannot trust their partners to safeguard their sexual and maternal health and fertility. In addition, they would like to see population policies and family planning services pay more attention to male sexuality and fertility and initiatives to support and promote greater male responsibility in such areas.

Concerned women and men both want to see policies that nurture the world's natural resources, not exploit them. They want to see pollution controls that restrain the gross polluters and waste producers, not restrictions that load disproportionate burdens on women at the household level. They want to transform economic policies that assign value to military expenditures and weapons of war but leave women's work and reproductive services uncounted and unvalued.

These wants are not unachievable daydreams. Creative effort on the part of women and men has begun to change attitudes and potentials. A good deal has been learned about what to do and how to do it. In the process, women are demonstrating that human and institutional behavior can be changed in ways that produce a cascade of environmental, population, developmental, and gender equity benefits.

2

The Game Is Not Fairly Divided

In Europe the late 14th century was a time of political turmoil, famine, and plague. John Bromyard, Chancellor of Cambridge University, foresaw the century's end as an apocalyptic time of moral reckoning, when the dreadful burdens of the poor would be lifted and the mighty humbled in a final Day of Judgment: "And with boldness will they be able to put their plaint before God and seek justice. . . . 'Our labours and goods they took away, to satiate their greed. They afflicted us with hunger and labours, that they might live delicately upon our labours and our goods. We have laboured and lived so hard a life that scarce for half a year had we a good sufficiency, scarce nothing save bread and bran and water. Nay, rather, what is worse, we died of hunger . . . And those robbers yonder gave not our own goods to us out of them . . . O just God, mighty judge, the game was not fairly divided between them and us. Their satiety was our famine; their merriment was our wretchedness; their jousts and tournaments were our torment.'"[1]

Today, as in 14th century Europe, deep-seated inequality exists in the social welfare and in people's access to secure livelihoods. Three important things have happened over the past six hundred years, however. First, the scale of inequity has become global, structured in the interaction between national economies. Second, the scale of our appropriation and disposal of the earth's material and natural resources is transforming the very conditions that support our existence. Third, huge gains in apparent economic efficiency have been won only by discounting the accompanying human costs and the progressive loss of environmental integrity.

These three trends are causally interdependent. It is not possible to change the direction or nature of one without also paying attention to the other two. It is thus problematic to argue for mutual self-interest in the environmental sphere as long as there is no parallel effort of will and policy that addresses global economic inequalities. The global environment has to work for all of us or it will not work for any of us. If the weak do not get stronger, the strong will not survive.

Unfortunately, the existing patterns of resource consumption and distribution around the world implicitly reflect a presumption that the strong can ensure their own survival by pursuing narrow self-interest. Further, such patterns foreshadow the possibility that, if the global environment will not accommodate both the weak and the strong, the weak will go to the wall. Under these conditions, the prospect that geopolitical instability will accompany global biological and physical transformation becomes a self-fulfilling prophecy.

No country, no currently dominant group, can be free of the effects of the changes that people already have brought about, wherever the point of origin. Uncomfortable though the thought might be, no one can guarantee a secure future. Further, people can minimize the disruption of change only by seeking solutions in concert with others. Self-interest means moving toward mutuality of interest.

The Economic Dimension of Environmental Change

Economic development must take place before poverty can be relieved. Some progress has been made in increasing the share that developing countries have in world economic output. According to 1993 International Monetary Fund estimates, industrialized countries now produce barely half of the total world output; that is, the gap between rich and poor countries is smaller than generally believed. However, persistent poverty threatens to undermine progress toward a sustainable environment. Most of the world's poor people—perhaps 80 percent of the poor in Latin America, 60 percent in Asia, and 50 percent in Africa—live in areas that are especially vulnerable to the kinds of environmental degradation that poverty causes. Economic growth in these areas is not an option but an imperative to relieve poverty-related pressure on the environment.

Although economic growth is a necessary condition for an environmentally sustainable future, it is not a sufficient condition. There are limits both to the amount of matter and energy that can be converted for human consumption and to the capacity of the earth to assimilate the waste generated by that conversion. Economic activity must adapt to the boundaries set by these two limiting conditions.

Further, for poor people's lives to improve worldwide, a different kind of economic activity is needed, including a more equitable and just distribution of resource rights and obligations. Moreover, as the worldwide DAWN network of feminist researchers and activists has shown, the underlying social causes of inequity and injustice lie in the inequitable relationships between men and women.[2] Because of this gender inequity, the human costs of poverty and environmental degradation fall hardest on poor women everywhere. As long as economic growth and care of the environment remain predicated on the exploitation of women's labor, time, and energy in the household, no sustainable future can come about. What is needed is not more of the same, more equitably distributed. A more fundamental re-shaping has to take place.

Economics without Gender Are Not Neutral

An important part of reshaping gender relations begins with the redefinition of what constitutes productive work. Masculine standards and norms have shaped what economists measure, what is valued, and how economic data are interpreted. Such supposedly neutral and objective economic conventions play an enormous role in determining economic policy. Yet, by not recognizing gender as the fundamental ordering principle of human relations, conventional economics and policies lock human society into inequitable and unsustainable economic activity.

Conventional economic data do not reflect women's real economic and social contributions. For instance, whereas the water industry is given an economic value, the work of a woman who gets up at 4 a.m. every day, walks 11 kilometers to a bore hole, and carries back to her home 30 liters of water in a tin balanced on her head is given no economic value and has no statistical existence in male constructs of economic activity. Grain that is processed in a grinding mill is given value; food that is processed domestically, as is most of the world's food, is given no value. Nor is women's contribution to the reproduction of the labor force through childbearing recorded in conventional economics. Women's wages for work that is the same or equivalent to the work of men are between two-fifths and two-thirds of men's wages. Research in contrasting cultural and work-site settings shows that the gap between male and female wage rates is largely a reflection of systemic discrimination rather than objective differences in productivity or other measures.[3] No useful understanding of economic, environmental, and population control activities can be developed as long as gender-biased measurement and valuation of economic activity persists.

Considerable effort by the United Nations development agencies and by specialist national institutes in countries such as Norway and Australia is going into making women's work and environmental costs and benefits visible in national statistical bases, survey data, and the United Nations System of Accounts. The World Bank's annual *Development Reports*, for example, now carry summary tables that disaggregate some of the conventional demographic, educational, and social data by male and female categories and attempt a first approximation of key environmental trends.

Important though this effort is, it does not address the fundamental gender biases in conventional economic theory and policy. Economists such as Marilyn Waring have explored the implications of ungendered economics, seeking to understand why and how women's fundamental contribution to the reproduction of family life, in its cultural, economic, biological, and so-cial aspects, is so profoundly undervalued and distorted. These economists see a connection between the gross waste of natural and economic resources in military expenditures, the economic exploitation of nature at the expense of other species, the feminization of poverty, and the subordination of women.

Concepts of power and aggression are strongly rooted in the masculine psyche and in patriarchy, the social expression of male dominance. Dominance within the household cascades through larger scale economic re-lations, compromising the achievement of the paramount human need to sat-isfy the basics of existence—a secure livelihood, food security, and a way of life that does not compromise the existence of future generations. Economic policies that are gender biased in their assumptions and effects can promote economic efficiency and growth but not equity between the sexes and envi-ronmental integrity. Economic reform is thus not merely a matter of tech-nical adjustment; it involves conscious choice among competing values.

Protecting the Quality of Life

Feminist economists argue that economic activity must be informed by values that do not compromise the quality of life of either men or women. The basic economic questions thus have to do with the kind of life economic activity is designed to achieve and for whom. These are not questions that can be answered merely by numerical estimation of the balance between people and the environment at the global level. Feminist economists rightly ask whose quality of life population control advocates are really concerned about. When polemicists argue that stringent fertility control among poor populations is the solution to global environmental problems (which in large part have been generated by the waste, pollution, and consumption patterns of industrialized countries), they are arguing for the protection of their own lifestyle at the expense of others.

From the point of view of many women, quality of life questions must begin with the gender inequities that structure people's interaction with the material world at the household level. Natural resources can no longer be treated primarily as inputs to production or as consumption goods in the market economy, with decisions about how much to use and when deter-mined by estimations of the market value lost by using a resource later rather than now. Nor is it sufficient to concentrate on the efficiency and produc-tivity of resource use, governed only by care that renewable resources are used at rates not greater than the rate at which they can continue to be gen-erated, wastes are produced at rates not greater than the rate at which they can be absorbed by the environment, and nonrenewable resources are de-pleted with optimal efficiency.

The economic decisions of today must take into account three additional considerations: the value of the nonmarket goods and services performed by women within the household, the value to everyone of natural resource goods, such as the carbon absorption capacity of forests and grasslands, and the value of the existence of future generations. From this perspective, conventional economic analysis fails to provide information about the nonmarket values that are needed to govern present-day decisions that affect the future.

For the tribal women of Chotanagpur in Ranchi, India, the links between poverty, environmental degradation, and gender-based inequalities are clear. If the women cannot secure their rightful access to land, their poverty will deeepen, and household welfare and natural resources will deteriorate. First, however, they must deal with the subtle and many-faceted gender-based barriers that prevent them from securing the land to which they are entitled. As related by Viji Srinivasan in a paper presented to the Workshop on Operational Strategies for Reaching Women in Agriculture, in 1986, they consider whether to borrow more money to pay a bribe to the man who is preventing them from planting trees on a barren hillside:

> Nibha thinks of their subsistence livelihoods and entreats them, "Don't borrow more. Talk to the man". . . Something flashes in Valeria's mind: "Let's go to the panchayat [village council]," she says. "Women are not permitted to attend the panchayat meetings," objects another. "Even when disputes involving women are discussed, we are not allowed." "The men say—bhago [go away] if we go near. The men say—what do women know about these matters—women cannot take proper decisions, women are not buddhiman [endowed with intelligence]." "But the scientists who say we cannot grow trees on this bare land are not always right either," put in another voice, "We can gain control over our lives if we try."[4]

The women of Chotanagpur are not asking self-interestedly for a share of a limited resource. They are asking for a reworking of the relationships between men and women and the way in which resources are managed. The two struggles are inextricably linked.

Debt as a Symptom and Cause of Persistent Inequality

The international debt crisis is no longer in the headlines but remains a major symptom and cause of injustices that underlie the population control and environmental debate. A national debt in itself is neither a sign of poverty nor wealth. Indeed, by far the largest debtor in the world is now the United States, yet it is not a poor country. Debt becomes problematic mainly in relation to a nation's capacity to service the loans and repay the capital. An inability to pay becomes doubly problematic when the debt is held by governments and institutions outside a nation's own borders, as is the case with most Third World debt.

The world's poorest countries are those classified by the World Bank as having a Gross National Product (GNP) of less than $500 per person. More than half the world's people live in these countries. Altogether, in 1992 these countries owed the institutions and governments of the industrial world $400 billion, or 40 percent of their combined GNP. In an effort to service their debt and adapt their economies to earn hard currency to repay the capital, the world's poorest countries must cut savagely into the expenditures essential to secure even the most basic standard of living. In 37 of the poorest countries, government expenditures on health and education fell by 50 percent and 25 percent, respectively, between 1980 and 1990. Overall, by the end of 1988, more was being paid out by the Third World in principal and interest, to the tune of $50 billion, than was being received as new finance (inclusive of aid).

For example, in 1992, the debt held by the countries of sub-Saharan Africa amounted to more than $160 billion, a relatively small proportion of Third World debt, but amounting to some 58 percent of African GNP. These countries were able to pay only a small fraction of the interest payments due. Nonetheless, the payments amounted to more than a quarter of all export earnings and cost more than the total expenditures on health and education. In sub-Saharan Africa, average incomes per person have fallen by about a quarter over the past decade.

In spite of this, for a long time the main focus of international efforts to relieve the debt problem of the Third World was the perceived threat to the solvency of the commercial banks of industrialized countries and the stability of the international monetary system. Considerable progress has been made in reducing or managing the large amounts owed to private banks, as well as the smaller amounts owed to governments. In the case of sub-Saharan Africa, Japan is the only bilateral member of the "Paris Club" of creditor governments that has not written off a portion of the debt owed. Because little of the debt would have been recovered in any case, the cost to the treasuries of rich countries has been small. The least progress has been made with respect to the debts of the poorest countries owed to the multilateral banks such as the World Bank and the International Monetary Fund. From 1988 to 1992 the multilateral banks' share of African debt grew from 19 to 28 percent. Loans from these institutions cannot be rescheduled or written off if debtor countries are to go on borrowing.

In what appears to be an imaginative contribution to the resolution of the crisis, some agencies have developed "debt for nature" swaps. Basically, an agency arranges to buy (or persuades banks to donate) part of the external debt, which is then converted back into local currency to finance land to be set aside in the debtor country as a conservation area. So far, Costa Rica, Bolivia, Ecuador, Mexico, and the Philippines have participated in such deals. However attractive they might seem, they perpetuate inequitable relationships. The people who already live in the designated areas rarely are consulted in advance of the deal. They have their own views about their environment being traded above their heads and being placed in a living natural history museum. Also, the swaps enshrine the historical exploitation that enabled colonialists to get rich by using the primary products of the Third World to build their own industrial capacity.

Debt for development swaps also have received considerable attention. The United Nations Children's Fund (UNICEF), for example, has persuaded a number of commercial banks to donate Third World debts to it. UNICEF in turn has exchanged the debt for local currency for use in projects benefitting women and children. While increasing the welfare of beneficiaries and improving social infrastructure, such as supplies of drinking water, these deals are insignificant in terms of their impact on the reduction of the debt burden.

Although the problems caused by external indebtedness have been eased for developing countries by a succession of debt management strategies, the overall problem has not gone away. Debt is ubiquitous in today's global economy. Injudicious lending, exorbitant borrowing, and wasteful expenditure continue to play their part in sustaining indebtedness. The fear that governments will spend unwisely in preference to servicing debt constrains further debt adjustment. The interaction among interest rate levels and inflation, the prices that Third World exports can command on the world market, economic stagnation, restrictions on trade, and a slowdown in trade compound the problem. However, at a meeting of heads of government organized by the Organization of African Unity (OAU) in Dakar in November 1992, a commitment was reached to direct the benefits of debt relief into basic education and health (including family planning), for example, with specific goals set for 1995 and the year 2000.

Poor investment prospects in turn have led to a slowdown in the amount of private investment reaching indebted Third World countries. By far the largest inflow of private capital over the past decade has gone to industrialized countries, mainly Japan and the countries of North America and Western Europe. The vast majority of Third World countries receive only a small portion of foreign investment, and in 1992 most of this went to only 10 countries (Argentina, Brazil, Mexico, Egypt, China, Hong Kong, Malaysia, Singapore, Thailand, and Taiwan). The only industries for which other developing countries can attract private capital are the resource-extractive industries in the logging and mining sectors. By the early 1990s less than 1 percent of private capital was flowing to the poorest group of countries.

Structural adjustment policies, or SAPs, have been an important part of the attempted solution. A SAP is a bundle of policies that are designed to remove market distortions, reduce government expenditures, and shift the structure of demand and production in order to stimulate economic growth and relieve the domestic impact of external debt. The main instruments include removal of subsidies, wage freezes, food price and interest rate increases, reduction of public sector employment and services, promotion of exportable goods and services, and the freeing of foreign exchange markets. Substantial financing from the multilateral and bilateral assistance agencies and banks has been made available for balance of payments support and lending to countries that adopt structural adjustment policies. By the end of 1988, 55 countries worldwide had adopted SAPs; by the end of 1989, the total included 28 countries in sub-Saharan Africa alone.

If publicly funded health and other services are cut back in conditions of economic stagnation and inadequate employment opportunities, however, the poor lose these services, as they are unable to pay for private sector alternatives. SAPs by and large have not brought the intended stimulus to growth and employment in the world's poorest countries. Almost every social indicator shows that, for these countries, the limits of adjustment have been reached. For example, progress in alleviating infant mortality, a precursor of declining fertility, has slowed or been reversed. According to UNICEF estimates, by 1992 some 210,000 children were dying every week because of cuts in services caused by the debt crisis.[5]

The true human cost, however, cannot be understood without probing a little deeper into the linkages between the domestic economy and the larger social and economic environment. It is here, in the detail of human interaction with the material world at the micro level, that the problems can be truly understood.

The Impact of Structural Adjustment Policies

The evidence of the effects of SAPs on people's welfare and livelihoods shows that, particularly in the poorest countries, the impact on men and women has been different and the impact on women has been largely negative. It is not possible to separate entirely the effects of the SAPs themselves from the effects of economic recession and economic contraction (which the SAPs were intended to correct), and, in some cases and for some sectors, the effects appear to be equivocal. Yet the overall effect has been to place even more demands on women's energy, time, and labor.

Principally, this occurs because rising prices and the removal of subsidies, coupled with few new jobs and the systemic forces that perpetuate women's inferior earnings and productivity in the informal sector, have increased women's need to generate cash. At the same time, the structural inequities that make this more difficult for women than for men have been left untouched.

The increased concentration of agricultural resources on export crops has provided more opportunities for wage employment in agriculture, while the rise in food prices has provided opportunities for some farmers to increase their profits. But the gains have been made at the expense of the women farmers' other tasks within the household or by increasing women's unpaid labor within the farm enterprise. The male bias in agricultural service provision and in access to farm inputs and markets has been left untouched, further compromising the capacity of women farmers to respond to new market opportunities. At the same time, the bias against small scale businesses in favor of export-oriented manufacturing and trade in services again discriminates against a sector in which female entrepreneurship is concentrated.

The net effect is to increase the demands on women with respect to household maintenance, food production, economic activity, and reproduction. At the same time, the reduction in social expenditures means that there have been no offsetting mechanisms to ease the additional pressures on women's time, energy, and labor. On the contrary, the reduction has imposed additional burdens as the responsibility for care falls back on the household sector. Increasingly hard pressed, women are less and less able to care for their environment or look after their farming activities in a sustainable way.

The consequences are numerous. As food prices rise, for example, women search for cheap food or substitute unprocessed food and spend more time in domestic processing. The effects do not translate into equal welfare losses for all family members: women bear a disproportionate burden.

As women extend their working day, the intergenerational effects are magnified. That is, children are progressively less well supervised, fed, and cared for. Here also there is a gender effect. School attendance among girls in particular tends to drop as mothers depend on their daughters to ease their own time constraints. The costs, in short, are absorbed primarily by females. There are limits, however, and the worsening health and nutritional data for women and children indicate that the threshold is quite close.

In short, because they are insensitive to gender relations and the workings of the micro economy, SAPs have undermined social equity, economic efficiency, and environmental sustainability. SAPs have damaged the very economic foundations that they were designed to strengthen. Mainstream economists and policymakers responsible for designing and implementing SAPs have created inappropriate definitions of productive work. They have neglected the time and energy constraints on women's productive labor as a resource that sustains the seamless web of domestic and public activities at the micro level, neglected the complex relationships that govern women's access to land, labor and capital, new technology, and services, and have assumed that extra unpaid labor is available at the household level for additional production or to take up the slack in social service provision.

The pressures on the local environment cannot be relieved as long as the SAP-induced burdens on women and the household economy press so hard. The international environmental agencies in the past have not been particularly sensitive to the experience of women living with these pressures. This lack of sensitivity makes it appear as if the developmental agenda and the environmental agenda are different: they are not. Politically and economically, they are codependent. For women in poor countries and for poor women everywhere, there is no environmentally sustainable future that does not include a greater measure of social equity and economic efficiency at the level of the domestic economy.

The Two Sides of the Fence: Codependence or Conflict?

The codependence of the developmental and environmental agendas is illuminated by three further elements in the debate. One is that the kinds of science and technology that inform the debate are reflections of a masculine response to nature, a response that seeks to dominate and control. The second is the misanthropic streak, or aversion to people, that runs through much of the discussion on conservation and preservation. The third and related element is the widespread expectation that women can, as it were, mop up global pollution and waste by better management of the domestic economy.

Control versus Nurturance

Many women perceive the drive behind modern science and technology as a search for ways to dominate nature, just as patriarchy seeks to dominate women. Feminists concerned with environmental issues point to the colossal ecological mistakes, such as the atom bomb and DDT, produced by a science and technology governed by the masculine qualities of control and aggression. They argue that control must give way to nurturance, a conviction that has led many women scientists in recent years into the emerging disciplines of biological agriculture, land care, *in situ* genetic resource conservation, and allied fields.

The drive to control has led to a rearrangement of nature. Perhaps as much nitrogen is being fixed from the atmosphere by chemical processes, for example, as is being fixed biotically. The evolved relationship between plants, animals, and their environment has been broken as natural materials have been shifted around the world. An estimated 40 percent of the plants and mammals now in Hawaii are exotics, for example, and at least half the flora of present-day New Zealand originated in other parts of the world.

This rearrangement of nature has enabled humankind to expand into and exploit almost every part of the world and to dominate all other species. It has vastly increased the efficiency by which matter is converted into products used by people. However, it has undermined the productivity of the natural resources on which human life ultimately depends and transformed the interaction of biological and socioeconomic relations in ways that threaten our continued existence.

Two pioneers of the view that control must give way to nurturance, Rachel Carson and Patricia Hynes, are women who first achieved recognition as professional scientists in patriarchal hierarchies. Before writing *Silent Spring*, a classic study of the effects of pesticides on the environment and the food chain, Carson worked for the U.S. Fish and Wildlife Service. Hynes has worked for the Hazardous Waste Division of the Environmental Protection Agency and as Chief of Environmental Management for the Massachusetts Port Authority. The scientific work of these two women, and their experience of working as women in scientific professions, deepened their insight into what is now expressed as *ecofeminism*, of science informed by nurturance and a more balanced sense of proportion, that is, an understanding that humankind cannot survive by apportioning a greater share of the world's resources at the expense of the existence of other species.

Nature versus People

As they explore the concepts of nurturance and proportionality, many women are led by consideration of the lessons of their own biology and their roles in family care and daily survival to two important conclusions. One is that people are a part of nature, not something separate from natural processes. The second is that people play a central role in the management of natural resources to meet human ends. In this sense, there are no natural landscapes: all landscapes are the product of human choices about how resources should be used or not used. These two conclusions combined lead to a third: that the preservation of biodiversity and respect for other forms of life are conditions for human survival.

Unfortunately, the interdependence of human survival and the survival of other species is being used to justify crude arguments for population control and the exclusion of people from certain areas. Arne Naess, emeritus professor of philosophy at Oslo University, was the first to coin the term *deep ecology* to express such a biocentric view of the world, based on the understanding that if people destroy other species, they destroy themselves.

Such a view must be tempered by the understanding that there are no solutions that do not involve people. Regulatory powers are not sufficient either to block damaging kinds of economic development nor to promote ecologically benign or sustainable development. Technological choices that might look right from the perspective of aggregate economic development can be ecological disasters that do little to meet the basic needs of poor people.

For example, a common approach to nature conservation is to exclude people from a valued ecosystem, demarcate a surrounding buffer zone in which only controlled exploitation is permitted, and to install a regulatory management system that relies on patrolling guards, fines, and other sanctions. This approach fosters friction, resentment, evasion, and corruption. It needlessly sets conservation against the livelihood of poor people. It turns out to be just another version of reliance on control rather than nurturance.

The Case of the Mudumalai Sanctuary

The Mudumalai Wildlife Sanctuary is an example of the approach of excluding people from a valued ecosystem. Abutting the borders of Tamil Nadu, Karnataka, and Kerala in southern India, the Mudumalai Wildlife Sanctuary recently was placed under the Nilgiris Biosphere Reserve in recognition of its fragile and rich diversity. Although the new designation does not preclude human activity, it does seek to restrict any influx of population and development that might harm the ecology of the area.

There are two settlements within the sanctuary. The western village is small, but the eastern settlement is a village growing to a town. An area of low rainfall, with low groundwater reserves and a single water course, the eastern village produces little more than one crop a year. The villagers' main source of income is the collection and sale of dung from their free-grazing cattle. A silk reeling farm, poultry farm, and large private farm are the only other commercial activities.

The flatlands surrounding the settlement form a natural funnel for migrating wild elephant herds as they pass between the gorge of the Moyar river and the hills to the south. But the enlargement of the settlement and the increasing development of surrounding estates, tourism, and road traffic restrict free passage to a corridor some 2 to 3 kilometers wide.

Energetic action by environmentalist groups recently blocked two economic development initiatives. The first proposal was to establish a large, modern tourist complex, which would have brought noise, commotion, and waste disposal problems to the area and made heavy demands on scarce water resources. Permission eventually was granted to build a modified version of the complex outside the sanctuary boundary. The second proposal was to build an electroplating plant. The plant would have used more water than the entire amount available for the settlement and channelled highly toxic effluent directly into the water course. Immediate local employment opportunities would have been limited because few local people possess any relevant skills. Both proposals violated numerous government regulations.

A third project, to develop a hydroelectric plant to meet the needs of towns and industry outside the sanctuary boundary, will probably go ahead. Clearance for the project was given in 1985, one year before the area was designated a biosphere reserve. The project requires extensive surface and underground engineering work, rehabilitation of an existing plant, housing for plant personnel, and a large population of transient laborers. Project authorities estimate that there will be an influx of three to four thousand people, requiring the development of an entire township. The proposed township site is a slope above the reservoir that supplies the existing settlement with its domestic water supply.

The additional pressure on grazing, forest, wood fuel supplies, and the impact on the elephants and other fauna caused by heavy vehicles using the road between the project site and the township have not been assessed by the project developers. Moreover, say the protesters, it is not even clear that the project is the best technical option, nor that it will be cost effective, whereas it is clear that it violates the provisions of the biosphere reserve.

While dispute over the hydroelectric project continues, a fourth initiative is causing concern. Hindustan Photo Films and the Ketti Rotary Club, with the intentions of promoting the welfare of the poor, proposed to establish a commercial fruit and vegetable farm for the tribal community, as well as an intensive cattle-keeping and dairy complex. The produce would supply the growing needs of the tourist market, as well as improve the tribal members' own nutrition. Land clearing has begun. Unfortunately, the site is directly in the migratory path of the elephants; an electric fence has been proposed to keep the elephants from destroying the produce.

The case illustrates the conflicts that arise when the environment, conservation, and human survival are viewed as opposing interests. Yet the search for strategies that reconcile what might at first appear to be mutually exclusive concerns needs another approach. All those affected, including the illiterate poor, women as well as men, must be fully involved in analyzing the problems and designing remedies.

Social Fences: Bringing People In

A contrasting approach based on nurturance and proportionality is to involve the people who live in an area in such a way that they themselves become a social fence, not only guarding against intrusion and degradation but actively involved in restoring the landscape's richness and productivity.

At its purest, this kind of bioregionalism expresses a vision of self-sufficient economic communities, federated within regions whose boundaries are defined by sustainable ecosystems. The vision is based on the concepts of restoration and reinhabitation. *Restoration* means the repair and care of damaged ecosystems and the protection and encouragement of a diversity of life forms. *Reinhabitation* means the discovery of the human activities a bioregion might support if people are to fit themselves to the environment. In practice, it means an approach to development that is decentralized, nonhierarchical, and democratic, as the following example illustrates.

By the 1970s, an extensive area in Tamil Nadu was experiencing serious degradation. Farmers sought to compensate for declining yields by cultivating the surrounding hills, allowing their cattle into forest reserves, and searching more intensively for fuel and other forest products. Water resources dried as the tree cover of watersheds was depleted and runoff increased. As agricultural wages and income fell, villagers increased wood fuel collection for sale to urban users and took out small timber to sell for urban construction.

With financial support from Sweden, in 1981 the Tamil Nadu Department of Forestry began working to rehabilitate some 500,000 hectares. The program's first phase concentrated on seedling distribution, creation of community multipurpose woodlots, soil and water conservation, establishment of fodder plantations, and tree planting along roads and canals, around reservoirs, and on designated wasteland. Villagers received direct benefits from the trees and fodder, and in employment income, but they did not become fully involved in decision making and planning. The program remained largely regulatory and directive in approach: encroachment and degradation continued.

A review of the experience led to the concept of *interface management*. Could the three thousand or so villagers living on the lower slopes become a social fence? Could an integrated approach to livelihood security and ecological sustainability be developed? In an experimental area of 5503 hectares, the program began working with villagers to demarcate three zones up the gradient: the upper slopes, to be untouched except for limited forest regeneration; the mid-slopes, to be accessed for small timber and minor forest products as supplementary income sources; and the lower slopes, to be developed for increased but sustainable economic exploitation, diversification of income, and expansion of biomass energy resources.

The villagers have become involved as "knowledge partners," contributing their experience to the choice, design, and siting of technology and infrastructure to control gully erosion, moderate water flow, entrap water, and conserve moisture. Villagers also have become increasingly involved in the provision of social infrastructure, support of community or group self-management, and the development of the responsiveness of *panchayats* (local government authorities) to ecological development. The social fence approach is strengthening the possibility of achieving sustained ecological conservation embedded in the dynamic of the social fabric.

Women and Global Housekeeping

Women throughout the world are applying the concepts of nurturance and proportionality to the problem of cleaning up pollution and waste. Every year the world's 24 leading industrialized countries consume an estimated two-thirds of the total resources used in that year. They have generated most of the pollutant gases that are changing the chemistry of the global atmosphere. They generate by far the largest proportion of the world's domestic and industrial wastes, including hazardous wastes. So far, they have been reluctant to compensate the rest of the world for the disproportionate impact of their consumption and waste generation.

Within this pattern of global inequity, women implicitly are being cast by economic planners in the role of global housekeepers. As domestic water rates rise to generate funding to clean up polluted water supplies, women in the home are faced with the real time, energy, and labor costs of using less water. Women, who are mainly responsible for the daily use and transformation of material goods and energy through the domestic economy, are being asked to generate less waste and use resources more sparingly.

Many women find the role assigned to them as global housekeepers troubling. Poor women are reluctant or simply not able to accept solutions that impose on them additional time, energy, and labor costs. In industrialized countries, women ask, for example, if working women were to give up the use of disposable diapers in order to reduce the amount of household waste entering the environment, whose time, labor, and energy would be used to wash the cloth diapers? If householders are to reduce their use of cars, who in the family will have access to transportation to shop and take children to school? Women in poor countries, and poor women everywhere, ask who pays the price in terms of providing additional household services if the cost of public transportation or basic medical, maternal, and other services increases and availability decreases?

In their own interest, women will seek to use less firewood, turn off electric lights, use less washing water, and so on, but most women do not accept that the burden of adjustment should fall disproportionately on their shoulders. Before they are asked to economize and use less, recycle more, and dispose of waste with care, they want to see proportionate action on the part of the profligate consumers, the gross producers of toxic and hazardous materials, and the exploiters of resources for profit who take no responsibility for the devastation they leave behind. Women's roles in the domestic economy, and the thriftiness with which they often must manage that economy, have accustomed them to the important ecological principle of parsimony: nurture what is there, recycle what is used, and avoid the production of toxic and hazardous wastes. As Vandana Shiva, a renowned Indian scientist, expresses it:

> Austerity in our culture used to be defined as living lightly on the earth, not hurting others, not living in a way that you must deprive others of their rights. Austerity today, in World Bank language, is a program to make nature and the poor pay more so that the rich can stay rich. . . . I have talked to tribals who are destroying forests in central India. Sal is a tree, it is a tree they worship, it is sacred to them, it is their mother, and they have tears in their eyes when they turn round and say that their mother is going to be killed by someone who is going to come and cut that tree, and the children are starving in the meantime because of the sal trees they have cut. The most irreversible destruction is that of destroying the cultural mechanisms that protect themselves and protect nature. Once these are lost where do we turn to for people who really know how to walk lightly on this earth?[6]

Finally, women are reluctant to accept solutions that they have had no part in devising, especially solutions that seek to manipulate a presumed but nonexistent domestic labor surplus in the name of the public good.

The Moral Dimensions of Policy

Women's perspectives on the issues of the environment and population control are influenced by the moral dimensions of the debate. Three moral issues in particular are of concern. One has to do with poverty as an affront to human justice. The second rejects the racial, eugenicist, and antilibertarian implications of population control advocacy. The third more directly challenges the assumed right of others to control women's fertility and sexuality in the common interest.

Poverty and Human Justice

Whereas the scale of inequity has become deeply embedded in global economic relations, international mechanisms for creating more effective links between economic growth and human development have not evolved. For example, immigration laws prevent the poor, who largely have only their labor to sell, from seeking the highest return on their labor through migration. The International Monetary Fund is not allowed to create and distribute liquidity among its members. No progressive income tax and expenditure policies allow the transfer of income and opportunities to those countries where they are needed. In brief, policymaking remains locked into considerations of short-term national advantage.

Most developing countries are not able to provide adequate safety nets for the vulnerable. Sweden, in contrast, until recently channelled about 30 percent of its national income to the poor, largely via income tax redistribution and social safety nets; in the United States, this figure is about 15 percent. Most developing countries, with larger populations and smaller budgets, channel between 5 and 15 percent of their national income to the poor. The only safety nets in place are food aid, official developmental assistance, non-government organizations, and charity, which are wholly inadequate to the scale of need.

The 24 leading industrialized countries together channel about 25 percent of their combined national incomes to meet the needs of the poorest and most vulnerable people in their own countries (including the 100 million people who fall below poverty line incomes of around $5000 a year). Their combined aid contribution to the needs of the 1 billion or so who are counted as the poorest of the poor in the Third World is approximately one-third of 1 percent of their combined national incomes.

Further, the flow of aid is often unrelated to the level of poverty. The 10 countries that together have more than 70 percent of the world's poorest people receive only about one-fourth of global aid. Much of the aid is ineffective in terms of alleviating poverty: the benefits of growth in national economies do not necessarily trickle down to the poorest. There are a few, but still far too few, international and national institutions that directly seek to increase the access of the poor to productive opportunities and credit.

At the same time, by the early 1990s, the world was spending more than $800 billion a year on the military and security. Furthermore, Third World countries with high military and security expenditures receive two times as much in aid as moderate spenders and four times as much as low spenders. Defense and security activities are large generators of pollutant gases, toxic chemicals, and other hazardous wastes and highly destructive of local environments.

These misallocations of resources and investment are attributable in part to the patriarchal views of the world held by conventional economists. It is a world that counts weapons of destruction as economically productive and women's domestic work as economically valueless. It is a world governed by the public decisions of men who choose to solve problems by force. It is a world in which women and children form the majority of the poor, the displaced, and the hungry. Such a world is not sustainable. The lack of global safety nets for the poor on the one hand and the gross expenditures on military and security matters on the other defy basic human justice, and the largest portion of those affected are women and children. The declaration of the Women's World Congress for a Healthy Planet submitted to the-development-related agenda (Agenda 21) of the United Nations Conference on the Environment and Development (UNCED) held in Rio de Janeiro in 1992 drew special attention to these links. The conference organizers chose to rule out discussion of the question of military and defense expenditures.

Population and the Controlistas

Those who advocate strong population control as the essential and key condition for sustaining the environment have become known as *controlistas.* Controlistas include many of the world's best-funded and most influential environmental agencies. Their arguments typically are based on simple arithmetic. The arithmetic suggests that, if rates of economic activity and incomes in poor countries were to rise significantly, the proportionately huge numbers of people in nonindustrialized countries would soon generate globally significant pollutants far in excess of the people of the already industrialized countries. Because economic growth is essential for poor countries, the only solution, in this line of argument, is to restrict population growth in poor countries. Erlich[7] has formulated the relationship as follows:

$$\frac{pollution}{area} = \frac{people}{area} \times \frac{economic\ production}{people} \times \frac{pollution}{economic\ production}$$

Poor countries are left to choose between a higher standard of living for a much reduced population or continued self-defeating population growth and environmental destruction until rising mortality brings population and economic well-being into balance. Aggressive fertility control is thus posited in the national self-interest of poor countries and the humane alternative to increasing misery and poverty.

Advocacy based on this line of analysis does not consider that industrialized countries contribute to global environmental change through consumption and waste generation. It assumes that current levels of consumption and emission in industrialized countries can continue unchecked. It ignores the empirical evidence that the relationship between population, area, and pollution is nonlinear and variable and is not determined, uniform, or stable. It is politically naive, setting the interests of the South against those of the North. It is implicitly racist in its operational consequences. It is eugenicist in its presumption that the lives of the poor are worth less than those of the better-off. It is totalitarian in its implications for human rights and specifically inimical to women's reproductive rights.

Others develop the controlistas' argument to suggest that the environmental crisis has been generated not by human carelessness but by human caring, which has allowed more people to survive. For example, Jonathan

Stone, Professor of Anatomy at the University of Sydney, expresses the view that advances in medicine and agricultural science have allowed too many people to survive as follows: "The view common to religious and humanist traditions, that human life is sacred and good, will soon be challenged by the biological reality that human life is destroying the ecology of the Earth, that we humans are a plague."[8]

Maurice King, a renowned pediatrician, recently upbraided the United Nations Children's Fund (UNICEF) for "premature investment" in keeping children alive and thus increasing the world's population.[9] These views are pervasive but wrong. One of the most powerful influences on voluntary restraint of fertility is parents' assurance that their children will survive. High mortality sustains high fertility; conversely, low infant mortality promotes low fertility.

Calls for restricting the number of children to 2.1 per woman to achieve global population stabilization are being freely advanced at scientific congresses around the world.[10] The World Bank lends its authority to the argument by urging that the number of people be brought into balance with the availability of natural resources.[11] The argument ends inevitably in calls for induced and involuntary population control, thus setting up the right of the strong and powerful to control the intimate decisions of the poor and vulnerable. It specifically ignores the gender dimensions of sexual power by which men control women's sexuality and fertility. Further, by formulating the necessity in terms of controlling women's fertility, it absolves men from responsibility for the outcome of their sexual behavior.

Women's Fertility and Family Planning

Much of the current argument surrounding the operational consequences of the controlista perspective has deep roots in nineteenth-century European history. The family planning movement gained credence amidst fear that rapid population growth, especially among the poor, posed a threat to order and welfare. Just as the emerging discipline of economics seemed to promise the possibility of prudent management of national progress, fertility control through contraception seemed to offer scope for prudent management of individual and social welfare. Information and services targeted at the poor, in the name of objectives identified by elites and held to be in the interests of society as a whole, appeared for the first time to be within technical grasp.

More positively, the nineteenth century also brought public recognition of women's sexuality, the idea of voluntary motherhood (largely to protect women's health), and the right of couples to control their fertility through the use of contraceptive devices. Opponents raised fears that information, education, and services would destroy family life and encourage promiscuity and prostitution. Religious objections to the willful prevention of conception and to pregnancy termination were also raised. The pioneers such as Margaret Sanger and Marie Stopes countered with more radical advocacy of women's right to manage safely their own sexuality and fertility. In order to secure the freedom to offer information and services, however, the nascent family planning movement had to become broader based among the medical profession and to win the neutrality if not the acceptance of moral and religious conservatives. Contraceptive services became clinic-centered and fell under the control of the health care establishment. With greater emphasis on family planning as an aid to safe motherhood, rather than on contraception as an aid for the safe management of sexuality, control of women's fertility became the main focus. The right of women to manage their own fertility and sexuality was downplayed.

During the years between the First and Second World Wars, renewed questions were raised, particularly in the United States, about the differential birth rates among the wealthy, the middle classes, and the poor. A case was made for the promotion of larger family size among the middle and upper classes in the interests of maintaining population quality and, hence, it was argued, industrial leadership. It gained wide currency and lingered on through the 1930s and 1940s, placing family planning practitioners on the defensive. After the Second World War, the baby boom muted concern for population quality in the United States and Europe, while public support for selective fertility control disappeared in light of Nazi atrocities and eugenicist experiments.

At the same time, however, there was renewed interest in the relationship between population growth and economic progress. Demographic studies and economic analysis seemed to show the importance of moderating the rate of increase in population, in order to allow time for economic growth to take off, and for early gains to accumulate as the basis for further growth. An increasing number of voluntary agencies began to promote or offer family planning information and services, domestically and internationally. By the late 1960s, family planning was firmly established as a central component of private and official international developmental assistance.

During the 1970s and 1980s the role of high rates of population growth as an impediment to economic progress once again came under question, and moral conservatism and religious fundamentalism reasserted themselves in debates on contraception and fertility control. Funding for family planning services and contraceptives decreased, and the presumed impact on population growth of family planning services and contraceptive use was challenged. In light of environmental concerns, however, the debate has swung around again to focus on fertility control rather than on maternal health or safe sex rationales for contraceptive services.

As far as many women are concerned, the fundamental problem is that women have been treated throughout as instrumental to the achievement of the goals of others. This is not to say that women have not benefitted from access to family planning services nor that women's interests and the public interest never coincide. Nonetheless, the right of women to manage their own sexuality and fertility safely has been subordinated and subsumed. Women's own views and priorities have been treated as micro variables in a debate that has been conducted largely in terms of macro level concerns.

The views of women's health advocates on these issues are clear but complex. Improvements in the efficacy and range of contraceptives, as well as their wider availability and accessibility, are seen as powerful tools in the liberation of women from patriarchal control, an important step in giving women control over their own fertility and as a potential opportunity for opening dialogue with population planners and the medical profession on wider issues of reproductive health.

However, women's health advocates also view modern contraceptive technologies, and the claims for their safety and efficacy, somewhat differently than does the medical profession. Contraceptives are always used in a context. The quality of clinical care, the degree of privacy and hygiene in the home, the nature of the woman's relationship with her partner, the degree to which a woman's concern to protect her sexuality or fertility is uppermost at a particular time, as well as other factors, all affect a woman's assessment of a contraceptive's effectiveness, safety, and appropriateness. Where she has neither information nor choice, contraception can be experienced as burdensome, threatening to her health, and coercive.

Many people also are concerned about the fact that men's responsibility for safe sex and fertility management is neglected. Women typically accept the health risks and burdens of contraception, because men can be irresponsible and uncooperative partners. Yet fertility reduction on the scale demanded by the controlistas cannot be achieved by better management of only female fertility. Important questions of gender relations and power are involved, which must be addressed by broader support for men to take responsibility for the consequences of their sexual behavior and for women's development. As the United Nations Population Fund stresses, the "extent to which women are free to make decisions affecting their lives may be the key to the future, not only of poor countries but of the richer ones too."[12]

Women's health advocates and feminists are asking additional questions with respect to the new reproductive technology. Many are disturbed that women's right and capacity to manage their own fertility is being subsumed in the biomedical management of fertility. Scientists are developing techniques to test embryonic cells, fertilized *in vitro*, for serious genetic disorders before they are implanted in a woman's uterus. They expect to be able to extend the list of diseases that can be identified by new genetic tests to include such health risks as susceptibility to high blood pressure and biological traits, such as eye color and sex. Such work opens up new eugenic possibilities. As the misuse of amniocentesis in countries such as India has shown, in societies with strong preferences for sons, the likelihood of abuse is high.

Others are asking comparable questions with regard to newly available contraceptive techniques such as the surgically implanted hormonal device Norplant. In the United States, the *Philadelphia Inquirer* ran an editorial titled "Poverty and Norplant—Can Contraception Reduce the Underclass?"[13] The *Inquirer* suggested that, because Norplant is a contraceptive requiring surgical removal and lasts 5 years, the welfare burden in the United States resulting from high fertility among the underclass might be reduced by providing incentives to poor women and teenagers to accept Norplant implants. The outcry from representatives of the black community and others has been condemned as "liberal fascism."[14] A radio talk show host apparently threw in for good measure the suggestion that all girls should receive N)rplant on reaching puberty, while others have suggested that the judiciary impose compulsory implants on women convicted of crimes such as child abuse.[15] Some international family planners have hailed Norplant "as a dream method for birth control programs."[16]

Sheldon Segal, who has been involved in the development of Norplant for decades, writes, "Those who suggest using Norplant for involuntary or coercive sterilization or birth control will find me leading the opposition. Our purpose in improving contraceptive technology is to enrich the quality of human life. Using Norplant, in this country or abroad, to toss aside rights and trample human dignity would be an intolerable perversion."[17]

Guarding the Moral Boundary

The compassionate response to the injustices that divide the world is to assert an ethic of responsibility and care, one that is sensitive to context and encompasses concrete relationships and values. Such an ethic focuses on nurturance, avoidance of harm, connectedness, and interdependence. It rejects policies that lead to consequences for others that would be unacceptable for the policymakers themselves. It rejects policies formulated solely on the basis of universalistic and abstract criteria by which a small and largely male elite seeks to determine the common good.

The social side of being human is constituted in terms of the concrete emotional relations of attachment and caring for children. By bringing that experience into the debate, women seek to avoid the tyranny of universalistic moral judgments about what is best for others. Concerned women and men together are asking for a new dialogue, a conscious engagement in a process of discovery of a mature morality to guide the difficult choices facing the world's people. The world cannot survive on difference and separation.

Nullis in Verba, or Don't Take Anyone's Word for It

Do We Know What's Going On?

The founding fathers of the Royal Society of London, one of the world's first scientific societies, took as their motto the Latin tag, *Nullis in Verba*. The motto translates roughly as "don't take anyone's word for it."[1] It is a most appropriate motto to keep in mind when analyzing what is happening to the environment.

If the debate on population control and environmental matters is at times bitter, vitriolic, or confrontational, it is partly because people do not agree about what is going on. Often there is no agreement on what to measure, how to measure it, or how to interpret what has been observed. Or, confronted by a mass of disordered information encompassing human, biological, and physical phenomena from many different fields, people lack a common language or framework for discussion. Misuse and abuse of information is common. The findings of local research studies, which typically yield wide-ranging estimates of the scale and magnitude of a problem, are lumped together to form national or even global trends, or the most dramatic is used as a proxy for the whole, yielding highly exaggerated claims.

Policymakers are uncertain about what constitutes quality in decision making when the information base is inadequate or disputed. Others worry that lack of or imperfect evidence for the potential for harm might nonetheless expose society to some as yet unforeseen hazard. Scientists worry that there is an inadequate basis for estimating the probability of risks that human society has never before experienced. Unsubstantiated beliefs, differences over the assessment of hazard and risk, and fuzzy concepts that allow wide interpretation all contribute to a debate in which forceful advocacy clouds more nuanced understanding. The larger the canvas, the bolder the colors; the subtle coloring that brings out the intricate and varied patterns of people's interaction with the environment is masked.

Further, developmental, population control, and environmental problems are complex in the general meaning that there seem to be many pieces of densely related data that need to be put together to make a complete picture. More important, they are complex because they are problems that, legitimately and rationally, may be viewed from different perspectives, yet their solution often demands that individual people act together. Corporate action demands shared perception, but shared perception does not emerge mechanistically from the logic of situations; it is shaped by the meaning people and their societies give to the world and to the flux of ideas and events within it.

A Closer Look at the Data

Many of the dramatic, even apocalyptic statements that are promoted and believed are not justified by the available data. Certainly, serious problems exist that need urgent attention. There are problems that, even if we do not know exactly what is going on, are serious enough to warrant corrective and remedial effort, even while further research and theorizing take place. None of these justifies the panic and loss of faith in human creativity that lead to policies of coercive control in the name of common survival. The development of a shared but critical understanding of the available evidence is an important step in building a sense of common purpose.

The Case of Nigerian Population Data

Some unsubstantiated beliefs arise from population census and survey data. The data for some developing countries are reliable and up to date; for others, they are much less so. Unfortunately, the larger the population base, the less accurate the data tend to be. China's population counts, for example, probably accurately capture the steep decline in fertility, yet demographers also reckon there is substantial undercounting of females, given the combination of government incentives and sanctions in favor of one-child families and the strong cultural preference for male children. Data from large, populous but poor countries, however, have a disproportionate influence on estimates of regional and global population size and rates of growth.

For example, in the mid-1980s Nigeria was estimated by the United Nations development agencies to have a population of 100 million people. The World Bank's 1991 estimate put the total at around 120 million.[2] The 1992 Nigerian census recorded a total of 88.5 million; some 30 to 35 million people appear to have been "lost" between 1991 and 1992. The differences in the totals are large enough to affect radically the calculations of important relationships, such as population densities and pressure on the land, as well as rates of population growth.

Demographers at the National Institute of Social and Economic Research in Ibadan regard the latest census figures as in the ballpark, subject to further statistical tests as disaggregated age and sex figures become available. They reason that the 1961–1962 sample census data, which were suppressed in favor of what are now generally acknowledged to be the wildly inflated 1963 census data (which were subsequently cancelled), did represent a fairly accurate baseline. The baseline data, if extrapolated, would yield a figure in the range of the totals recorded in the 1992 census.

As another example, consider the case of the 1991 census figures for India. India rightly prides itself on its unbroken series of decennial censuses beginning in 1881. It has been a matter of concern for the central government that, since the beginning of the century, the censuses have shown that the proportion of females to males in the population has been decreasing. The 1981 census seemed to give some ground for hope that the trend was reversing, but according to the 1991 census data, the overall ratio again has declined, to 929 females per 1000 males, and especially in the large Hindi-speaking states, the ratio appears to have declined precipitously.

Although there are reasons to think that measures taken in recent years to improve the status of women in India are having a positive effect, there are also grounds for thinking that the declining sex ratio in such states as Uttar Pradesh and Bihar record only too accurately the real condition of women's lives and the extent of discrimination against them. There are also grounds for arguing that there might have been substantial undercounting of women and girls in the 1991 census in the states that showed the steepest declines in the sex ratio. In fact, on the basis of the statistics alone, no one can be absolutely certain where the truth of the matter lies.

Disputed Risk Assessment

It is hazardous to extend uncritically the level of risk accepted by one scientific discipline to other domains. The standards incorporate different judgments about what constitutes acceptable risk. Those whose lives are directly affected by a problem typically have different perceptions of risk than those who study a problem from the outside. Further, the concepts of risk and hazard are often fused, adding to the confusion. Strictly speaking, an estimate of hazard defines the potential for harm, while an estimate of risk defines the probability that harm will in fact occur. There is great danger in population control and environmental debates that the two concepts, and the particular way in which they are being used, are not clarified. For example, Stephen Schneider, head of Interdisciplinary Climate Systems at the National Center for Atmospheric Research in Boulder, Colorado, reports on an apparently irreconcilable difference between himself and Andrew Solow, a statistician from Woods Hole Oceanographic Institute.[3] Their difference centers on estimates of the probability that the next century will be 2°C or more warmer than this century. Schneider testified to the House of Representatives that he thought the probability "high," and Solow testified that he thought the probability "low." Both were looking at the same data. Further discussion between them revealed that Schneider considered a 50 percent chance to be a high probability, whereas Solow considered a 50 percent chance to be a low probability, a 95 percent chance to be a moderate probability, and only a 99 percent chance to be a high probability.

Risk Assessment and Reproductive Tract Infection

Gender-biased assumptions also color assessments of hazard and risk. The case of reproductive tract infection (RTI) is intimately related to the acceptance and effectiveness of family planning programs. Most family planning programs and mother and child clinics in developing countries do not offer services related to the diagnosis and treatment of infection. It is a common belief that the risk of dying in pregnancy far outweighs the risks of neglecting reproductive tract infections and justifies the priority given to maternal rather than reproductive health services.[4] According to UNFPA data, the risks of maternal death in developing countries indeed are unacceptably high: In Africa, one of every 21 women dies as a result of pregnancy or childbirth, one in 38 in South Asia, and one in 90 in Latin America.

In 1988, Judith Wasserheit, then Chief of the Sexually Transmitted Disease Branch at the Atlanta Centers for Disease Control, surveyed the data relating to reproductive tract infection among men and women in developing countries. A more general version written by Dixon-Mueller and Wasserheit concluded: "in allocating scarce human and financial health care resources to developing countries, policymakers, program planners, and international donor agencies have generally given low priority to RTIs. In part this is because of the mistaken belief that RTIs are not fatal, that they are too expensive and too complicated to treat, and that in most countries they affect only small and specialized segments of sexually active adults such as prostitutes. Each of these assumptions, however, can be challenged."[5]

First, the prevalence of reproductive tract infections among the general population is much higher than is generally believed. Data from Africa, Asia, and Latin America relating to family planning clients, gynecology clients, women giving birth in clinic settings, and community-based surveys (i.e., not including clients of sexually transmitted disease clinics or those with acute pelvic inflammatory disease), for example, yield gonorrhoea prevalence rates ranging from 7 to 66 percent (median, 24 percent) among high-risk patients, and 0.3 to 40 percent (median, 6 percent) among low-risk patients.[6]

The consequences of gonorrheal infection in women and the likelihood of complications among infected women[7] can be summarized as:

Upper tract infection, if untreated	10%–40%
HIV transmission, possible increased risk	2- to 9-fold
Miscarriage or stillbirth	5%–40%
Fetal death	15%–67%
Congenital infection of infant	30%–45%

Upper tract infection in turn can lead to pelvic inflammatory disease and infertility, ectopic pregnancy, chronic pelvic pain, and to low birth weight or premature delivery.

These are not trivial inconveniences, nor are they tragedies only for individual women: their potential for harm is much wider. Ectopic pregnancy, if undiagnosed, is a leading cause of maternal death. Chronic pelvic pain is disabling to the point that women can no longer carry out their work effectively, leading to loss of welfare and care for the family as a whole. Low birth weight and premature delivery lead to higher rates of infant death, up to 15 to 67 percent, some three to five times the rate for uninfected mothers. High rates of infant death in turn maintain people's need and desire to have more children. As Oladipo Ladipo, a leading Nigerian obstetrician and gynecologist, has stressed, infertility is a "total disaster" in any society in which a woman's status is expressed largely in terms of her ability to bear healthy children. Typically, a woman's infertility leads to rejection by her partner, social ostracism, and loss of access to land or other productive resources with which to support herself and any previous children. It often leaves little means to a livelihood other than prostitution and, thus, promotes the spread of infection.

The harm spills over into other policy areas. Undiagnosed infections may cause problems in the use of contraceptives, which women may attribute to the contraceptive itself. The belief that contraceptives are a cause of infection is widespread among women and a major reason why they do not continue using the technology. According to two surveys reported by the UNFPA in the State of the World Population 1992, 50 percent of Filipino women believed the pill causes sterility. Thirty-one per cent of women cited fear of side effects and dislike of methods known as their main reasons for not using contraceptives in the 1988–1989 Third National Survey in India.

Assessing Impacts and Costs

As in other areas of life, although it might become accepted that the hazard and risk associated with reproductive tract infections is high, this alone does not make the case for priority attention in the allocation of public resources. Two American public health economists, M. Over and P. Piot, estimated the public health significance of RTIs compared to other diseases.[8] They developed the concept of age-adjusted "healthy life years lost" (HLYL) per person to estimate that sexually transmitted diseases (HIV, syphilis, chancroid, chlamydia, and gonorrhoea) are responsible for approximately 15 percent of the burden of disease in urban areas with high prevalence of sexually transmitted diseases (defined as greater than 5 percent prevalence of gonorrhoea among sexually active adults or greater than 10 percent of seroprevalence of syphilis among pregnant women). Using the HLYL measure, they estimate that sexually transmitted diseases rank third after measles and malaria among common diseases in developing countries in terms of their socioeconomic impact. If the estimate is restricted to the economically productive period of a person's life, sexually transmitted diseases rank second only to measles in terms of their impact on health.

The cost-effectiveness of treating reproductive tract infections compared with other diseases also appears to be high. Schulz et al. estimated the cost of immunizing children against childhood diseases compared with the cost of treating common reproductive tract infections. They found that in the Gambia, for example, the costs (in 1990–1991 prices) of immunization in terms of "childhood death prevented" were measles, $40.83; pertussis, $99.85; and neonatal tetanus, $152.53. The direct costs per child for full immunization were $5 to $15. Data from a number of countries suggested in comparison that $1.40 "would avert one case of gonoccal opthalmia neonatorum [which results in blindness if untreated] and $12 would avert an adverse outcome associated with syphilis during pregnancy."[9]

A Closer Look at Fuzzy Concepts

The debate about sustainable development, the environment, and population issues is not only plagued by disputes over the facts, assessments of hazard and risk, and the cost-effectiveness of alternative interventions. The debate suffers from a remarkable lack of clarity about key concepts. The term *development* is itself far from clear, let alone such concepts as sustainability. The particular case of the term *desertification* illustrates the more general problem.

The Case of Desertification

In 1987, the United Nations' Desertification Control Program Activity Center estimated that 35 percent of the earth's land surface was desertified. This figure recurs in alarmist texts as an indicator of the irreversible degradation of the world's drylands as the result of human activity. In its original context, however, the figure unambiguously refers to the entire arid region of the world, at least half of which is classified as quite arid and not in danger: it is already too arid for any form of agricultural or pastoral use and has been so for thousands of years. The World Resources Institute's 1990 estimate in *The State of the World's Resources* was more moderately expressed: "By some estimates, 10 percent of the land surface of the planet has been transformed by human activities from forest and rangelands into desert; as much as 25 percent more is at risk."

Even though cautiously worded, the WRI's estimate hides substantial controversy over what exactly desertification might be, whether it is advancing or not, where it might be occurring, and what causes it. Current orthodoxy favors the view that naturally dry areas are undergoing extensive transformation through both anthropogenic and biological and physical change, and that these changes are degenerative, leading to lower levels of natural productivity. These views have been given substantial political currency through the pleas for action to combat desertification by African governments at the 1992 United Nations Conference on the Environment and Development.

Populist versions articulate the orthodoxy in terms of an advancing desert. Whether or not the changes are irreversible depends mainly on two things: the specific biological and physical trends that are beyond human control and that occur irrespective of human activity and the willingness of governments, and the people who live in such areas, to devote sufficient time, capital, and effort to restoring degraded landscapes and easing the pressures that led to degradation in the first place.

Desertification as Degenerative Change

Some writers have used the term *desertification* to include any area undergoing degenerative change, including water-logged irrigated areas. The World Bank's estimate that more than a third of irrigated land in India and a quarter in Pakistan are affected by waterlogging and salinity often is included in figures of desertified land. Used in this sense, the term refers to processes that tend to turn any natural resource into wasteland, recalling the original Egyptian hieroglyph from which the word *desert* is derived, meaning abandoned or forsaken.

In population control and environmental debates, the focus of concern invariably turns to degenerative change in developing countries, yet there are grounds for arguing that the debate is out of focus. The most recent global assessment of soil degradation sponsored by the United Nations Environment Program estimates that more than 3 billion acres of land, or 11 percent of the earth's vegetated surface, have undergone moderate or worse soil degradation over the past 45 years as a result of human activity.[10] The most prevalent cause of land degradation was found to be overgrazing, accounting for 35 percent of all degraded land. Destructive agricultural practices were found to account for 28 percent of total land degradation, with two-thirds of the damage occurring in the United States.

Desertification in Relation to Poverty

A related and more generally accepted orthodoxy is that the world's drylands increasingly are being put to uses to which they are inherently unsuited, under pressure of increasing poverty and population growth. A study by Kates and Haarmann,[11] however, shows that considerable definitional difficulties exist, even at the macro level, in determining the extent of either drylands or poverty, let alone establishing the degree of overlap between drylands and grasslands as environments where poor people live. Different authors have enumerated poverty, drylands, and grasslands in different ways. For example, the "poor" can be counted in terms of income, food availability, or nutrition status as absolute measures or in relation to other concepts such as "energy intake deficient for maintenance" or hunger. Kates and Haarmann show that the numbers of poor in sub-Saharan Africa may be counted as 120 million ("extremely poor"), 156 million ("poorest of the poor"), 325 million ("living in absolute poverty"), 141 million ("energy deficient for maintenance"), or 239 million ("energy deficient for work"), depending on the data source and definitions used.

Nonetheless, statistical data based on local studies indicate that: (a) the incidence of dryland environments and poverty are closely associated; (b) the concentration of drylands is highest in the least developed countries (78 percent of savanna grasslands are located in low-income countries; low-income countries together constitute about half the total area of all developing countries); and (c) the proportion of the poor (variously categorized, and excluding China) in the total population is highest in sub-Saharan Africa, which contains a disproportionate share of the world's drylands and grasslands. Even these gross associations, however, remain suggestive rather than certainties. The United Nations and FAO desertification data and maps for Africa in particular are known to be inaccurate and, to some disputed extent, based in part on estimates, difficult-to-interpret satellite images, and patchy verification on the ground. Counting the poor is a similarly contentious exercise.

Desertification and the Chain of Causality

It is remarkably difficult to pin down any single, specific chain of causality when discussing desertification. The heart of the matter is that rainfall in dry areas is highly variable in amount among years. Many but not all dry areas are also areas of low soil fertility; vegetative growth responds accordingly. As Farouk El-Baz, former adviser to Egyptian President Anwar Sadat and Director of the Smithsonian Institute's Center for Earth and Planetary Studies, has persuasively argued, sustainable exploitation of dry areas, as herders and dryland farmers well know, requires sensitive adjustments to the fluctuating vegetative cycle and availability of water. The relationship between the numbers of people and the health of the ecosystem can approximate stability only where water can be conserved and products can be stored or traded to even out the fat years and lean years.

Anything that weakens or disrupts people's capacity to respond flexibly to the vagaries of dryland conditions tends toward environmental degradation. Kates and Haarmann identify from case studies three typical sequences of displacement, division, and degradation:

1. Displacement and disruption of proven coping mechanisms, that is, the relationships and structures that maintain livelihoods through fat and lean years, as a consequence of activities that may, for example, reduce the extent of grazing land or access to water, change price relations or labor availability, or undermine community and family management and leadership.

2. Displacement from areas of higher productivity to areas of lower inherent productivity, with subsequent inappropriate or excessive use of resources, as a result of changes in the allocation of resources among potentially competitive groups.

3. Degradation and displacement as a result of extreme climatic events, with potential for recovery of assets and income impaired by 1 and 2, above.

Whereas it is useful to sort and group experience as a way of gaining insight into patterns and processes, it must be recognized that many combinations of events and pressures stimulate the sequences identified. Population growth and population densities may be part of the picture, but only a part, and their precise contribution is specific and cannot be generalized.

Certainly in some regions the area classified as arid or semiarid can be shown to advance over the period of a few decades or longer, but long time series data and satellite images also show areas of retreat in accordance with long-term oscillations in rainfall patterns. Certainly in particular pastoral locations evidence exists of overgrazing, to which increases in the number of humans and livestock contribute. However, changes in the productivity of grasslands typically occur around settlements and water points and in consequence of changes in boundaries, not as a general phenomenon in relation to overall human population densities or rates of population growth. These changes can be, but are not necessarily, degenerative or irreversible.

Certainly population pressure can lead cultivators to move into areas of more marginal rainfall, but they do so under specific conditions of economic history and current developmental policy; the incursion is not inevitable. Indeed, the combined effects of drought, war, changes in land use, and the migration of men leave an increasing number of arid areas in sub-Saharan Africa depopulated. Male herders, followed by women and children, move to urban areas or settle and diversify away from extensive grazing into livestock farming on the margins of cultivated areas.

In arid areas where high male migration is taking place, conservation efforts can make matters worse rather than better. Antidesertification measures can impose additional and disproportionate burdens on the women who are left behind, as they are expected to contribute more of their labor time to such activities as carting stones and watering trees. The efforts they make to hold back "the disappearing earth, men and water"[12] can incur high opportunity costs, reducing household welfare overall, while doing nothing to change the underlying gender inequities.

In fact, gender relations, of all social changes, have proved to be the least responsive to the changing conditions of drylands and savannahs. Developmental activities have tended to reinforce existing gender inequities, as the example of cattle fodder banks illustrates. Scientists expected that the fodder grown in specially planted pastures along the Niger river in West Africa would be managed as a fodder bank, grazed by pregnant and lactating cows to increase milk production through the dry season. Cattle keepers, however, kept the pastures free from grazing until late in the dry season, reserved the grazing land for weak or sick animals, and then grazed the entire herd on the remaining pasture at the end of the dry season. Subsequent studies revealed that the farmers' strategy halved normal cow and calf mortality. It also increased the returns on animal sales rather than milk sales. Men control cattle and grazing while women have the right to the income from milk sales. Men bought the inputs for the fodder banks from cattle sales; feeding cows to increase milk sales was not a high priority for them.[13]

Macro, Meso, Micro, Wrong: Spatial Dimensions of the Debate

The question of spatial scale is another key element in sustainable development that is poorly understood. Growing evidence shows that many natural resource systems are sensitive to scale. That is to say, demand can no longer be met on the basis of the resources that are locally available; local resource use must be linked to larger systems of survival if degenerative change is not to occur. The historically familiar ways in which particular societies in the past have kept within, or extended, the threshold available to them include war, migration, technological innovation, intensification of land use, trade, and modification of the social rules governing sexual behavior and procreation.

The problems are that (a) the scale of demand has become so large that such historic means of accommodation and adjustment are near exhaustion as the means for survival of particular societies (there is no larger system of survival than the earth itself); and (b) change in the earth's biological and physical systems brought about by excessive demand on natural resources threatens the survival of all societies, not just the ones that are reaching their local thresholds.

Questionable Assumptions Concerning Scale Effects

Many sociological phenomena have nonlinear scale effects, that is, the effects do not increase directly in line with the scale of interaction. Mainstream developmental analysis of economic growth, however, tends to assume linearity as well as equilibrium and uniformity of rate. That is to say, the process of scale-sensitive transformation is held to occur more or less smoothly at a steady pace along a path from one equilibrium state to another. For example, the demand for housing does not grow smoothly over time in proportion to the increase in population. Demand surges ahead when prices seem attractive in relation to the price of other goods; demand may drop sharply in response to tax changes or employment prospects. Demand can be affected independently by changes in the formation of families and by expectations about home ownership (most Germans, for example, expect to live in rented homes). The assumption of equilibrium states is especially pervasive: the debate is littered with references to the need to bring the global population and the environment into balance.

Further, large-scale phenomena are explained as the linked series of innumerable small changes. The old nursery rhyme begins with the warning that for the loss of a nail the horseshoe was lost, and for the loss of the shoe the horse was lost, and so on to the loss of the battle, all for the sake of a horseshoe nail. Linear metaphors of a chain of cause and effect, of one small thing leading smoothly to large outcomes, are deeply embedded in our thinking. A hierarchy of relationships and a hierarchy of scale are implied. Linear metaphors of how the world works are not just intellectual tools; they often serve as normative guides to the creation of institutional relationships and practice.

Yet there is little in the historical record to validate assumptions of uniformity and equilibrium. On the contrary, the historical record suggests that societies as a whole can never be described as being in a state of long-term equilibrium with their environment. The causal pathways linking the events of daily domestic life to broad societal change are really not known in any predictive sense.

Significant Implications of Scale Effects

Complex questions of scale give rise to consideration of how humankind organizes its economic relations to form a dynamic whole. People have developed unprecedented knowledge, power, and the capacity to manage, direct, and concentrate economic resources, in the process apparently shifting upwards the level at which management of scale effects is necessary and possible.

For instance, by controlling variability and reducing complexity in natural systems throughout the world, the reliability of agricultural production has increased. It is by no means obvious, however, what the implications are in terms of sustainability. Can reliability be equated with resilience over the longer term? Recorded history shows previous cycles of simplification, concentration, and dominance, such as the great irrigation civilizations of the Tigris and Euphrates basins or the Pharaonic empires of the Nile, but the gains have not been sustained. Modern technologies and command of physical matter allow people to extend control over biological and physical resources in a truly global economy. No one knows, however, if this adds to or subtracts from the stability and resilience of organized human society.

These reflections are not trivial. On the one hand, population polemicists call for global population control on the presumption that intervention at the global level is the decisive point of leverage. On the other hand, innumerable local initiatives operate on the presumption that if problems are dealt with on the local level, global problems will go away.

Global policies in the end must translate into lower level decision making and behavior change that are sensitive to context. In the case of population control issues, policies must address one of the most intimate and sensitive spheres of human behavior. It is, moreover, behavior that is embedded in local, not global, circumstances and expectations.

This Year, Next Year, Sometime, Never: Problems of Time

Questions about how relationships change over time are as problematic as questions of scale. Perceptions of how complex interactions change through time are colored by culture. Metaphors of time, in turn, appear to have a profound influence on policies for sustainable development.

For example, one thread in the Judeo-Christian tradition is an understanding of genealogy as the vector of history played out against immanent, stable, natural laws that govern the repeating cycles of life and the oscillations of the seasons and the years. As Ecclesiastes says, "One generation passeth away, and another generation cometh: but the earth abideth forever."[14]

By the middle years of the 19th century, Lyell, Darwin, and others were developing new insight into the deep time of geology.[15] The stratigraphy of rock formations began to be read as the record of time as a cyclical process operating under immanent law, while fossils were read as the tracks of time as an arrow through the geological record, that is, as both the genealogical transmission of inherited characteristics and as the evolution of function in response to changing conditions.

Geological inquiry brought further challenging insights: multicellular life forms emerged comparatively late in the complex physical and chemical evolution of the material world. Within remarkably stable parameters of global temperature and chemistry, geologically abrupt cooling and warming periods have taken place. The history of life has been interrupted by at least a dozen episodes of mass extinction (the cause of which is still debated). The human perception of an enduring earth is in this perspective unduly influenced by the short time period of human existence.

Linking Time and Energy

Further profound but puzzling developments in the meaning and nature of time have been made in the area of quantum dynamics, which links energy to time. The second law of thermodynamics states that the physical organization of energy becomes increasingly disordered through time. Earth scientists, however, who point to phenomena in biological rather than astrophysical time, argue that life on earth, left to itself, manages to balance incoming and outgoing energy so that the disorganization of energy in the earth's systems does not increase through time; order is continually renewed.

It is important to the population control–environmental debate to understand the biological mechanism. The sun is a huge source of high-energy visible light photons. Plants, as they grow, capture and convert this energy through photosynthesis of the photons of visible light, thereby absorbing carbon dioxide. Plants (including trees) then separate the oxygen and carbon, using the carbon to build up their own substance while releasing the separated oxygen. People, in turn, consume the energy needed for their existence as carbon-based food derived from plants and as oxygen. Over their lifetimes people consume no more energy than they emit as heat, excreta, and carbon dioxide. Plants and people thus do not add energy to the earth's system, but they are continually replacing the highly organized energy received from the sun with disorganized energy, which eventually is radiated back into space as heat in the form of infrared photons. The earth is thus in biochemical terms not a closed energy system nor a static one. By radically changing the mix and quantity of plants and people, humankind now has in its power the capacity to influence the energy exchange process.

When social scientists study population and economic data, however, the perception of the link between time and energy again changes. The Brundtland Commission[16] estimated that by the late 1980s, humans had already consumed 40 percent of the energy produced by land-based photosynthesis. The commission further calculated that a sevenfold increase in world economic activity would be needed to give every person alive in 1987 a standard of living equivalent to that of the average American. Such an increase in economic activity would appropriate an even greater percentage of terrestrial photosynthesis. Apocalyptic visions of the future, trading off economic growth and earth system equilibria in terms of population size, appeared inescapable.

Such visions are based on metaphor and cannot be independently verified. Indeed, one of the conclusions to be drawn from these reflections on space, time, and energy is the profound influence that metaphor has in shaping policy response to the challenge of sustainability. Jessica Mathews, Vice President of the World Resources Institute, for instance, implicitly calls upon the Judeo-Christian metaphors in her assertion that achieving sustainable economic growth "will require the remodelling of agriculture, energy use and industrial production after nature's example—their reinvention, in fact. These economic systems must become circular rather than linear."[17]

Women and Metaphors of Change

Women's economic and familial responsibilities place them at the point at which population control and environmental issues meet in daily life. Women have unique roles as mothers in bearing and raising children, distinct, though complementary, to the roles of men as fathers. They are in many countries responsible for preparing food, collecting wood for fuel, fetching water, and cultivating the land for food and other commodities. They trade, brew beer, rear and sell small livestock, and make and sell food products and handicrafts to raise cash.

The distinctiveness of these roles increasingly is recognized in the rhetoric and action of sustainable development. In terms of the impact of their roles in sustainable development, however, women are variously cast in the literature, to use Rocheleau's vivid phrase, as victims, villains, and fixers.[18]

As victims, women are the ones who must walk farther to find fuel, as loggers destroy the forest, and farther for water as the loss of forest cover dries up the streams and wells. They are the ones who, in whole or in part, are responsible for feeding their families and are left to cultivate vulnerable lands as good land is taken into male ownership. Women are the ones whose reproductive health and fertility are threatened by bearing children and by living where waste dumping and industrial pollution have made land cheap and rents low for people who have little money, few jobs, or meager education. They are the ones who become the health providers and teachers of last resort, as family and community care disintegrates under the pressure of poverty and as public services are cut back.

Other analyses identify women as villains because of their child-bearing roles, linked to fertility trends, and because their responsibilities for fuel, water, and agriculture position them as resource consumers. In aggregate, the small individual activities of women have a large impact on the world's water supplies, tree cover, and farmlands. Women also are seen by others as the fixers who will rescue the world from its folly, put an end to poverty, instill peace, reduce population growth, save the environment, and reduce inequality.

Women thus are linked to three contrasting, indeed contradictory, metaphors of change. The labels, notably, do not encompass the relational nature of gender. Women are treated as if they were actors independent of their relationship to men and to the context in which they live. In addition, the labels leave no scope for self-determination, the potential for women to change gender relations and shape the future on their terms. In asking whether we know enough about what is going on to reach for crisis-driven policies, it is well to remember how profoundly the debate is marked by contrasting metaphors and models of the nature of reality.

Food and Agriculture:
Is There Room to Maneuver?

Newspapers feed on predictions of global famine. Influential figures such as Lester Brown of the Worldwatch Institute, Washington, D.C. speak persuasively of the future collapse of agriculture, as poverty, greed, and environmental malpractices despoil the natural productivity of soil, water, and biodiversity. Food supply and hunger are melded in images of an inexorable race in which the finishing line is calamity. Shocking pictures record the fate of thousands of destitute people, mainly women, children, and the old, crippled by hunger and disease. If today's prosperity cannot feed today's people, what hope is there for the future?

The question cannot be answered as it stands. It is necessary first to clarify a series of more basic questions, such as: What is food?

Food, Food Supply, and Food Security

Two fundamental aspects of food underlie the current population control-environmental debates. One concerns food as power, food as a card in international and agrarian politics. Nations no less than individual families have reason to fear the dependency that might result if they can neither produce sufficient food nor command the means to buy as much as they need.

The other aspect concerns food as the means to alleviate hunger. In fact, many of the debates about the world food situation are disguised debates about hunger and the most effective ways to deal with hunger. The confusion between the two begins when it is assumed that hunger will disappear if sufficient grain is produced and traded on world markets.

Framed in these terms, the debate narrows down to two constraints: the biological, physical, and technological constraints to production, specifically to the production of grain, and the efficiency and effectiveness of markets in moving grain between surplus and deficit producers.

The difficulties with this way of posing the problem are (a) only some types of grain enter international markets; (b) not all food is grain;

(c) only a small proportion of the food produced is ever marketed internationally; and (d) access to food is a function not only of supply but also of effective demand. Increasing the supply of food does not in itself necessarily increase the capacity of people who are hungry to acquire food.

Food Is More Than Grain

The focus on grain is reasonable because cereals are the world's most important foodstuffs as a source of energy. They can be stored for long periods of time, and they are a concentrated source of nutrients. To equate food with internationally traded cereals, however, is to miss a large proportion of the local grains, roots, tubers, leaves, animals, insects, fish, tree products, and fungi that are consumed as food and traded in informal markets.

Tef in Ethiopia, grain amaranth in many parts of Latin America, and wild fonio and cram-cram in West Africa are all important components of local consumption and trading incomes. Bananas and plantains are economically the second most important crop in Africa after cassava; 90 percent of them are grown in backyards and consumed and sold locally. Cola nuts are responsible for up to 37 percent of a household's cash income in western Cameroon; shea nuts and processed shea nut butter play a similar role, especially for women, in west Africa. More than 175 of the 200 or so large, wild herbivores in the world have not been domesticated, yet they are an important source of meat. Of all foodstuffs consumed in northern Zambia, dried caterpillars give the highest protein for weight values. Although viewed with disgust by other Zambians, caterpillars are seasonally important dietary and trade items. A 1979 dietary study in Lushoto, Tanzania, found that wild vegetables appear in 32 percent of all meals.[1]

Furthermore, the focus on grain simply ignores the substantial contribution of root crops and tubers. Only potatoes and cassava products are important items in international trade; the remainder are held back because they do not store well and they are bulky. Yet, particularly in Africa, root crops and tubers make a substantial contribution to dietary calories and an important if lesser contribution to protein consumption. The admittedly somewhat shaky data, which are thought to underestimate considerably the true levels of production and consumption, indicate that root crops and tubers are the single most important source of food for the majority of people who live in sub-Saharan Africa. They provide 15 percent of the dietary calories for Africa as a whole. For Nigeria, which is home to about a fifth of the continent's people, the contribution rises to 30 percent, while Zairians derive more than half their calories from root crops and tubers.[2] These examples might seem quaint, but the point is far from trivial; sources of food are many and diverse and range far beyond the limited number that are internationally traded in formal markets.

Food Supply

Comparable fuzziness surrounds the data on food supply. The term itself is not very precise. The FAO defines *supply* at the country level as the total amount of foodstuffs produced in a country, added to the amount imported, adjusted for changes in carryover stocks from one year to the next. This definition excludes all food gathered from the wild and an additional unknown quantity of the hard-to-measure foodstuffs, including roots and tubers and the produce of home gardens.

Supply defined in this way indicates nothing concerning wastage or use. Only in countries such as the United States do marketed grain figures approximate total grain production. In most cases, food supply figures give no indication of the portion remaining for human consumption after wastage, replanting material, livestock feed, and other nonfood uses have been deducted. Yet *supply* is often wrongly equated with *availability as human food*. Once the appropriate deductions have been made, there remains the question of who might have access to the amount available.

Bearing all these cautions in mind, global production of marketed food crops in a favorable weather year currently is estimated to exceed demand by about 20 percent.[3] (Demand is here calculated on the basis of number of people times standard dietary requirements, not as an economic concept.) Developments in agricultural technology have reduced year-to-year variation in output to a considerable extent, to about plus or minus 10 percent.

The global figures hide regional production variations, which are critical to any assessment of supply. Regional production deficits are heightened by the poverty of nations unable to afford to import sufficient food when years of poor rainfall lead to higher prices on world food markets. As a rule of thumb, it is estimated that the price of grains traded on world markets increases by 7 percent when exportable yield drops by 10 percent.

Twenty-one countries are more or less consistently net cereal exporters, but only three countries account for more than 80 percent of all traded cereals: the United States, Canada, and France. The United States alone produces more than three-quarters of the world's traded soybeans and more than half the world's traded maize.

Over the past 10 years eight countries more or less consistently have imported more than 5 million metric tons of cereals a year: the former Soviet Union, Japan, China, the Korean Republic, Egypt, Mexico, Iran, and Italy. Of these, China is by far the most significant: it is already the world's biggest importer of wheat. Nonetheless, by far the majority of countries, for most years, consume mainly what they produce themselves.

Policy decisions and political changes typically are important influences on food supplies. Unfortunately, these influences are often overlooked by polemicists and the media. The FAO's announcement that there had been sharp declines in world cereal output in 1991 compared with 1990, that harvest returns were lower than consumption requirements for 1990-1991, and that carryover stocks would be drawn down to their lowest levels since 1976 led to screaming headlines that a world food crisis was at hand. Yet the sharpest falls in output were in the United States as a result of changes in agricultural policy and in the Soviet Union as a result of political developments.

Stocks of Food

Stocks are not the same as reserves, though the two are often confused. Different countries define stocks in different ways, so it is hardly surprising if there is confusion. Generally speaking, stocks are aggregate cereal surplus, calculated on the basis of last year's carryover stocks, plus the current year's production and imports, minus domestic use and exports. Because the centrally planned economies did not publish information on the level of their carryover stocks, however, and the new regimes are not yet able in every case to make accurate data available, the formulation of a global figure is problematic. Further, because marketing years are not the same everywhere, nor for every type of grain, global carryover stocks are calculated as an average. The average does not represent the actual stocks held at that time.

The United States, Canada, and the European Community are the world's major holders of marketed grain stocks. The stocks are physically held not only by governments but by trading companies, processing firms, cooperatives, and farmers themselves, among others. The level of stocks anyone holds often reflects a mix of both economic and political concerns. In the United States, for example, government-held stocks are released to the international market almost wholly on the basis of political considerations.

Grain Reserves

Cereal stocks are held in considerably higher quantities than cereal reserves. Reserves are held as short-term buffers to meet needs at moments of temporary crisis. Their level generally does not fluctuate in response to economic supply and demand. They are not intended to deal with longer term problems of deficient production or purchasing power. Because the level of reserves is relatively low, it is easy, but misleading, to make an alarmist headline out of them.

Food Aid and Cereal Imports

The major part of food aid shipments consist of cereals. The level of cereal shipments as aid in any one year varies considerably but seems to have little direct connection either with the level of stocks or with need. For instance, during what were supposedly the world food crisis years of 1973–74, cereal aid actually declined and carryover stocks increased.

Trends in food aid and cereal imports often are read as indicators of increasing dependency. However, the concept of dependency in this context simply adds further ambiguity to an already confused picture.

The Middle East and North Africa, sub-Saharan Africa, Latin America, and the Caribbean have roughly tripled their imports of food aid over the period 1974/75–1989/90. Recent changes in the former Soviet bloc and eastern Europe are adding greatly to the current demand for food aid in these areas. Over the same period, 1974–90, sub-Saharan Africa's cereal imports have almost doubled and the Middle East and North Africa's have more than tripled.

Neither the food aid nor the cereal import figures necessarily indicate any increasing dependency. For example, based on World Bank and FAO data for 1989 and 1990, current total grain imports to sub-Saharan Africa amount to just over 13 percent of total cereal production in sub-Saharan Africa, a proportion that has held at roughly the same level throughout the 1980s. If expressed in terms of cereal imports and food aid per person, food imports and food aid overall are negligible. It is mainly in terms of particular African countries' decreasing ability to pay for imports, or persistent political disorder, that the trends give rise to real concern.

The World Food Situation and Food Security

Reference to the "world food situation" is usually made in terms of the marketed grain figures. The limitations of these figures as a measure of food availability have been mentioned already. Use of the concept *food security* does little to clarify matters. At the global level, it has no meaning: the world is years away from assuring that all people have reliable access to sufficient food to satisfy their hunger. This is a distributional issue that people so far have been incapable of solving or unwilling to solve.

It is true but misleading to use data regarding global consumption per person as an index of global food security. Based on aggregate production data divided by numbers of people, consumption per person in developing countries rose by 70 percent over the period 1968 through 1985. This is by no means a small achievement; it is probably unparalleled in human history. But it tells us little that is meaningful about who the hungry are or how many people have access to too little food to maintain dignity or even life itself.

At national levels, food security is assessed typically in terms of economic capacity to meet aggregate food requirements. That is, food security is expressed in terms of an economic assessment, which in itself says nothing about the distributional, access, or quality aspects of food.

Trade and income data help to flesh out the picture. Trade and income are important mediators of access and hunger, at both the national and household levels.[4] Nations that are too indebted to import food, and households (including farm households) that have too little income through self-employment or wages to purchase food, experience hunger and malnutrition even where food supplies overall are abundant.

It is only at the household level that economic and need-based assessments, quality considerations (including aesthetic ones), and the sociocultural factors that govern access to food (such as a person's age and gender) are incorporated into definitions of food security. This is unfortunate, as it is these aspects that are central to the determination of the level and distribution of actual hunger and malnutrition.

Famines: A Matter of Entitlement

Famines are popularly regarded as the simple and inevitable outcome of population growth in conditions of sudden crop failure or a more gradual failure to increase production in line with population increase. Amartya Sen, however, showed in a classic study published in 1982 that it is the breakdown of people's entitlement to food, rather than an overall shortage of food, that has been critical to the onset and duration of the world's major famines.

A number of triggers may, alone or in combination, lead to the loss of entitlement for particular social groups, households, or individuals. These include war and violence, migration, resettlement as a result of drought or the development of, for example, large-scale reservoirs, land reforms, and the intrusion of cash relations into more personal forms of exchange. In the absence of adequate employment or welfare rights, food aid can ease the pain until local entitlements can be recreated.

Nor are famines the inevitable consequence of drought. In 1987, two-thirds of the sown area in India experienced deficient rainfall, one of the worst droughts in this century. Rapid assessment surveys of a cross-section of households were undertaken in the five worst-affected states to assess the nutritional impact on children, men, and women. Overall, average energy intake fell to about the predrought level of landless laborer households, well above energy intake levels in the droughts of 1965–67 and 1973. The number of households subsisting on starvation diets was far fewer than in previous droughts, and virtually no households were found to be subsisting on foods gathered from the wild.[5]

Widespread hunger and its consequences were avoided because the government swiftly mobilized the interventions prepared for just such an emergency. Food-for-work schemes maintained entitlements to food among the poorest. Distribution mechanisms moved reserves to where they were needed. Stocks were released onto the market in response to adroit price management.

The Relationship Among Women, Food, and Agriculture

Much of the discussion on the relationship between world food supplies, hunger, and population growth is conducted only in the aggregate terms just presented. This distorts impressions in two ways. First, the debate becomes dominated by the perceptions of the handful of industrial countries whose populations are distanced from self-provisioning. Notwithstanding rapid and increasing rates of urbanization, the majority of the world's people are based in agrarian economies where self-provisioning continues to play an important role.

Second, at the microeconomic level at which self-provisioning occurs, agricultural surplus and consumption of the foodstuffs that farmers themselves produce are not simple linear functions of production. It is impossible to understand how hunger is distributed in this microeconomic world without understanding how gender relations condition women's access to food.

Production, Consumption, and Surplus at the Household Level

Few societies today are self-provisioning in the literal sense. Producer families survive by manipulating employment opportunities, agricultural production, food stocks, and food reserves, on the basis of both monetary and in-kind transactions. Many of the in-kind transactions occur within the domain of the household. They include an implicit (and in some African societies, explicit) remuneration for all those tasks, such as cooking, cleaning, fetching water, and child-rearing, that are necessary for the maintenance and social reproduction of the household. In most societies these tasks are considered female tasks, but women's management of the domestic domain does not mean they get an assured or better access to food. On the contrary.

Particularly, but not only, in South Asia, nutritional, health, and sociological research shows that adult men in self-provisioning households tend to have preferential access to whatever food is available.[6] As the amount or quality of food deteriorates, the differences in male and female health and nutritional status increase. Research further reveals that even in better-off households, women and girls can have a lower nutritional and health status than men and boys. At the extreme, they might even be "excluded from domestic subsistence," a somewhat guarded way of saying that, when times are hard, women and girls get kicked out of the home to fend for themselves. None of these intrahousehold gender differences are picked up in economic analyses based on theoretical per person consumption data.

The concept of *surplus* also has more nuances at the level of the microeconomy. What is sold to the market does not necessarily represent a true household surplus. Take, for instance, the extreme but common case of poor farming families indebted to a landlord. They may not in any real sense possess what they produce. It is committed in advance against what is needed to produce the crop, for sale at harvest prices, that is, at the lowest prices. They must buy back their food and other needs later in the year on terms dictated by those who command economic and social power. If they have insufficient cash to purchase these goods, they must commit their labor in payment.

Unfortunately, here another difficulty arises. Whether remuneration is given in cash or in kind, labor markets are not neutral with respect to men and women. That is, the wage rates for men and women, even for the same job, are not equal. Typically, female agricultural laborers are paid between one-third and two-fifths of the going male rate. The difference typically reflects neither productivity nor physiological differences between men and women but are an expression of unequal gender relationships that structure both women's entitlement to food and work and the degree to which they experience hunger.

Even at less extreme points on the self-provisioning continuum, marketed food typically represents the product of a complex set of adjustments and calculations within the household, in which biological need is only one factor to be considered. Households may choose to squeeze consumption in order to secure other benefits. These benefits are not necessarily immediate. Parents might choose to sell more food to the market in order to pay school fees for their children, for example. At any point above consumption necessary to maintain the required level of work, food need is a variable and not an absolute standard. It is the mechanisms for allocating the costs and benefits within the household that determine which of its members go hungry.

Seasonal Variations and Gender Inequalities

Seasonal variations of various kinds are an essential consideration in the calculaions of self-provisioning families. Even in conditions of abundance, adequate mechanisms simply may not exist for smoothing and harmonizing the peaks in demand for labor, in prices, in food needs, and availability throughout the farming year. The case of labor illustrates some of these gender-based complexities and consequences.

There is a tendency to lump male and female labor together when measuring and analyzing labor peaks. Doing this misses an essential part of the dynamic. In most agricultural societies, labor is allocated between men and women on the basis of social norms about what work men and women should do. The more rigid the norms, the more constraining to production seasonal labor peaks become.

The effect is most marked in areas where there is a single rainy season in which agriculture is possible. Both women and men extend their working day in order to get the crops in and growing well, peaking again over the harvesting period. The work needed to keep the home going and look after children, however, does not go away. Women must work an even longer day than men to keep up, skimp on agricultural production activities, or skimp on other tasks, with negative consequences for the well-being of the whole family.

Further, as household food stocks and cash reserves are typically low at the beginning of the planting season, women may receive no compensatory increase in their food intake. Instead, they run down their bodily reserves.

Unfortunately, the time of peak labor demand in farming also often coincides with the extra demands made on women's bodies from pregnancy and nursing, as a result of conceptions begun around the time of the previous year's harvest. Although the potential to reproduce exists all through the year, there is indeed a marked periodicity in births, particularly in single-rains agricultural societies. Harvest times operate at a number of levels to induce this effect. For example, better nutrition has measurable effects on male and female physiology—menstruation may resume for example after a time of amennorhea induced by the stress of hunger and hard work. Weddings often are timed to coincide with the availability of plentiful food. Seasonal laborers return home. There is less work to do, more time to celebrate and relax together. Unless the seasonal nutritional deficit is made up as food becomes more available, women may enter into a spiral of increasing deficit.[7] The high levels of anemia among women even in well-stocked self-provisioning societies are in part a measure of this effect and are in turn a major determinant of high levels of maternal mortality.

Responses to Weather Variability

Many areas of developing countries are characterized by high variability in rainfall within and between years. The greater the variability, and the risk that soil-moisture conditions will not be favorable for raising crops, the more likely it is that farming systems are based on loss-minimizing strategies and activities.

Such strategies include diversification of production sites and mix of production activities; diversification of agronomic and management practices; a more flexible use of resources; development of infrastructure such as contour embankments to conserve and stabilize moisture and soils; diversification of income sources; and maintenance of social and economic support networks.

These responses are not, or not only, technical responses. Men and women make separate adjustments and adaptations to their activities. Many of the adaptations and adjustments in agronomic and management practices on the farm involve women in more work, for example, collecting grasses and other green matter from roadsides for composting or for feeding livestock.

The degree to which these adjustments are complementary or discriminatory depends in part on the degree of flexibility in the gender division of labor. In Java, men are not embarrassed to take over child-care and domestic chores when women can earn cash at some gender-specific agricultural task, such as weeding.

In Tanzania, by contrast, men have been heard to complain about having to wait all day for food because the women are away from home fetching water.[8]

Women will trade off their allocation of time against other resources. They might decide, for example, to convert some part of the household's food stock to beer and use the cash from the beer sales to buy a goat if the rains falter. Less positively, a husband may seize his wife's jewelry, clothing, or cooking equipment for sale to tide over a period of stress, long before he is forced to run down his own assets.

Not surprisingly perhaps, surveys based on community assessments of vulnerability to the variability of weather pick out the households where women have little or no education and households headed by women as among the most vulnerable. Because their margins for flexible response are so narrow, women in such households are the least likely to maintain their membership in self-help groups and other support networks when weather is unfavorable to food production, and they are the most likely to suffer hunger even where other households survive unscathed.

Institutional Factors in the Gender Relationship

Insensitivity on the part of the developmental community to the gender-structured dynamic of the microeconomy has meant that modernizing institutions and opportunities at times impose additional unforeseen stress on women. The case of rural schools in eastern and southern Africa illustrates the general point.

Until recently, primary and secondary school terms were timed to match the agricultural seasons of the colonial authorities' home countries. For the most part, the school holidays did not coincide with the rainfall patterns of eastern and southern Africa. Yet labor use studies show that children might contribute on average up to 57 percent of the total hours worked within the farm household. Girls tend to contribute slightly less time to farm work than boys but contribute more time overall when other activities are also counted. Girls' work tends to support their mothers' activities while boys' work tends to support their fathers'.

In a provisional analysis of the labor that might become available through better timing of the school terms, the best case scenario released 23 times more labor than the worst case.[9] In the region as a whole, fewer girls than boys attend school, and it is hard to determine in gender terms exactly where the additional burden of child-labor foregone might fall. Nonetheless, if they are to be meaningful, analyses of trends in food production and consumption in Africa must be sensitive to these complexities. An analysis of the timing of the payment of school fees adds to the difficulty of planning the school year. In some parts of Kenya, for example, second-term fees must be paid in the middle of the peak labor period, before crop income becomes available, when family food stocks are at their lowest. When payment of school fees for all children, and specifically for girls, is considered a woman's responsibility, the mismatch between the demand for payment and the time when women have access to income can be a major reason why girls, in particular, drop out of school.

Surveys in the Mochudi District of Botswana in the late 1970s showed that during the plowing season, nearly one-third of primary school children were caring for themselves without the help of an adult, while their parents were absent cultivating the land far from the villages where the schools were located.[10] The incidence of burns and cuts among children treated in the clinics peaked during that month, school performance dropped, and many of the children became malnourished. Their mothers in particular attributed the growing delinquency among children to these periods of enforced separation.

Implications of Gender Relations for Overall Food Supply and the Incidence of Hunger

For one reason or another, the debate on population growth, food, and agriculture has not yet come to grips with the critical importance of the basic dynamics of gender relations in the microeconomy. Yet it is there, buried within the structure of rural microeconomics, that the socioeconomic forces that govern supply, hunger, and nutrition are generated. The implications of gender relations for food supply and hunger are further explored in Chapter 10.

The Technical Room for Maneuver

The evidence for a continuing technical capacity to maintain agricultural surpluses is equivocal. The big picture, as far as it can be painted today, appears to give scant grounds for optimism. In fact, however, the information for assessing whether it might be technically possible to sustain agricultural surpluses is limited and unsatisfactory. The Intergovernmental Panel on Climate Change (IPCC) at present concludes with caution that the weight of the evidence favors a continuing margin of surplus, even under the business-as-usual scenario that might lead to a doubling of carbon dioxide emissions by the year 2025, and a world population of 9.4 billion.

The IPCC recognizes that the maintenance of actual, achieved, aggregate food surpluses hinges on the interaction between biological/physical and socioeconomic forces. It is an interaction that cannot be separated from political and trading relationships and the creation of nonfarm livelihoods. How the socioeconomic and political dynamic will in fact unfold as the years go by is contingent on how exactly changes in global climate patterns might in turn change regional temperature and rainfall patterns, and how fast; and that is exactly what we do not know.[11]

The Impact of Climate Change on Agriculture

Existing regional models alert us to the sensitivity of present food surpluses to changes in rainfall and temperature. It has been estimated, for example, that a 1 percent reduction in rainfall could increase drought-related losses in the United States corn belt by about 50 percent.

Recent studies of the sensitivity of food output to changes in temperture and rainfall suggest that declines of 10 to 15 percent in grain yields in Africa, tropical Latin America, and much of India and southeast Asia are likely to occur, assuming a doubling of carbon dioxide concentrations in the atmosphere. It is not easy, however, to disentangle the net effects on the basis of current information. Elevated levels of atmospheric carbon dioxide also incerease the rate of growth of many agricultural plants and trees, offering the prospect of intensifying agricultural production. Increased atmospheric carbon dioxide levels, however, also depress the protein content of some pasture grasses, wheat, and legumes.

Further, estimates of the consequences for crop yield at global and regional levels tend to ignore the crucial role that crop mix has on food supply at the local level. For example, whereas yields per hectare for cereals as a whole in sub-Saharan Africa are only 40 percent of the world average, yields per hectare equal or exceed the world average for sorghums and millets, which are better adapted to drought conditions than maize or wheat. The importance of crop mix to agricultural production totals is well illustrated by the contrasting experiences of Mozambique and Zimbabwe during the 1992–1993 drought in southern and eastern Africa.[12] In Mozambique, cereal production in 1992 dropped to one-third of its 1990 level. Maize, which accounted for nearly 55 percent of cereal production by weight, fell by more than 70 percent. The tonnage of roots and tubers produced, however, is about three times that of cereals, and their production fell by only a quarter. Overall, food production declined by 27 percent. In Zimbabwe, which is commonly regarded as a more efficient and productive agricultural producer than Mozambique, overall food production fell by 50 percent, largely because of the much higher reliance on cereal production (and on maize and wheat rather than millets or sorghums). The choice of crop mix is largely influenced by policy rather than determined by technical necessity.

Whereas it is not possible on the basis of currently available information to tie large-scale changes into more specific understanding of agricultural effects, there remain a series of agricultural concerns that can be raised:

1. The degree to which the variability of rainfall within crop seasons, between agricultural regions, and across years becomes less stable and more extreme;

2. The frequency with which unusually severe highs and lows in rainfall and temperature might occur;

3. The likelihood that critical levels of warmth or moisture are crossed in the present margins of cultivation and livestock herding;

4. The extent and severity of pest and disease outbreaks as pathogens move into new areas;

5. The pace and continuity of climatic change.

Other global changes also are thought likely to impact on agriculture. The depletion of the ozone layer already is affecting the protein quality and growth of some of the world's most important food crops, as well as pastures and natural grasslands. Neither the eventual extent of these effects, nor the balance between beneficial and harmful effects, is as yet clear.

Agriculture's Contribution to Global Problems

Agriculture in its turn is contributing to global environmental change. Agriculture as a whole is estimated to contribute 35 percent of total methane emissions, principally via rice paddies and ruminant animals, as well as a substantial percentage of nitrogen dioxide emissions.[13] Both gasses contribute to atmospheric warming. The total contribution of agriculture to warming trends is estimated to be around 15 percent. Other agricultural activities with global effects include the use of methyl bromide to control pests in fruit and vegetables. Methyl bromide has been identified recently as contributing to ozone depletion and has been included in the latest global ozone protocols. Less directly, intensive use of nonrenewable resources, such as nitrogen fertilizer on grasslands, has led not only to economic inefficiency but also to substantial loss of nitrogen to the environment and loss of biodiversity.[14] Over-application of pesticides has had serious and sometimes fatal impacts on human health.[15] Moreover, pesticides fail to control harmful insect populations in the longer term and lead to resistance. For example, in the mid-1980s in Indonesia and in the late 1970s and late 1980s in Thailand, infestations of the brown planthopper, a pest of rice, surged as pesticides eliminated the planthoppers' natural enemies. Agriculture is estimated to claim two-thirds of all water removed from rivers, lakes, streams, and aquifers.[16] Technically achievable water savings would relieve water scarcity significantly. For example, reducing the amount of water used in irrigation by one-tenth would free up sufficient water approximately to double domestic water use worldwide.

Agriculture's Contribution to Local Environmental Problems: The Netherlands Case

The extent of the contribution of modern farming to environmental problems is not generally given much weight in popular debates on the future of agriculture: the focus is on trends in developing countries. It is instructive therefore to look at the case of the Netherlands.[17]

Netherlands agriculture by any economic measure is a success story. Over the past decades, the Netherlands has been either the second or the third largest exporter of agricultural products in the world. The environmental cost is huge, however. For the sake of brevity, the cost is illustrated here with data from pasture and livestock production, a part of the agricultural industry in which Dutch farmers excel. Grassland (predominantly managed artificial pasture but including managed natural grassland) and fodder maize account for 65 percent (1.3 million hectares) of the cultivated area and one-third of the total area.

The area of grassland and fodder maize represents the direct *economic* area of exploitation. The *ecological* area of exploitation includes the land in other countries used to grow crops imported to the Netherlands as cattle feed and the land used to deposit manure and absorb ammonia (ammonia currently is generated at 234 million kilograms a year, 90 percent of which comes from keeping animals, and cow manure at 1.5 kg per square meter of land), phosphate, and nitrate. Other ecological costs include the eutrophication of groundwater and the drastic loss of biological diversity in Dutch grasslands over the past 50 years.

In 1984, the Benelux countries (Belgium, the Netherlands, and Luxembourg) imported 12 million tons of cassava chips from Thailand, principally for use in livestock (including pigs and poultry) concentrates. The chips contained 90,000 metric tons of K_2O. Total use of potassium fertilizers in Thailand in 1984 was 75,000 metric tons for all crops.[18]

Long-distant nutrient flows such as these, subtracting fertility from one production system and concentrating it in another, are inherently unsustainable. The need to move rapidly toward production systems that are "competitive, safe, and sustainable" has been accepted by government and farmer organizations as both urgent and necessary.

Although agriculture's contribution to local and global environmental problems cannot be eliminated altogether, it is reducible. It is not clear, however, if the changes necessary on environmental grounds would increase or decrease the potential to generate continuing agricultural surpluses.

Agriculture in Relation to Natural Resources

A series of larger scale trends in the availability and quality of natural resources underlie the direct agricultural concerns listed in the previous section. Agriculture depends ultimately on the light, water, soil, and genetic resources essential to primary plant production. Any change in the amount or quality of these four, singly or in combination, changes the assessment of agricultural potential.

The dimensions of the problem often are stated in physical terms. For example, hydrologists identify water-scarce countries as those where the known annual supplies are less than 1000 cubic meters per person. On this reckoning, 26 countries, home to 232 million people, already suffer from water scarcity. Eleven of these countries are in Africa, and hydrologists predict that by 2010 another six will become water-scarce.

There are a number of difficulties with this way of reckoning. Not everyone in countries with ample water per person in fact has access to adequate amounts of water or water of acceptable quality; not everyone in a water-scarce country suffers from water-scarcity; not everyone in a water-scarce household suffers equally. Poor women and children everywhere stand the last in line. Where they are responsible for bringing water to the household, it is they and not some gender-neutral person who must search farther and deeper for diminishing supplies.

To express the problem in physical terms is sometimes to fall into a determinist trap. FAO data, widely cited as proof of an impending crisis, provide a handy example. In 1984, the FAO published an analysis that linked food security to the availability of land climatically suited to rain-fed agriculture. Overall, the FAO concluded that only about 63 percent of the land area of developing countries was suitable for rain-fed agriculture. The overall picture was broken up as follows between broad regions of the world: 85 percent of the land area in South America, 84 percent in Southeast Asia, 64 percent in Central America, and only 53 percent in Africa. Southwest Asia was found to be in the worst case situation, with only 18 percent of its land area suited to rain-fed agriculture, the rest being too dry, too cool, or too mountainous. Twenty-two percent of the land area in developing countries, with 11 percent of the world's population, was judged incapable under prevailing technology use and management of producing sufficient food to support its inhabitants.

Yet millions of people are in fact farming in these areas. While there is plenty of evidence of deterioration, it is by no means universal nor evenly spread through the FAO's maps, while the evidence for food deficits as a function of production shortfalls is, as we have seen, not very convincing. This is not to say that there are no problems, or that these problems are not related to questions of the availability and quality of the natural resource base. It does suggest, however, that the question is not rightly posed.

Restating the Relationship Among Natural Resources, Agriculture, and Food Supply

Farmers in rain-fed areas have evolved complex and often ingenious mechanisms for concentrating nutrients and water at the point where crop production is to take place. For instance, the movable stockyards placed to hold cattle overnight on crop lands in the infertile Barotse sand areas of western Zambia concentrate nutrients from daytime free-range grazing of the natural vegetation, with virtually no losses.

As the need and demand for cash have increased, however, crops are being grown more intensively: more nutrient is being removed from the soil and the manuring requirement is increasing. At the same time, as the population has grown, the area available for free-range grazing is declining, and the amount of manure available is no longer sufficient. The crunch comes when farmers do not have access to or cannot afford to buy fertilizers to make up for the emerging nutrient deficit.

One of the reasons why the farmers do not have large enough cash incomes to buy fertilizer is because the overall efficiency of their farm enterprises remains low. Application of purchased fertilizer might raise or at least help to maintain yield, but it also raises management costs. One of the reasons why efficiency is low, and higher management costs difficult to support, is that much of the food farming is in the hands of women, a trend that is growing as young men search for urban or mining wages. The productivity of women's labor and women's access to cash income is even more constrained than that of the men. A much higher proportion of men than women in western Zambia have at least some access to agricultural training, credit, and simple farm machinery and equipment.

Thus, what might appear to be a difficult physical problem determined by measurable relationships among observable quantities turns out to be a rather complex and fuzzy problem caught in the dynamics of gender relations. The challenge for the future, then, is to face up to the present discordance in the way biological, physical, and socioeconomic forces interact with each other.

Food, Agriculture, and Population Growth

The call for a more reflective examination of the data and the concepts and the way they are handled in debates needs to be applied tenfold to statements about population in relation to food supply.

What Malthus Actually Said

In 1798, before empirical data were in hand, that is, 3 years before the first British census was taken and some 40 years before births and deaths began to be registered in England, Malthus argued:

> Population, when unchecked, increases in a geometrical ratio. Subsistence increases only in arithmetical ratio. ... By that law of our nature which makes food necessary to the life of man, the effects of these two unequal powers must be kept equal.
> This implies a strong and constantly operating check on population from the difficulty of subsistence. ... Among plants and animals its effects are waste of seed, sickness and pre-mature death. Among mankind, misery and vice."[19]

The plotting of population against food supply has proved to be a popular exercise ever since. Yet Malthusian checks on population have not occurred on any important scale for the reason already noted, that food production is not linearly related in any direct way to surplus, consumption, or hunger.

Plotting the Limits in Population Terms

In its 1984 *World Development Report*, the World Bank estimated that if average farm yields rose from 2 metric tons of grain equivalent per hectare to five metric tons, the world could support a maximum of 11.5 billion people. In the same year, the FAO published the results of a massive study of the "human carrying capacity" of lands in developing countries. It concluded that by the year 2000 the world could support four times the projected population of 6.4 billion and that there was plenty of scope for absorbing even higher populations in the next century, even though some 64 countries would be unable to feed their own populations from their own lands.

Estimates such as these are not without their uses for planning purposes; they give a sense of the magnitude of effort needed to increase food production. But the gap between the two estimates signals their sensitivity to the assumptions built into the calculations. Both essentially are linear extrapolations from existing trends. They miss all the dynamism of real life systems, with their unaccountable time lags and lurching thresholds, and the unexpected impulses that take systems in uncharted directions as new relationships are formed.

Changing the Boundaries of the Debate

Consider the following four recent news items selected at random:

□ There is emerging evidence that the effect of elevated levels of atmospheric carbon dioxide might be to lower the protein content of some important plant groups, including some pasture grasses, legumes, and wheat (*New Scientist*, May 30, 1992, Letters).

□ A study commissioned by the U.S. Environmental Protection Agency of three models of the impact of global warming on farm output, food prices, and the numbers of hungry people reported that, on all three counts, tropical countries fared worse than temperate countries in each of the models (*The Economist*, May 23, 1992, International section).

□ Genetically engineered wheat has been produced for the first time, by biologists at the University of Florida, opening the way for the development of varieties with greater resistance to drought, pests and diseases, and weed competition (*New Scientist*, June 13, 1992, Technology section).

☐ Experts at the Harvard School of Public Health warn that the number of people infected with HIV will shoot upwards in the next few years, with populous countries such as Pakistan, Bangladesh, Egypt, and Nigeria, as well as most of Asia, being particularly affected (*New Scientist*, June 13, 1992, p. 9).

Any one of these forces for change has the potential to alter radically both the big picture, that is, the overall trend of events, and the context in which individual men and women make their decisions. Whether in fact they do so depends in a fundamental sense on three unique human capacities: the capacity to respond to circumstance, to exchange information and experience widely and to transmit the accumulated stock of knowledge to the next generations, and to develop rules for or ways of thinking about the world that allow for the purposeful management of events.

Making Sense of It All

To make almost any simplification about anything as rich, complex, and dynamic as the state of the world's food and agriculture is to enter onto polemical ground. It is evident that there are problems, but the definition of the problem depends on where you stand in the system.

It is another commonplace that men and women occupy different positions. This is not to say that they stand in necessary opposition to each other. Nonetheless, whether looking at production, consumption, need, or effective demand, there are marked differences, conditioned by inequalities in gender relations that are becoming increasingly dysfunctional for human survival.

Unless women and men become partners in the development of new ways of thinking about the world and how to manage its resources for survival, future prospects look grim: not because of some neo-Malthusian inevitability, but because women's labor and energy are the key point at which biophysical processes are carried over into socioeconomic processes. At present, that point is weak and becoming weaker, bearing too much of the load. Deliberate effort to strengthen and enhance women's roles is thus a necessary part of the search for sustainable futures.

5

Energy and Trees:
Where Do Women Really Fit In?

The story of trees as a source of energy is a fascinating illustration of how the wrong policy conclusions can be drawn from looking at too broad a picture over inappropriate time scales and from too narrow or too selective a point of view. There is widespread agreement that a problem exists. In some countries current rates of forest loss are great and increasing. In the Brazilian state of Rondonia, for example, some 1200 square kilometers of forest were reported destroyed by 1975, rising to more than 16,000 square kilometers by 1985. Comparable rates of forest clearance occurred in the recent past in such countries as Australia and New Zealand when the world's natural forest reserves still seemed abundant; today, natural forests are a scarce and dwindling resource.

Within this broad consensus, however, there is considerable disagreement about what sort of problem exists with the use of trees as energy, and for whom. There are at least three versions of the story, based on contrasting views of what the fundamental challenge is really all about.

Contrasting Perspectives

The Environmentalist Perspective

The environmentalists' version weaves together concern for the loss of biodiversity from the destruction of tropical forests, preservation of forests for the purpose of absorbing carbon dioxide emissions, degradation of soils as forest land is put to other uses, and the loss of forest plants and animals of economic value. The direct and potential economic value of forests is substantial. One-quarter of all prescription drugs are estimated to be derived from plants, and more than half of the world's species of plants are thought to grow in tropical forests.

The driving force behind the environmentalist story is a concern for biological resources as the basis of economic activity and the means of human existence. Inasmuch as some two-fifths of the world's people depend on trees as their main source of fuel, however, environmentalists tend to see people as part of the problem.

The Developmental Perspective

The developmental version of the story is concerned with the link between poverty and the use of resources. It illustrates how unequal economic relations encourage poor countries and poor people to exploit trees as natural capital in order to gain current income and the means for daily survival. The developmental focus is on trees as livelihoods.

The poverty-driven consumption of trees can be extremely rapid, but it may have little to do with the exploitation of trees as fuel. In the Ivory Coast, a heavily indebted west African country, for example, timber exports by the early 1980s formed 13 percent and more of all export earnings. Today, after more than 20 years in which the average annual rate of decrease in forested area has exceeded 2 percent, commercial logging of the natural forest is a dying industry.

The Demographic Perspective

The demographic version of the story is concerned with the dynamics of growth in human numbers in relation to forest depletion. The rate of forest cutting is presented as a simple function of population growth. In this version, the mechanisms connecting the two trends are considered immaterial. This is unfortunate, because it is precisely in the detail of these mechanisms, as we shall see, that the complexity and nonlinear nature of the relationship is revealed.

Unclear Policy Choices: An Illustration

Because there is no agreement on how to define the problem, the policy proposals flowing from analysis are unclear, as the following example illustrates. Two billion people in developing countries are thought to depend on fuel wood and other biomass as their only source of energy. Some part, perhaps around 30 percent of total deforestation, might be due to the use of trees as fuel.[1]

The carbon emissions consequent to deforestation are substantial: 1.7 million metric tons in 1986 due to tropical deforestation alone.[2] At the same time, carbon emissions from fossil fuels were estimated by 1988 to be more than 5 billion metric tons, of which approximately 4 billion were emitted in industrial countries.

What is the appropriate policy response? Seek alternative, cheap, accessible energy sources, at site, for present fuel wood users? Abandon all fuel wood development programs? Enforce compulsory contraceptive use on all fuel wood users? Control fossil fuel use in industrialized countries? Or is there some other option?

Environmental Colonialism

The kinds of policy questions just discussed cannot be answered on purely technical or economic grounds. The political relations between states influence the choices that are made. For instance, the connection that has been made between trees as carbon sinks and the carbon emissions of industrialized countries illustrates how policy gets caught up in longer-standing international developmental debates.

On the one hand, it has been estimated that around four-fifths of the land-based store of carbon, around 1.5 billion metric tons, is held in forests (although this calculation almost certainly underestimates the contribution of grasslands as carbon stores). About two-thirds of the total land-based store of carbon is held in tropical forests. On the other hand, industrialized countries are estimated to generate some four-fifths of total carbon dioxide emissions.

Industrialized countries, however, have relatively and absolutely small areas of forest. Even though the forested area in temperate countries is in fact increasing, not decreasing (Sweden, for example, has 50 percent more land under forest today than 50 years ago), there is insufficient area available to absorb the carbon dioxide emissions of industrialized countries. Industrialized countries, therefore, have an interest in preserving or renewing forests elsewhere as carbon sinks. The Dutch Electricity Generating Board, for example, in consultation with the Ministries of Agriculture and the Environment in 1990 proposed replanting 250,000 hectares over 25 years in South and Central America to offset the carbon dioxide emissions from the two coal-fired power stations scheduled to open in the Netherlands in 1994 and 1997.

A. Agarwal and S. Narain, two leading Indian researchers, have made a persuasive case against the "environmental colonialism" that locates both the problem and the solution in developing countries.[3] They locate the problem of carbon emissions squarely in the energy demands of industrialized countries, which are vastly in excess of the carbon sinks available within their own territories. They propose a system of tradable emission quotas, calculated in proportion to a country's share of the global population, with the sum of all quotas not exceeding the global availability of carbon sinks.

That is, they propose an allocation of emission rights based on the availability of carbon sinks in proportion to population, rather than in proportion to current levels of energy consumption. Present arrangements provide little incentive for already high-energy consumers to reduce their consumption. On the other hand, Agarwal's and Narian's proposals give little reason for developing countries to check their population growth. Expressed like this, policymakers on either side of the argument are faced with an unpalatable and politically unacceptable choice.

Unequal Consumption

Undeniably, the pattern of global energy consumption reflects the historic advantage of the early industrializers and the present disadvantage of developing countries. In discussing the pattern, it is easy to mix up the many different units of measurement that are currently in use. Some, such as barrels of oil a day, or tons of oil equivalent a year, or kilowatts, are not, strictly speaking, units of energy at all: they are units of power. That is, they measure the flow of energy per unit of time. Units of energy include the kilojoule, calorie, British Thermal Unit, barrels of oil equivalent, and tons of coal equivalent. However, energy can be expressed also as a given amount of power during a given time, as in kilowatt-hour.

Nonetheless, however much the data may be jumbled around in the popular debates on population and the environment, a clear pattern emerges. The pattern has seven marked features:

1. Industrial countries are the main consumers of commercial energy (coal, oil, gas, and electricity). With only 15 percent of the world's population, the 24 leading industrialized countries consume some 55 percent of the world's commercial energy.

2. Commercial energy forms an increasing percentage of the energy consumption of middle-income developing countries and a rising percentage of the consumption of many low-income countries.

3. Relatively little commercial energy is used in rural villages and farms in low-income countries.

4. Little commercial energy is used in low-income countries because little is available and then only at a very high cost. Costs are absolutely high and relative to incomes.

5. Most poor people, both rural and urban, rely on fuel wood and charcoal. The poorest rural people also use crop residues and dried dung.

6. Such biomass energy sources are used at very low levels of energy efficiency.

7. Such biomass energy sources carry high costs to human health.

The problem of trees as domestic fuel is in large part a problem of poverty, of nations as well as people. International and domestic policies to alleviate poverty are thus a necessary part of the solution.

Consumption of Fuel Wood and Charcoal in Low-Income Countries

The global data on fuel wood and charcoal consumption are not reliable, not only for the reasons given above but also because much of the consumption is not directly observable. The information that is available is derived from small-scale surveys and from aerial and satellite imaging.[4]

Nonetheless, it is evident that sub-Saharan Africa is the only area in which the average annual growth in the rate of consumption of fuel wood and charcoal is increasing. The region has the highest rate of increase in population and among the highest rates of deforestation. Further, it is the only region of the world in which fuel wood and charcoal consumption are increasing as a percentage of all energy consumption. Population control lobbyists frequently use these data to justify their case. The lobbyists argue that high rates of deforestation are caused by high rates of fuel wood and charcoal consumption and that the rate of consumption is driven by high rates of population growth.

The data in themselves do not justify such a simple interpretation. For example, people who use wood fuel rarely cut down whole trees: the major causes of deforestation in sub-Saharan Africa are commercial logging and urban expansion. Logging, as in the Cameroon, Ghana, and the Ivory Coast, is linked to high rates of national debt. The debt has relatively little to do with population growth in itself and much more to do with economic policy, trade, and domestic expenditure choices. Urbanization, though linked in part to population growth, is linked also to migration from rural to urban areas. Then again, the main reason why the proportionate consumption of fuel wood and charcoal is increasing is that people and nations are becoming less able to afford the price of commercial energy.

Further, the highest rates of deforestation are not in sub-Saharan Africa but among the middle-income countries of East Asia and the Pacific, an area of relatively low consumption of fuel wood and charcoal but high rates of commercial logging. Indeed, if the data are disaggregated to country level, Malaysia, with little foreign debt or need for foreign aid, and a falling rate of population growth, has one of the highest rates in the world of forest destruction through logging. Even so, it is often forgotten that the major part of the tropical timber trade occurs within the country of origin.

The Energy Consumption of Industrialized Countries

The energy consumption patterns of industrialized countries are no more uniform than those of developing countries. Nor are the levels of energy use of the most profligate consumers necessary for economic prosperity. Japan, a country of high population density, used 6 percent less energy in 1988 than it did in 1973, even though its economic output grew by 46 percent over the 15 years. By 1991, Japan had achieved an 81 percent increase in real output for the same amount of energy as it was using in 1973. The 1991 amount was 30 percent less than that of the United States.[5]

The extent to which economic growth and high levels of energy use can be decoupled depends a great deal on policy reforms in the energy sector and changes in energy pricing. Negotiations over the options involve difficult political choices to accommodate the different ways in which countries organize their way of life.

An Illustration

One reason why the United States as a whole lags behind its competitors on the energy front is its huge fleet of vehicles. By 1990, the fleet formed an estimated 36 percent of the world's total, consumed 4 billion barrels of oil a year, or roughly 16 percent of the world's oil production, and produced 1 billion metric tons of carbon dioxide, as well as other polluting gases.[6] Given these figures, it is hard to understand the selective focus on controlling the birth of children in developing countries as the solution to carbon dioxide emissions.

Drawing the Threads Together

When the different parts of the story so far are drawn together, the picture that emerges is that population growth in itself is only part of a much more complex set of problematic, scale-sensitive relationships and of time-sensitive patterns of demand for energy. A reduction in the rate of population growth, or in total numbers, cannot in itself fix the problem of deforestation or inequities in energy consumption. One might as well argue that the United States should reduce its vehicle fleet and increase its efficiency of energy use.

The appropriate and effective policy response cannot be derived from the macro picture. The big picture indicates only the scale of the problem at the global level. Policy interventions must deal with the dynamics of daily life in particular settings.

An Illustration from Costa Rica

The impact of population growth and rising income levels on air pollution, solid waste, urban growth, and deforestation in the Central Valley of Costa Rica has been studied in some detail.[7] Rising incomes were found to make the greatest contribution to air pollution via vehicle fuel consumption; lower rates of population growth were calculated to reduce the number of vehicles in circulation by less than a quarter.

The contribution of population growth to solid waste was also low, although more than its contribution to air pollution. Its contribution to urban growth, however, was found to be overwhelming, via physical expansion into agricultural lands, opening of new land to supply urban consumers, and increased demand for fuel wood, leading in turn to deforestation of the urban perimeter. The study concludes:

> The results clearly indicate that reducing population growth is neither a necessary nor sufficient condition for environmental conservation, but lower rates of population growth could have substantial positive impact on the urban environment.[8]

A conclusion, however, that urbanization in itself is everywhere the culprit would be premature and probably wrong. In many other developing countries urbanization is taking place at unprecedented rates, but its impact on the surrounding landscape is variable. Where impacts are negative, the causal mechanisms must be properly understood in terms of local pressures.

Contrasting Examples

Researchers at the Center for Science and the Environment in New Delhi estimate that between the early 1970s and the early 1980s, the forested area within 100 kilometers of India's 41 largest cities shrank by a third. As in Costa Rica, physical expansion and land-clearing for agriculture accounted for some of this loss, but by far the most important factor was the commercialization of the urban biomass fuel market. Increasing the availability of other forms of energy, at affordable prices, could alter the situation dramatically.

Similarly, in the Sudan, Gambia, and the Senegal, supplying the urban fuel market represents an important source of cash income for rural people. The opening of road and river communications has stimulated this market and increased the pressure to cut live trees and make charcoal. (Rural people, in contrast, harvest dead wood to meet their own fuel needs.[9]) In the Gambia, the policy response has been to ban the use of charcoal altogether.

Expanding the Room to Maneuver

The examples just cited link back to our earlier discussion of poverty as the constraining factor in policy choice. Poverty constrains both the range of choice and the opportunity to choose appropriate policies. In both industrialized and developing countries, however, new technologies and energy policies are beginning to expand the room to maneuver.[10]

In Europe, the head of the U.K. Energy Technology Support Unit, which advises the Department of Energy, recently estimated that up to 30 percent of Britain's existing electricity needs could be generated from renewable sources, given appropriate policy support. Denmark is already a significant generator of wind energy, and the European Wind Energy Association figures that 10 percent of Europe's present energy needs could be met by wind generation within the next three decades. The use of trees, crops, and crop wastes as biomass fuel is also a serious commercial option. Even in population-dense countries such as The Netherlands, NOVEM, a Dutch energy and environmental organization, estimates that up to 12 percent of existing Dutch energy requirements could be met from biomass and waste.

In the United States, two researchers at Princeton University, David Hall and Robert Williams, have calculated that natural gas used to generate electricity was marginally less costly than biomass in reducing carbon dioxide. Both natural gas and biomass were found to be more cost-effective than hydroelectric, nuclear, and advanced coal technologies. California is already the world's leading generator of wind energy, and one enthusiast thinks that North Dakota is windy enough to meet more than a third of the country's energy needs.

Some developing countries are moving quickly in similar directions through their own efforts. The Belgundi Group of companies located near Belgaum, in Bangalore, India, for instance, derives all its energy from agricultural wastes and residues and operates an 8 megawatt biomass power plant to supply steam and power to enterprises in its Energy Park at Belgundi. The World Bank is helping Indonesia and Mexico to install 10 kilowatt wind turbines. In conjunction with local solar-power grids (and back-up diesel generators), the turbines provide sufficient renewable energy for a village of several hundred households for an investment of as little as $200,000.

In sum, technological innovation, policy reform, and price adjustments in the energy sector would soften considerably the hard choices. A stark trade-off between population control and forest survival and drastic reductions in energy consumption is not necessary.

Trees as Domestic Fuel

The presumed relationship between the use of wood as fuel and population growth is peculiarly subject to myth making, both in the sense of generating narratives that become the basis for policy and intervention and in the more general sense of generating popular but unjustifiable beliefs. One of the starkest examples is the belief that a rapid rise in the population of the Himalayas has induced widespread deforestation, largely through wood fuel consumption.[11] The removal of the tree cover is held, in turn, to have caused substantial loss of soil and brought about climatic changes, including reduction in rainfall and intensification of flooding in the Gangetic and Brahmaputra river basins.

Revising the Myth

Numerous studies in the early 1970s appeared to validate this analysis. Ten years later, however, researchers argued that there was little evidence of mass deforestation and no evidence of imminent ecological collapse in the Himalayas. Although crown quality has deteriorated and the mix of species changed, net deforestation remains unproved. The local studies of fuel wood consumption per person that had been used to create the myth were shown to vary by a factor of almost a hundred.[12] Whereas the evidence did support the view that there are serious problems of poverty and resource management warranting urgent intervention, specific studies of particular elements in the myth suggested a set of relationships with many more nuances.

For instance, it was shown that a loss of tree cover in itself does not necessarily lead to greater soil erosion. Low vegetation and ground cover hold soils in place rather than mature trees. Researchers noted that increased population, in fact, tends to stabilize hillsides, as an increasing proportion of the steep slopes are terraced for agriculture. Conversely, trends such as a reduction in the availability of labor, brought about by the migration of men or an increase in the proportion of children going to school, can lead to the abandonment of sound resource management.[13]

Researchers developed a more sophisticated understanding of high mountains as inherently unstable geophysical landscapes. At the macro scale, say at the level of a watershed, catastrophic events such as heavy rainstorms tend to overwhelm the effects of human activity. In contrast, human affairs tend to be decisive for changes on the scale of a hillside and smaller.

Monsoon rains wash huge amounts of sediment from the Himalayas into the Ganges-Brahmaputra delta in Bangladesh, but the Himalayan mountains are readily erodible, and the sediment may have little to do with any changes in the scale or nature of human activity. Researchers in India and Bangladesh argue that it is poor economic planning and agricultural development in the floodplains, coupled with widespread poverty, that give rise to the huge downstream loss of life and the devastations caused by the annual floods. Engineering works, dams, and drainage channels executed in the name of development might have worsened rather than alleviated the problems, by blocking natural drainage systems and encouraging cultivation in natural wetlands.[14]

Studies conducted in association with the International Center for Integrated Mountain Development (ICIMOD) have considerably strengthened the empirical basis for understanding specific mountain conditions.[15] Clearly, it is time that grandiose statements about the nature of the energy supply and deforestation problem, and what needs to be done, give way to more subtly tailored interventions.

End-Use Analysis

One way of coming to grips with the detail is to undertake end-use analysis. The end-use approach starts with the consumer of energy, by sector. In the household sector, cooking generally is the dominant end use, although various other end uses, such as space and water heating, lighting and cooling, can be important. The specific mix of end uses depends on factors such as the income status of the household, the cultural setting, and of course, the climate.

Each end use, in turn, can be further disaggregated by need. Under cooking, for example, factors such as cooking technology, the type of fuel used, energy consumption levels, and sociocultural preferences might be included. This kind of analysis captures the complexities and interdependencies of the ways in which users make their choices.

Gender-Sensitive End-Use Analysis

End-use analysis of wood fuel in fact shows there are strong, interactive, class, seasonal, and gender effects. The analysis can lead to some unexpected conclusions. For instance, one study in Karnataka, India, found that better-off farming households met half their energy requirements from firewood taken from their own land and the remainder from firewood purchased in the market.[16] Wage-dependent households used two-thirds of the amount of fuel used by the better off and gathered more than 90 percent of their requirement in the form of twigs and branches from wayside trees, shrubs and field edges, agricultural waste (including dung), and crop residues. In other words, contrary to popular belief, in Karnataka it is the better off, not the poorest, who are the main consumers of fuel wood. Other studies also show that the poorer the population, the greater the reliance on crop residues and gathered wood as fuel and the greater the proportion of households headed by women or dependent on women's income.

The composition of the fuel available in the form of waste and crop residue varies seasonally. One study records how poor women used millet stems through the end of the harvesting season, then pigeon pea stems, and then through the agricultural slack season relied on gathering, cutting, and drying a weed, *Ipomea fitulosa*, supplemented by whatever fallen wood they could find.[17] Another study details these links carefully for poor female-headed households in Mokhotlong, Lesotho.[18] The type of fuel used and the time spent getting it vary according to the seasonal availability of dung. Slow-cooking protein sources are not used equally throughout the year but are depleted during the cold season when the slow-burning compacted dung from the cattle yards is available. During the summer the population relies heavily on wild vegetable protein sources, which require more time to locate and gather but which can be rapidly cooked, using the horse and cattle dung picked up on the high pastures, kindled with quick-burning resinous and woody shrubs. It is fuel seasonalities and not crop availability that determine which foods are eaten when and the food preparation equipment that is used.

Implications for Women's Health and Welfare

The reliance on trees, shrubs, animal and crop waste, and weeds for fuel has serious implications for women's health. The World Health Organization has estimated that three to four hundred million women are at risk from the toxic fumes they inhale, such as benzopyrene, a cancer-causing chemical; women may inhale the equivalent of twenty packs of cigarettes a day.[19] They also risk their physical and reproductive health carrying firewood, typically in loads up to 25–35 kilos over 3–5 kilometers, although numerous developing countries have enacted legislation setting the maximum load for women at 20 kilos. One study in Nepal, which measured the actual amount of firewood carried by women, showed that women transported an average of 7000 pounds of firewood a year.[20]

For the poorest, the work burden on women can be truly crushing. As a poor woman in Chotanagpur, India, is reported to have said:

> We get up at 4 a.m. at the first cock-crow. We light the *chullah* [stove], wash vessels, then go to bring grass and water for bullocks and cows, collect cow-dung, make [dung] cakes and collect dry leaves for fuel, which takes at least three hours, bring drinking water; then we cook food, feed animals, milk the cows, go for work in the fields or in brick-carrying. In summer we collect dry leaves for fuel for at least three hours. In winter we go to the jungle, if possible (it is ten miles away), and stock some fuel wood for the rainy season, some of us husk the paddy ourselves. Then, when we come back from construction work, we cook food again. By that time husbands come home, some drunk, and say "why haven't you prepared food?"[21]

There is another way in which poverty, women, and fuel wood interact. At the worst extremes of rural poverty, men in search of cash leave their families to work as migrant farm laborers or on the fringes of urban economies. The pressure on the time and energy of the women who are left behind increases, and women work more hours in a day. One study in the Himalayan region of Uttar Pradesh found that even during the peak agricultural season, with women working as many as seven hours in agriculture and animal husbandry, the amount of human energy used to collect fuel and fodder averaged two and a half times the amount used in cultivation.[22] Such conditions sustain the need for children to ease the burdens on women.

Implications for Agricultural Productivity

Where no labor is available, women without land may take to cutting the forest illegally and carrying firewood on their heads to sell in towns or to middlemen. Low agricultural productivity, worsened by the outmigration of men, may lead to further land clearing to expand the area farmed. Increasing deforestation in turn affects how women allocate their time, agricultural labor, and the family's food consumption. One study in Nepal found that the farther women had to go to find firewood, the less firewood they used, and the less time they spent on agricultural tasks.[23] Where deforestation was severe, the time spent by women in agricultural labor dropped by 40 percent.

Cereal farming in the study area showed high marginal returns to additional labor. Dry season crops such as wheat, maize, and mustard had the highest returns to women's labor, but because the dry season was also the time women had to devote the most time to fetching firewood, the conflict for their time was particularly severe. The conflicting demands on women's time and energy had adverse consequences for the nutritional status of preschool children.

Cook Stoves as the Solution

Over the past twenty or so years, the suggested solution to the problem of local fuel wood scarcities has been twofold: to introduce fuel-efficient, time-saving, improved cook stoves and to plant trees for firewood. Insofar as fuel wood shortages are, as we have seen, symptoms of much broader problems, these micro remedies have not had the desired results. Let us take a look at the details of some of these interventions.

Programs to provide improved cook stoves for women are often seen as the main way in which women and forestry are interrelated, a perspective that parallels the assumption that population control means controlling women's fertility (rather than, for example, male sexuality). As one exasperated field worker wrote in 1984:

> In talking to forestry development experts in the United States, Europe, and West Africa, usually when I ask about the involvement of women in forestry activities, the standard response is "cookstoves." It is an automatic, programmed response, like a knee-jerk response. Rarely does anyone offer any information about other ways in which women are involved with or affected by forestry activities.[24]

Low Energy Efficiencies

The focus on cook stoves is not without justification, however. Traditional stoves, variants of three-stone cooking on open fires, waste up to three-quarters of the energy generated. Wood and charcoal stoves of improved design introduced in Kenya offer fuel efficiencies of 29 to 38 percent, compared with 12 percent to 19 percent from unimproved stoves, at a cost (for initial purchase and fuel savings) that can be recovered in 2–3 months. New clay stoves introduced in Burkina Faso save 35 percent to 70 percent in fuel, thus saving 2.5–5 hours of fuel collecting time a week, at a cost in construction labor that could be recouped in 2–4 weeks.[25]

Overall Impact of Cook Stoves

In both these cases, the cook stove programs were successful in that the improved designs have become widely disseminated. The overall impact on deforestation of even successful programs has been slight, however, because savings at the national level are inconsequential compared with the trees lost from commercial logging and from land clearing for urban expansion, agriculture, and grazing.[26]

Many programs, however, perhaps the majority them, have been far from successful. There are many diverse circumstantial reasons why this has been so, but the single common cause of failure is that the designs have not met women's own specifications.

Reasons for Failure

We have seen, for example, that the type of fuel used often varies with the season, so cook stoves need to be efficient at burning different types of fuel if they are to meet the needs of poorer women. Also, even though the costs might appear low to outsiders, women often do not control sufficient income to purchase improved stoves, while their husbands do not see any reason to spend scarce cash on relieving the pressures on women's time, energy, or health. Further, although the smoke from unimproved stoves is an irritant, it might serve important functions in terms of curing food or in pest and insect control. In some climates, the role of stoves in space heating is important; in others it is not. In some communities, the stove must accommodate a multiplicity of small dishes, in others one or two big pots must be balanced on the stove. Additional concerns might include the safety of young children, the height at which cooking tasks are carried out, and the construction materials and skills available.

Lessons from the Cook Stove Experience

Women's use of and need for improved cook stoves is not one undifferentiated whole. Opportunities for innovation exist and can bring a range of worthwhile local benefits, but these opportunities cannot be captured from above or by central direction. In every local situation, women themselves need to be involved in analysis of the problem that an improved stove might

overcome, the design, the testing of options, and in discussion of the manufacturing and dissemination possibilities.

Tree Planting as the Solution

The experience with tree planting is not so different from that of cook stoves.
The World Bank estimated 10 years ago that there would need to be a five-
fold increase in the rate of forest planting to meet wood fuel needs in developing countries. The Bank estimated that a fifteenfold increase would be
necessary in sub-Saharan Africa. The presumption that the need for firewood was the a main cause of deforestation led to many programs for
planting trees for wood fuel. Social forestry in the community and agroforestry on farms became popular with the aid community and nongovernmental organizations. The justification for the interventions, species selected for planting, and the presumed motivating force to engage
community participation were largely externally derived from the macro
analysis.

Understanding Complexity

Subsequent reviews and field studies of widespread project failure led to a
growing realization that things were not so simple. In many communities,
for instance, whereas women have rights to harvest wood from trees, they
have no rights to land on which to plant trees and no rights of tree ownership. Men and women often exploit different species of trees and shrubs or
harvest trees growing in different locations. Further, both men and women
typically favor species that offer a mix of benefits, rather than a single benefit
such as firewood. However, men and women typically have their own distinct
knowledge about these benefits and their own preferences, in line with their
gender-specific tasks and responsibilities.[27] One thing the studies showed
conclusively was that women are related to forestry issues in many ways that
go beyond cook stoves and wood fuel.

Villagers Make Their Own Analysis

Further field studies showed that village men and women can offer a sophisticated analysis of the multiple causes of deforestation. One field study in the
Ivory Coast recorded in detail how villagers understood changes in their
landscape in terms of complex chains of linked causation.[28] An increase in the
number of households occurred as extended families split up under economic
pressures; the number of people increased, as better health care led to fewer
child deaths and as traditional patterns of child spacing broke down.
Agricultural techniques changed, such as the mix of crops grown and the

proportion of crops to animal husbandry, as male labor became seasonally scarce as a result of migration and the schooling especially of boys. Changes came about in the practice of seasonal controlled burning of grasslands and forests, as village self-management weakened in the face of migration and modernization. Fields were extended because of recurrent drought and low productivity; it became necessary to locate fields farther away from the village, to avoid the depredations of the increasing numbers of livestock. Increasingly men appropriated land, leaving less available for allocation to women under traditional rights of use. The impact of the money economy and the gradual transformation of firewood into a commodity for sale also had an impact on the villagers' lives. The demand for wood fuel increased from rapidly growing towns, swollen by rural migrants; and the demand for wood as construction timber grew.

Leading to More Sensitive Design

As understanding has developed of the complex reality within which women and men exploit forest resources, so the design of interventions has become more sensitive, more participatory, and more effective. Interventions become facilitative of activities controlled by the local users of trees and managers of the landscape. Project experience, however, is not the only reason for this shift in perspective. Over the past twenty years, women themselves have been moved to protest and action. Women at the grass roots level have become involved in the fuel wood problem, which is not only or even primarily about trees as fuel.

The Green Belt Movement

The Green Belt movement was started in 1974–77 by Dr. Wangari Mathai among women's groups in Naivasha, a dry area of Kenya, and has spread to many other African countries. The Director of the Zimbabwe Forestry Commission noted in his 1992 survey of rural energy that two-thirds of households interviewed were already planting trees on their own initiative. In 1985, about 80 schools in one densely populated, semiarid district in Zimbabwe began tree nurseries. One school nursery subsequently grew 20,000 trees in one season, the majority of them local species identified by villagers as the most suitable to meet a range of local needs. Wangari Mathai's own interest began when she saw how poor women in urban slums fed their children easy-to-cook but not very nourishing food because of shortages and the high prices of wood and charcoal. Because she had a background in the biological sciences, she saw clearly that there could be no long-term agricultural future for the country and no livelihoods for rural people, unless the land's water, trees, and other natural resources were cared for:

We needed to do something within our reach. We didn't have a lot of money, but we had a lot of hands, so we decided to start with what we could do and that was to plant trees.[29]

One of the groups involved, the Nyakinyua Gitiri Women's group based in Murang'a, in 1989 received a United Nations Environment Program award. The forty-four women in the group raised more than 60,000 tree seedlings over six years. They started by using their existing skills in handicrafts and goat-rearing to raise money to set up a tree nursery. They chose an area near the local market town, an area highly prone to soil erosion. The chairperson of the group, Mrs. Yudita Wanjiru Mareko, explained:

> At that time, there was also wanton cutting down of trees for firewood and most slopes looked fairly naked—a situation we felt had to be arrested before it got out of hand.[30]

They persuaded the local administration to donate a 0.3 acre plot and acquired 8,000 seedlings of various species in order to meet the different uses their potential customers might have for trees. By 1989, they were handling 35,000 seedlings a year. The seedlings are sold (or donated if need be) to local farmers, schools, and local officials and for planting on public land.

The Chipko Movement

Equally renowned is the Chipko movement, which began with an incident in 1973 in the Chamoli District in Uttar Pradesh, India. A group of women decided that they would not let a manufacturing company, which through corruption was allotted a license to cut a forest reserve, cut down a single tree. They stood by the trees and joined their arms around the trunks as the cutters approached. News of their successful defiance spread among women in neighboring areas. Supported by Gandhian volunteers, the women organized themselves into larger groups, held demonstrations, went on marches, and challenged the all-male village leaderships to preserve the forests. In one incident, an exasperated forest official is reported to have shouted:

> "You foolish women. Do you know what forests bear? Resin, timber, foreign exchange." One woman responded in the same tone: "Yes, we know what forests bear. Soil, water and pure air."[31]

Over the next ten years, women's groups in Chamoli District planted more than two million trees, with survival rates of around 90 percent, an astonishingly high figure according to Forestry Department officials. The movement has inspired similar efforts elsewhere in India, such as the Appiko Movement in the Western Ghats region of Karnataka, and the Girnar Movement in

Gujarat and Goa. Many less well known initiatives have been taken, and the story of one of these is told in the next section.

The Bankura Story

In West Bengal, India, at the beginning of the 1980s, a few desperately poor, frequently hungry, tired, dispirited women came together to discuss their lives with members of a women's research team.[32] As a result of meeting together, the women realized their problems were not the result of individual failures and that there might be benefits from trying to do something together about their own situation. Researchers from the Center for Women's Development Studies (CWDS), Delhi, helped women from three villages to register as the Bankura women's society.

On the basis of the group's analysis of what they might do to help themselves and their families, the women struggled to obtain a donation of land from the private landlords. The landlords themselves lacked resources to develop the by then thoroughly degraded hillside, bare of trees. Accustomed to rearing silkworms on the leaves formerly gathered from the forest that used to grow on the hillside, the women knew they could earn an income if only they could get some rights to land and get the trees to grow again.

Once the land was secured and registered in the name of the society, women researchers from the CWDS again helped the women, this time to make contact with officials controlling government funds to cover the labor and costs of establishing the plantation. The women helped in planting saplings on 9 acres, then tended and watered them. The survival rate was 98 percent, compared with the Forestry Department's 55 percent. The leaves were ready for harvesting a full 18 months ahead of normal maturity in the Department's own plantations. The society secured the silkworm eggs from the Silk Board in the nearest town, and soon the women were selling high quality cocoons to the Department of Sericulture.

Over time the Bankura women's society has diversified its activities. The women have been able to buy simple equipment to make improved leaf plates, bowls, and cups for sale in the local market; they have begun making rope from grasses planted on other reclaimed plots; they have started to trade in various seeds; they have financed bulk purchase of paddy for husking to meet their own household needs; and they have planted fodder grasses and begun keeping small stock (pigs, rabbits, and ducks). The process of innovation continues, and although not all new ventures are successful, the impetus for change has not stopped. Women have made contact with organizations able to provide training in management and entrepreneurial skills.

They also have evolved a system of spearhead teams, which make contact with women in other villages, tell their story, and encourage other women to begin their own societies and activities. One woman recalls how she went with a Sericulture expert to visit one village. He was appalled at the state of the bare, eroded land pledged by the village to the women's society:

> "Nothing will grow here," pronounced the Sericulture expert. On the way back I walked through the hamlet. Many naked, half-fed children with diseased skin came out. They were not washed because their mothers had no time. Women look famished. They spoke little, but when they did, it was in despair. "This hillock *can* give us an income, we want to plant it, you must help us."[33]

The women took the risk and the saplings grew. By 1988, there were 12 registered societies, each the registered owner of small plots of donated land, with a total membership of 1500 women. The movement continues to grow, and the experience of working with the women, supporting their activities, and helping them to achieve their visions and ambitions is enabling and inspiring other agencies and groups to begin their own movements. The women of Bankura and neighboring districts are beginning to shape and control their own future. As one village woman said,

> "We have learned that actually it is the land that owns the people. We have worked hard to give the land a green cover, and in return it has clothed us with authority. We are advancing together. The journey has begun."[34]

The End of the Story

We can draw five important lessons from this exploration of energy and trees. First, none of the three original versions of the story captures the richness and complexity of reality. None of the proponents can claim a monopoly on the truth. Second, obvious policy prescriptions can be wrong; unless informed by nuances and a localized understanding of how biomass energy is used, energy supply and consumption policies will miss their mark. Third, the relationships among the use of wood fuel and charcoal, population growth, and deforestation and other environmental harm are not linear, direct, or necessary. Fourth, price adjustments, energy policy reform, and technological innovations are softening the policy trade-offs and expanding the room to maneuver. Fifth, apparently powerful interventions such as the provision of improved cook stoves and planting trees will not have a major impact as long as larger distortions in energy use and supply exist. They will not work at all unless users are involved from the beginning in defining the problem, through to the development and application of solutions.

Women enter the story as the prime users of fuel wood, charcoal, and cookstoves and as managers of the landscapes from which fuel wood and other biomass fuels are collected. They are the ultimate end users at the opposite end of the energy supply chain.

Further, there is a direct and necessary connection between the amount of energy women themselves expend in managing the household fuel economy and the amount of energy women have available for managing other domestic tasks and agricultural activities. A reduction in the amount of external energy available to a household translates into pressure on the energy levels of women themselves.

Women around the world are showing that they need not be the helpless victims of the larger distortions. They are seizing the initiative. They show that transformations are possible at the local level. Given appropriate policy support, these local transformations could be expanded to have an impact on the larger picture.

The Education of Women and Girls: The Best Bet

A Price Worth Paying

In its 1992 review of the environment and development, the World Bank concluded that improving education for girls "may be the most important long-term environmental policy in the developing world." Education helps women to manage natural resources more efficiently and to achieve a greater part of their income through paid employment rather than through exploiting natural resources.

Better educated women also have smaller families and healthier and better-educated children. Countries that had achieved near universal primary education for boys by 1965 but in which enrollment rates for girls currently lag far behind have about twice the infant mortality and fertility rates of countries that have less educational discrimination.

Female Education: High Social Returns at Affordable Cost

Societies benefit in four ways from investing in the education of girls and women: overall, the number of children borne by each woman falls; the productivity of female labor and employment increases; women on the whole live longer; the number of maternal deaths and the number of children who die before they are one year old decline.

How Education and Fertility Are Linked

The ways in which the education of girls and women bring about a reduction in fertility are not fully understood. The links nonetheless appear to be, in their essentials, constant, irrespective of cultural, political, or economic circumstance. It is this constancy that justifies the expectation that investment in the education of girls and women anywhere in the world will slow down the growth of population.

Female education and fertility are linked both directly and indirectly. When girls are enrolled in school through the secondary level, for instance, they tend to be older when they marry for the first time (among girls who are married young, the age at which they begin having sexual relations with their husbands is later). The age of first marriage in most, though not all, societies strongly influences the age at which women have their first child. The risks of maternal and infant mortality associated with too-early childbearing in conditions of poverty are diminished.

In-school education, even of the dry, rote-based kind, tends to impart to girls a strengthened sense of self-worth and of accomplishment, which is independent of childbearing and motherhood. Education helps women to demand, acquire, and make use of information, including information on family planning and child care. It tends to strengthen their capacity to earn higher levels of income, whether they are self-employed or earn wage income. Women's control over income in turn tends to increase their role in family decision making and lessens their dependence on their children's labor for survival and security in their old age. In these and other more subtle ways, education partially eliminates the link between women's status and repeated maternity as proof of fertility and provides women with a degree of control over their own sexuality.

The Costs of Educating Girls Compared with Family Planning

In 1992 the World Bank analyzed the costs of educating women and girls as a means of fertility reduction. Econometric studies conducted by Bank researchers showed that an extra year of schooling is associated with a reduction in fertility of approximately 5–10 percent. On the basis of a sample of 45 countries, which included 71 percent of the world's low-income population, researchers simulated the effects of increasing the secondary school enrollment of girls from the 1965 average to 30 percent of total enrollment. Their model showed that 9.1 million births a year could have been avoided. At a 1990 cost of $30,000, educating 1000 girls for an additional year would prevent 500 births (at a cost of $60 for every birth prevented). Evaluation of typical family planning costs suggests an approximate cost of $65 for every birth prevented. Educating girls, therefore, is at least as cost effective in reducing fertility as are family planning interventions.

The Link Between Educating Girls and Economic Activity

The link to productivity and economic growth is also well established. Nearly 10 years ago, a leading policy analyst, Constantina Safilios, examined the statistical relationship between socioeconomic development and women's status in 75 developing countries.[1] She showed that women's literacy and access to paid employment were key determinants of women's status. Women's status in turn was shown to be a key determinant of fertility and child survival.

The data then available did not clarify fully whether education or employment was the most important investment. While acknowledging the role that women's education played in preparing them to compete in the employment market, Safilios concluded that policies should focus on increasing women's paid employment as the means by which parents would recognize the value of educating girls. Subsequently, World Bank data have made clear that investment in the education of girls and women is the key to achieving higher rates of employment among women, greater productivity of women's labor, and higher financial returns.

The Effects of Female Education on Mortality Reduction

The effects of the education of girls and women on child and maternal mortality is no less dramatic than its effects on fertility and economic prosperity. Education has a significant impact on reducing maternal mortality, an enormous benefit to women and their families in low-income countries, where maternal deaths are the leading cause of female mortality. Health care interventions are estimated to cost some 60 percent more than an additional year of schooling for 1000 women, to achieve the same reduction in overall female mortality. Numerical estimates of the impact that the education of girls and women has on reducing child mortality place the reduction at between 5 and 10 percent for each year of schooling.

The Gender Dimension: A Price To Be Paid

Eliminating educational discrimination in low-income countries, the World Bank estimates, currently would cost only about a quarter of 1 percent of the countries' gross domestic product (GDP), or one-tenth of their defense spending, or 1 percent of their investment in new capital goods. An increasing number of countries consider that to be a price worth paying. Over the past several decades, both poor and not-so-poor countries have begun to invest more heavily in raising the primary school enrollment of girls. In 1985, however, the latest year for which reliable figures are available, the number of girls enrolled in primary schools in low-income countries still amounted to only 41 percent of the total. In Afghanistan, Benin, Guinea, Nepal, Pakistan, Somalia, Yemen (People's Democratic Repuclic), and Yemen (Yemen Arab Republic), enrollment of girls was a third or less.

Wastage and Attrition in the Formal School System

Getting girls into primary school is only the first hurdle, however. If no special measures are taken, more girls everywhere drop out of school, and at an earlier age, than boys. In some areas, notably sub-Saharan Africa, more girls repeat classes and, on average, achieve lower final test scores than boys. The proportion of girls entering school is thus a poor predictor of the proportion who complete their primary education.

The difference between boys' and girls' educational chances sharpens at the secondary and tertiary levels. The enrollment of girls in secondary school in Africa is 34 percent, in Asia 39 percent, and in Latin America 45 percent. These figures imply that in Africa, for example, only 10 percent of the age group (and only 5 percent in Sahelian countries) attend secondary school. Tertiary enrollment in Africa falls to 21 percent of the total and in Asia to 33 percent, while in Latin America it remains at 45 percent.

The high levels of wastage and attrition have serious implications for the efficiency of the entire school system. On the one hand, school costs are spread over fewer pupils. On the other, private and public economic rates of return are diminished. If current provision cannot, for whatever reason, attract and keep girls in the educational system, two of the basic justifications for educational investment are defeated, namely, its effect as a multiplier of intellectual and social capital and its ability to spiral the economies of scale from one school cohort to the next and from one generation to another.

Issues of Gender Equality

Unfortunately, analysis of case studies of the causes of gender-based educational discrimination suggests that many of the causes are subtle, intransigent, and resistant to simple policy interventions. The underlying reason is that the education of women touches deep-seated male sensitivity to issues of gender equality.

Gender-based attitudinal barriers are consistently undervalued in economic and educational studies of the measures necessary to raise the enrollments of girls and women. Few governments are convinced that gender inequalities matter, and they are politically more inclined to show concern for geographic or class-based inequalities in access or provision. While recognizing an argument in social justice for equal opportunity, men repeatedly express their fear that to move too fast or too forcefully would alienate the very parents and teachers whose support is required to implement reforms.

In recent years the response of educationists who are women has become more explicit about the implications of educational equality for power relations between men and women. Basically, they say that there can be no economic or social progress while women remain powerless and that educational opportunity is a means of self-empowerment that can have high private and public returns.

Groups such as the newly established Forum for African Women Educationalists are lobbying to put women's education at the center of their national agendas. The forum is made up of women Ministers of Education and Permanent Secretaries and women Regents and Vice-Chancellors of universities and represents a formidable new force on the African educational scene. However judiciously they frame their arguments, they are clear, at least among themselves, that there is a gender dimension to the price to be paid for educating women. If societies want to secure the high social returns that can be achieved only by educating women, then men will have to accept adjustments in the relations between men and women.

Women activists are clear, too, about the implications. For investments to be effective, the way in which educational opportunity is presented must connect to the social and economic reality of girls' and women's lives and status. Progress toward educational equality is not just a matter of expanding the number of places in school or hiring more teachers who are women, though both might be necessary components in particular settings. Further, attitudinal barriers, including the low self-image of many women, which may prevent them from pushing for education, must be tackled directly. In addition, the content of education and the setting in which it is offered have to change.

The Inertia of Existing Systems: The Case of Bangladesh and India

In both Bangladesh and India, governments have made an effort over many years to raise women's very low standard of literacy and to enroll more girls in school. The poorer the women, the less likely they are to have received any formal education at all. Impressive gains have occurred, but the overall number of illiterate women is increasing, and the gap between male and female educational standards is not closing and in some areas is even widening. Education as such seems to have failed to break the weight of tradition or shift the huge, inert educational bureaucracies into meaningful action.

Systemic Discrimination within Society

The educational trends reflect systemic discrimination in these societies as a whole. In both countries, there are substantially fewer females than males in the population, and as the latest 1991 Indian census suggests, the rate of decline might even be increasing. From their earliest days of childhood, women's health and nutrition status is less than that of men, and women have higher rates of mortality. In both countries there are strong statistical associations among the areas of acutest poverty and natural resource depletion, the lowest levels of female literacy, low and declining male:female ratios, and the highest rates of fertility.

The failure of educational policies to break through the gender gap so far has both demand and supply aspects. Poor women lack the capacity and the will to demand education. Educational facilities for their part fail to deliver a service that attracts and retains girls and women. The reasons are many, interdependent, and complex.

The Influence of Demand Factors

As a rule, girls and women are caught up in the daily struggle for food, fuel, water, fodder, and wages; they have little time or energy available for schooling. Their socially defined roles and the norms governing their behavior discourage critical thinking and inculcate passivity and deference to the views of others. Their work, and their acceptance of pain and suffering as their lot in life, isolates them from other women and teaches them to accept failure in their own lives as personal failure. Robbed of their confidence to think and learn without fear of failure, they are paralyzed by their own poor self-image.

Lacking the ability and will to demand education for themselves, and dependent for their status and welfare on their husbands and sons, older women often perpetuate the underachievement of girls by demanding their presence to help in the house and field and to care for younger children. In societies in which girls take a dowry from their house on marriage, fathers are reluctant to invest in their daughters' education, only to lose them to another household: "The daughter is like the husk of the rice which is thrown away, but the son is like the grain of the rice which is kept in the home."[2]

Where poverty presses hardest and households are dependent on wage labor to survive, parents themselves may push girls into the earliest possible marriage for economic reasons. By sending a girl away to join her husband, parents reduce the number of dependents in the household who must be fed and clothed.

The undervaluation of girls and economic and cultural preferences for sons have important implications for family planning. A national survey in India in the late 1980s investigated the association between fertility levels and the number and sex of surviving children.[3] The survey showed that parents who had one or more surviving sons were much more likely to be using family planning than parents who had only daughters. Rural parents who had three or more surviving sons were more than twice as likely to be using family planning as parents with only one son and more than three times as likely as were parents with three or more daughters. Where the preference for sons is strong, couples tend not to use contraception to limit family size until they have the desired number of sons. Further, couples in countries such as India and China may resort to amniocentesis testing, followed by selective abortion, as a means to regulate the ratio of sons to daughters.

The Influence of Supply-Side Factors

On the supply side, too, the barriers to the education of girls and women are strong, interlocking, and complex. The teaching profession is a male-dominated structure, staffed by those who are inclined to think that women's disadvantage is a facet of poverty, which affects both men and women equally. They are inclined also to think that the high dropout rates for girls in school and for women in adult education classes is the fault of the girls and women themselves and of the social order. Male district adult education officers have said such things as: "How can they understand anything before they can read and write?," "They are not punctual—they always make excuses that they have other things to do," and "If their husbands' don't allow them to come, what can we do?"[4]

The Director of Adult Education in Karanataka is rightly proud of the fact that more than a third of the state's adult education centers are specially for women, but 40–50 percent of the women who initially attend drop out after a few classes, and a further 25 percent drop out before they complete the course. The timing, the location of the classes, the sex of the instructor, the content and relevance of the courses, the methods of teaching, the materials used, and the language used to give instruction all serve to alienate women.

Nor do the women take particularly kindly to the expert-driven, top-down approach of many officials, whose distaste for working with women, let alone women of lower caste or tribal status, simply reinforces women's sense of humiliation, fear, and ignorance. As far as poor women are concerned, education becomes a tool of oppression, not of liberation. Control over the educational agenda and the power to determine what women need and should respond to remain with men. A well-intentioned male literacy campaigner based in Lucknow, in Uttar Pradesh, felt he was doing the right thing in a participatory way but lamented, "First we try to motivate them and make them aware of their felt needs, but they do not respond."[5]

The Search for Alternatives

The governments of both Bangladesh and India have tried to overcome some of the limitations of government service by contracting nongovernmental organizations to conduct literacy and adult education classes. The contractual relationship on the whole has not been satisfactory; the government retains a supervisory and regulatory role that permits only linear expansion of the scale of its existing effort, not growth in terms of greater impact on the system.

In Madhya Pradesh, India, under the stimulation of a dedicated woman State Secretary, a lien on the electricity rate generates money for the Women's Development Fund, which offers scholarships to every girl 15 years old and older who stays in school to her 18th year. Whereas initiatives such as these have helped at the margin, none has tackled the formidable bundle of interlocking factors that constrain supply and demand.

Two more recent and remarkable programs, the BRAC schools program in

Bangladesh and the Mahila Samakhya program in India, are beginning to change the overall system of education provision. By working through educational instruments to improve women's status, these programs are reeducating the system itself to become able and motivated to increase the participation of girls and women. The link finally is being made between where women are and what education and literacy services provide. The programs also show that educating women need not rest on long-term justifications: the positive private and public benefits quickly become apparent.

The nonformal schools of BRAC, a Bangladesh nongovernmental organization, and the government-sponsored Mahila Samakhya program in India, which is described in the following chapter, attempt to do just that. They focus on the empowerment of women and girls as the key to unleashing a creative process of change. At a meeting of women's group facilitators of the Mahila Samakhya program, one woman said:

> If we believe what people say about women, it is like living in the dark. By working with this program, I have come into the light, and because I myself no longer believe that women must live in the darkness, I can help other women to come into the light.[6]

The BRAC Schools Program, Bangladesh

To understand the magnitude of the achievement of BRAC's schools program and how it has come about, it is useful first to set the scene.

Background to Bangladesh

A nation of more than 115 million people living on the delta of three of the world's largest rivers, Bangladesh is one of the most densely populated countries in the world, with over 8600 people for every 1000 hectares. Despite a continuing high rate of population growth, at more than 2 percent a year, Bangladesh nonetheless has proved it is not condemned by history and geography to be the eternal disaster that many predicted when it won its independence in 1971. Over the past 20 years, maternal and infant death rates have fallen, the mean age at which girls marry has risen to just over 18 years, an increasing percentage of boys and girls attend school, and apart from the acute needs occasioned by floods or cyclones, agricultural output has increased above the rate of population growth.

Yet Bangladesh remains one of the poorest countries on earth. Gross national product per person is only $210. Fifty-five percent of the population is estimated, on the basis of income data, to live in absolute poverty, with insufficient means to satisfy basic food requirements. Maybe twenty-five million of the rural poor earn 60 percent or less of the poverty line income, according to a 1992 study by the prestigious Bangladesh Institute of Development Studies.[7] More than half the rural inhabitants own less than a third of an acre of land, do not own their homestead plot, and have no secure rights over their flimsy houses of palm thatch. Fuel, whether from trees, animal wastes, or crop residues, is in desperately short supply. In both the countryside and the towns, employment opportunities are insufficient to provide the growing labor force with work throughout the year.

In such conditions of poverty and inequity, the flow of cash in the rural economy is low, and social instability is high. More than a fifth of all women are divorced, separated, or widowed. Forced by circumstance to take responsibility for their own and their children's survival, in a culture that cherishes the seclusion of women and enfolds them in the protective norms of the family, an increasing number of poor women are defying custom in order to better their lives and secure a future for their children. "The pain of hunger pushed away their veil."[8]

The Educational Situation of Girls and Women

The government of Bangladesh has given high priority to the principle of universal primary education and adult literacy. Some 85 percent of rural women are illiterate, however, and among the poorest women, illiteracy is probably universal. Although primary school enrollment of both boys and girls has been rising, a large differential persists between boys and girls. Further, while no more than 15 percent of all schoolchildren pass the primary stage, probably fewer than 3 percent of girls complete primary school. The dropout rate is highest in the first year.

As in India, the reasons lie both in the gross inadequacies in what is supplied and how it is delivered and in the gap between what the schools offer and what is seen as relevant, worthwhile, and appropriate by pupils and parents. An early study by Shamima Islam, based on research conducted in 1976–1977, also noted the weak support for the concept of women's right to education.

Background to BRAC

In 1972 F. H. Abed returned to Dhaka from a banking career in Britain to contribute to relief and rehabilitation activities, as the new state of Bangladesh emerged from its struggle for independence. The visionary and passionate response of Abed and his wife, Ayisha, led to the creation of the Bangladesh Rural Advancement Committee (BRAC).

Through 20 years of experimentation and creative evolution, BRAC has initiated and supported an integrated program for the rural poor. By the turn of the century, the program will be active in nearly a quarter of Bangladesh's villages and an expanding proportion of her urban slums.

At the middle of 1992, BRAC's activities included 8666 schools, 5230 for 8- to 10-year-olds and 3436 for 11- to 16-year-olds, with more than a quarter of a million pupils, of whom more than 73 percent were girls. The intention is to increase the number of schools to 50,000 by the end of 1995, a demonstration of cost-effective community-based education of girls and women on a scale that is beginning to make a difference to the entire educational and social system. As Jharna, a field worker in the education program, says, "Men are not challenged by poverty to change; they only have to 'permit' their wives and daughters to work. It is women and girls who will have to carry radical social change on their shoulders and prepare the future generations."[9]

BRAC's Core Values

To understand how BRAC has come to this point, a few preliminary clarifications are in order. BRAC's core values reflect an unshakable belief that even desperately poor people can be trusted to make socially beneficial decisions—that is, decisions that benefit themselves *and* the public good, as long as opportunities are structured to enable them to do so. BRAC further believes that the way in which the new opportunities are developed is the key to the creation of a multifaceted process of empowerment that can over time bring about self-sustaining change in the structures of oppression and poverty. These beliefs are based on a recognition that in a society as vast and complex as Bangladesh, and in an environment that is physically and climatically highly variable and unstable, a process of change that is driven by experts must be ineffective. The puzzle-solving approach of science based on detail and quantitative exactitude will always be swamped by greater uncertainties about the nature and performance of the human and biophysical system. The situation-improving approach of professional service activity, on the other hand, must be sensitive to the small adaptations people make to circumstance that make the difference between life and death for millions of poor Bangladeshis. Such sensitivity is not possible unless the knowledge and experience of the poor themselves enters into the process of identifying, shaping, and managing the new opportunities. The evaluation and creation of future states, which are unknown and unknowable, must be driven by the values and priorities of the poor themselves.

The expansion of BRAC's activities thus has been incremental, self-reflective, and experientially based. Its ambition to do more has grown as its capacity to do more has grown and as the need for more to be done has become evident. Although there have been moments of tension between BRAC—and the nongovernmental sector as a whole—and the government, BRAC has sought to become complementary with the public sector in order to develop what is supplied and what is demanded as coherent systems.

BRAC's Achievements

BRAC's values and beliefs are embedded strongly in its mix of program activities. According to data in BRAC Quarterly Reports for 1985–1992, achievements include:

□ Mobilization of male and female savings and credit groups in which peer discipline makes up for lack of collateral. With further training support, the groups are encouraged to evolve into village organizations that take increasing responsibility for their own further development. Women form nearly 70 percent of the membership and take some two-thirds of the loans disbursed, with a greater than 95 percent repayment record. Trading, livestock rearing, and paddy husking account for 80 percent of the borrowing by women. By the end of December 1991, total savings (for both men and women) amounted to more than $6 million.

□ Specialized income-generating activities, such as poultry and sericulture. These activities are evolving into vertically integrated industries largely controlled and managed by women, who take loans and receive technical and management training:

The *poultry* activities are reserved for destitute women, who make up an estimated 3 percent of the total population, in order to provide a continuing means of livelihood when their entitlement to the government's wheat ration ceases. In 1989–1990, in collaboration with the Directorate of Livestock Services, the Directorate of Relief and Rehabilitation, and the World Food Program, BRAC trained and issued loans to 20,000 women (of a total of 40,000) who specialize in raising chicks for sale to other women, rearing improved cocks and egg-laying hens, providing vaccination and other basic veterinary care, and collecting eggs for sale or working in chicken feed centers. Their net earned income was nearly $1.25 million. The net monthly income of, for example, an individual chick rearer was $9. By the year 2000, the program will have reached up to 30 percent of the women entitled to the wheat ration.

The *sericulture* activities provide opportunities for women to lease land to plant mulberry saplings for sale, receive an income from guarding and caring for mulberry trees planted along roadsides and canals and from selling the leaves, rear silkworms, mature the worms through to the cocoon stage, and, increasingly, process the cocoons and the silk thread through to finished textiles. Nearly a million women participate, and more than five million trees have been planted; by the year 2000, it is estimated that there will be more than two million women participants and some 25 million trees planted. A silkworm rearer's net income is about $12–15 a month, for about 10 days' work.

□ A range of health activities, which, in association with government services, includes the development of mechanisms for mass immunization, the spread of knowledge about oral rehydration therapy for the home treatment of diarrheal illness, improved maternal and child care, and motivation to adopt family planning.

□ A paralegal program, which trains village men and women to provide legal awareness training to groups on request, in return for a small remuneration paid by the group members. The training covers Muslim family law and marriage, inheritance, land law, and citizen's rights. Early monitoring of the effects of the training suggests that one of the most immediate results is to encourage parents to honor the legal age of marriage for girls (18 years).[10]

Women within BRAC

The brief sketch of some of BRAC's key programs illustrates the degree to which women stand at the center of BRAC's concerns and achievements. Although within BRAC an increasing number of women hold field program staff and junior and middle management positions, the organization remains male dominated. That so much has been accomplished largely through male staff is a tribute to the sincerity with which BRAC as an organization has been willing and able to challenge society's patriarchal norms. Twenty years ago, men in the village would not let the women talk to BRAC staff; ten years ago, even BRAC staff were troubled by the idea of women field officers riding bicycles as they carried out their work in a *purdah* culture. Today, women field staff ride motor bikes, and women group leaders themselves ride bicycles.

At an internal workshop for women program and management staff, an older woman who had joined BRAC in its early days reminded the new, university educated recruits, "I used to work in a coir factory where you had to hold your sari in front of your face when a man addressed you—but you could be asked any day to raise your skirt to your waist."[11]

Others recalled how even 10 years ago they had to sleep in cowsheds at the district administration headquarters because no accommodation was available for women and how this only strengthened their determination to overcome all difficulties in the search for ways to alleviate the miseries and indignities of poor village women. Today, as Zarina, another workshop participant optimistically claimed, "We are not dependent on anyone else: now we can find our own way."[12]

BRAC's Initial Experience in Providing Education

BRAC began experimenting with adult education in literacy as it began mobilizing and supporting credit and savings groups. It found that reading and number skills in themselves had little relevance to the group members' lives. Through analysis and discussion with their members, BRAC realized that while there were many occupational and management skills the groups wanted to learn, literacy and number skills were only tools for achieving other goals in life, not ends in themselves. Further, BRAC workers came to understand the force of parents' desire that their children have opportunities to learn that would help break the cycle of poverty. A common village folk saying underlines the point: "Don't pour water on the top of the tree while cutting the roots."

BRAC began to study the kind of education that was really available in local schools. The staff wanted to understand why parents regarded these institutions as part of the fabric of corruption and oppression, rather than a potential liberating force. In 1980 it reported a typical case:

> In Shantigarh Union there are sixteen primary schools, all registered with the government. Out of these, eleven are government-aided. . . . Seven government-aided schools are hardly running at all, with often half a dozen students, never more than forty, and rarely more than one teacher in the school, the rest doing politics and business. One unregistered school has been closed for years, though the teachers are still drawing rations. This situation, where half the schools in the Union are not functioning in any real sense, and about twenty privileged men draw subsidies . . . for doing nothing, has been going on for several years. . . . A school is, in practice, an enterprise of the teachers.[13]

Further, the content of the lessons appeared to be geared entirely to exam-based qualification leading to a clerical, bureaucratic, or professional career. Teaching methods were based on dreary learning by rote. Books and other learning materials were in short supply. There was no accommodation in the class scheduling to the seasons, with the varying hazards of the climate and the demands of agriculture. There was no recognition that from the age of 8 years or so, the children, especially the girls, of poor families contribute up to 4 hours' work a day to family survival. There was nothing to help older girls manage the onset of menstruation. The design of school buildings and the facilities provided did little to promote hygiene or offer security and privacy to girls. Girls had few role models in the schools: the majority of teachers were men. Despite the government's recommendation of a 50:50 quota, relatively few women qualified as teachers, and women themselves were unwilling to take the risks associated with being posted away from home.

As far as village girls and women themselves were concerned, the situation often could be even worse.[14] In December 1986, I visited a registered primary school close to the Union (subdistrict) administrative headquarters in

Mymensingh district. None of the teachers were present when I arrived during school hours. I eventually discovered some twenty small girls shut up in a dark, dirt-floored shed behind the school, with six or seven older girls and women. They were making brooms, baskets, and mats from rushes and palm fronds, supervised by a man who turned out to be a senior teacher at the school and the brother of the Union Chairman. Caught in an embarrassing situation, the man was persuaded to leave. Then the women told me that the chairman charged them for issuing the food ration cards to which they were entitled as destitute women. He demanded that they and their children work free for his brother, the teacher, a certain number of days a month before he would issue the ration, and he always gave short measure. Worst of all, the women, and two of the girls still in their early teens, pointed to a number of their younger daughters, claiming the chairman and his brother were their fathers.

Learning the Lessons of Experimentation

Through the early years of the 1980s, BRAC, along with a number of other nongovernmental organizations, donor-funded projects, and government agencies, struggled to find ways to remedy the situation. A range of interventions were tested.

□ Did the provision of scholarships encourage more girls to enroll and stay in secondary school (it did) and in primary education (it did not significantly), and if they did so, what would be the effect on fertility? Research showed that even among secondary school dropouts, the fertility rate was considerably lower than among young women who had only a primary education; the rate among those who completed primary schooling in turn was somewhat lower than for those who never attended school.

□ Would provision of school meals encourage girls to enroll and stay in primary school and could women's groups provide the meals as an income-generating activity? None of the experiments were sufficiently persuasive to be continued.

□ Was the cultural devaluation of females a sufficiently strong explanation of the low enrollment/high dropout rates? Research suggested it might be a powerful but not a decisive factor.

□ Was the fact that girls at puberty mostly are married and take up residence in another's household a powerful disincentive to parental, or specifically paternal, investment in the education of girls? Again, research suggested this could be an important but not decisive factor.

□ Was the need for the labor of girls in homestead and other tasks decisive? Research suggested that it was an important but not an insurmountable problem.

□ Could schools, reconceptualized as *places of learning*, increase their at-
tractiveness if particular aspects were adapted, including location,
timing and duration of lessons, lesson content, learning materials and
teaching methods, the facilities, the sex of the teacher, the size of the
class, and the mix of boys and girls in the class? All these were tested,
singly and in combination.

The overwhelming evidence from the experimentation was that neither
cultural, familial, nor economic factors posed insuperable barriers to increasing girls' access to educational opportunity. Suitably attractive, relevant,
and worthwhile education could be provided in the community at affordable
cost. The key was to reformulate concepts of education and educational provision so that the system becomes driven by the energy of girls and women
themselves and accountable to them.

Women's Advocacy of Education

At the same time, Bangladeshi women activists and researchers began to formulate a woman-centered vision of the education of girls. They argued that
it is an indivisible component of basic human rights, a tradition in Bengali
history and a duty under Islamic law. Further, they showed that one of the
strongest benefits for girls themselves of time in school is the time to mature, as individual people and as members of society, away from the pressures that push them straight from childhood into adult roles as wives and
mothers. They noted that many of the data relating to illness and death in
pregnancy and childbirth, abortion, and sexually transmitted infections
were particularly adverse for young girls and women in the 12- to 24-year-
old age group. Anything that helps to delay the age at first marriage and first
pregnancy thus has enormous benefits for women themselves, their families,
and the community.

The Next Steps in Nonformal Provision

In 1984 BRAC began to shape what has become its Nonformal Primary
Education (NFPE) program, for children 8–10 years old who had dropped
out of or never entered government schooling. It offered a second chance for
some, a first chance for others, beneficial in itself but also potentially a bridge
to the formal school system. The key components were:

□ an innovative 3-year primary curriculum, based on continuous assessment;

□ materials based on identified needs and interests of rural children;

□ class duration and timing adapted to family survival needs (2.5
hours a day for the first 2 years, and 3 hours a day in the third, 6
days a week, for an average of 270 days per year, the exact timing

determined by the teacher and community in response to local circumstances);

□ community-based schools housed in typical village structures on land rented from the community;

□ community participation in planning, staff recruitment, and management; a school committee of two parents, a community leader, and the BRAC Program Officer to supervise the school and monthly parent meetings, mostly during the day to encourage mothers to attend;

□ new materials and techniques for primary teacher training;

□ development of a paraprofessional cadre of teachers living within the community, staying with their class through the 3-year cycle.

Beginning and Growing

At the end of the first 3-year cycle, BRAC had more than 400 schools with more than 12,000 pupils. The cycle was timed to coincide with the government school year so that BRAC graduates could pass immediately into the formal system. On the completion of a cycle, the schools close or, where there remains a need, accept a further cohort of pupils. An evaluation by the respected Bangladesh Institute of Education and Research in 1988 showed that 90 percent of students completed their studies, with an average attendance rate of greater than 90 percent. More than 90 percent of the graduates joined Class IV in the formal system (compared with 60 percent of primary graduates enrolled in the formal system).

In 1988, classes for older children, 11–16 years old, were started in response to parental demand. Primary Education for Older Children (PEOC, or Kishor-Kishori) was designed to help those who were not able to enter or stay in school at an earlier age. The 3-year program was condensed, initially to 2 years and later to 18 months, and the content and materials were adapted. Special effort was made to encourage married girls also to attend.

BRAC and the community select the children from the poorest landless families, with a goal of enrolling 70 percent girls. By June 1991, the target had been exceeded: 72 percent of the younger pupils and 76 percent of the PEOC pupils were girls. More than 80 percent of the teachers were women. The teachers are appointed under contract and receive a small monthly stipend, beginning at about $11 a month, rising to $12.50. With few other local employment opportunities for women, this sum represents a useful, year-round income in a respected occupation and in itself contributes to changing social attitudes and opportunities. Not surprisingly, the teacher dropout rate is less than 2 percent.

Teachers are typically between 20 and 30 years old and have children of their own; therefore, the teacher's pupils and their parents are her own neighbors. As one of the teachers explains:

> Here we all know each other and the school is right in the village. The parents know me and they know where to find their children. If I am sick, my children run to tell the school committee so everyone knows what is happening. And if a child gets sick in class, I can send someone quickly for her parents to come. If a pupil doesn't show up, the others can tell me where she is or I can see her parents later. It's very safe."[15]

Learning, Not Teaching

The aim of the BRAC NFPE schools is to impart literacy, number skills, and social awareness by using materials and examples relevant to village life. The social awareness component emphasizes health, nutrition, hygiene, sanitation, safety and first aid, ecosystems, family life, the community, the nation, and the larger world. Simple approaches to science are also introduced. The methods of teaching encourage pupil participation and pupil-to-pupil learning, the development of comprehension rather than repetitious drills, and child development through physical exercise, games, dancing and singing, storytelling, and craft activities.

The methods of teacher training, reinforced by refresher training throughout the 3-year cycle, similarly are designed to stimulate creativity and self-confidence among young women and men who are only a few years distant from their own more stifling experience of primary education. Selected from the village where they will teach, they share the burdens and humiliations of poverty and oppression of other landless villagers, so teacher training methods must not only impart curriculum knowledge and teaching skills but also build a positive self-image.

Notwithstanding the stress BRAC places on developing alternatives to the stiff methods of the formal system, the schools must prepare their pupils for entry into Class IV in the formal educational system. Teachers, therefore, are provided with guideline routines and class management manuals that help prepare their pupils for life in the formal system.

Further Developments in Kishor-Kishori

Both the schools for younger children and the Kishor-Kishori (KK) schools continue to evolve during the current phase of expansion. Expansion plans sketch the framework, assess the management and training requirements, and elaborate the costs: they do not set out a blueprint for blind replication.

The Link Between the Kishor-Kishori Schools and Other BRAC Programs

One particularly interesting development is the link between the girls-only KK schools for older children and two other BRAC programs: the Women's Health Development Program (WHDP) and the Rural Development Program (RDP).

The WHDP currently operates in ten districts. Its objectives are to reduce maternal and infant mortality by 50 percent by a mix of village-based initiatives, drawing on previous experience with mass immunization, oral rehydration therapy, family life education, training of village midwives, and maternal and child health care. BRAC previously had shown that by mobilizing, training, and supporting community-based organizations, such as mothers' clubs and village health committees, poor, illiterate women and men can take increasing responsibility for maintaining their own health and administering their own treatment on a scale that makes a difference, without loss of quality. The RDP supports savings and credit activities and income-generating enterprise development. Both the WHDP and the RDP seek to establish effective working relations with government services and field personnel in a supplementary and complementary fashion.

By linking the WHDP, RDP, and KK schools for girls, BRAC hopes to amplify the effects of each in ways that translate individual benefits into socially desirable outcomes. The original design envisaged a 3-year lead-in period, beginning with the WHDP and the phased start of RDP activities. Women, however, are asking for an accelerated start to RDP activities to ensure that they have access to the means to carry out the things they are learning under the WHDP.

Knowledge and skills acquisition is reinforced, as mothers are encouraged to bring their babies to the KK school once a month. Each pupil becomes responsible for three mothers. Under the guidance of BRAC's NFPE Program staff, pupils weigh the babies and maintain their growth charts and are encouraged to talk about motherhood and family relations. Meanwhile, the WHDP program staff discuss with the mothers any problems raised by them, such as the hygienic management of menstruation, reproductive tract infection, contraceptive technology and use, child health and nutrition, and how their own bodies are made and function.

A young female gynecology intern who advises the program in Bogra district has been struck by the importance of creating a private arena for girls and women, a space outside the home in which they feel free to express their intimate fears and to ask questions without being made to feel stupid or ignorant (as government clinic staff are apt to make them feel). "No one in the village has any privacy. The family is always there. You cannot bypass the men but the future generation depends on the capacity, knowledge and education of our girls and women. We have to provide a place where they can talk."[16]

The Impact of BRAC on Government Provision of Education

The government recently has introduced compulsory primary education in a major effort to improve the quality of educational provision, under the General Education Project. With the support of the international donor community, it plans to build 20,000 new schools by the year 2000, accompanied by a range of new investments in curriculum development, teacher training and upgrading, and school management. Substantial though the General Education Project investments are, even under the most optimistic assumptions about improvements in enrollment and decline in dropout rates, it is estimated that some 32 million children in the 6- to 10-year-old age group, the majority of them girls, will drop out of or never enter primary schooling.

An explicit goal is to increase the proportion of girls who enter and remain in primary schooling. Within the limitations of government provision, the General Education Project draws to a considerable extent on the BRAC experience. The General Education Project will:

1. Collect, analyze, and use gender-sensitive data and monitor progress in the enrollment and retention of girls

2. Facilitate the recruitment of women teachers, for example, by emphasizing recruitment, training, and deployment within their own locality

3. Improve buildings to ensure appropriate washing, dormitory, and other facilities for girls and women teachers

4. Start a satellite schools program to bring flexibly scheduled classes closer to girls' homes for the first three grades

5. Address women-in-development topics, eliminate discriminatory language in new textbooks, and move to less authoritarian teaching methods and away from rote learning

6. Develop a new teacher training curriculum to upgrade teachers' knowledge and skills in such topics as nutrition, health, environment, and population education

7. Introduce a gender-sensitive population and family life component

8. Extend the secondary girls' scholarship program

9. Collaborate with the nongovernment sector in (a) administration of a school improvement fund to make schools more attractive and secure for

girls, and (b) nonformal delivery of primary education "along lines similar to those pioneered by Bangladesh Rural Advancement Committee"[17]

The impact of BRAC on the overall system has been more profound than this one explicit reference suggests. BRAC staff, in fact, are working closely with the local educational authorities as government provision expands.

In three districts where there are already 159 BRAC schools, for example, BRAC training is being provided to headmasters and their assistants, education officers, and adult education officers. The purpose of the training is to show how to set up school management committees and other mechanisms to involve parents and other community members in school programs and administration.

Making Sense of It All

A number of important points may be drawn out of BRAC's experience. First, the economic and development rationales for investing in the education of girls and women are irrefutable. Second, anyone interested in slowing or halting the rate of population increase should be on the side, unequivocally and enthusiastically, of the proponents of girls' and women's education. Third, boosting the participation of girls and women is achievable now.

If education is really going to make a difference on a scale that changes whole systems, however, questions of gender equity cannot be avoided. Deliberate effort is needed to change societal attitudes, women's own self-image, and the concepts in which gender relations are shrouded.

Men cannot, will not, or merely hesitate to take on this task alone. Without women's energy and commitment and insight into what needs to change and how it can be done with sensitivity while preserving harmony, the mere expansion of educational opportunity will fail to reap its full reward.

7

The Mahila Samakhya Program, India

The sound of bandits' gunfire echoes through the dry, bare hills of Manikpur Banda, Uttar Pradesh. Bonded labor, feudal oppression, and acute poverty bite deeply into the dignity of the people who live here. The women's voices are raised in a lilting song:

> We are hungry, we are naked;
> We work all day yet we go hungry;
> Now, we are not going to take this nonsense anymore!
> Go, announce this to everyone! [1]

In Sabarkantha District in Gujarat, women sit in a circle on the ground with their heads bowed. Their faces are concealed by the dirty ends of their ragged saris, which is how they have been taught to behave in the presence of men. Their husbands and the village council sit facing the women. "Tell me who you are," demands one of the men. Slowly at first, and then with increasing confidence, one woman and then another stands fully upright, removes her head covering from her face, and says her own personal name in public.

In claiming their own identities, in standing upright without shame, in speaking out loud without humiliation before men, in raising their voices in defiance of oppression, the women of Manikpur Banda and Sabarakantha are taking the first steps on the Mahila Samakhya path.

The Mahila Samakhya Program

The Mahila Samakhya program can be summed up as education for women's equality. It seeks to equip women with the tools for learning. Once women take those tools into their own hands, they are able to make choices and play a greater role in shaping the future for themselves and their families. Unlike traditional supply-oriented education programs, literacy and achievement in school are seen as the means, not the ends, of education.

The Beginnings

Improving women's access to educational opportunity in India is not a simple matter of expanding capacity. In Bihar, for example, 95 percent of children between 6 and 11 years old already live within 1 kilometer of a school. Yet Bihar has the highest dropout rates over the first 4 years of primary school of any state in India and fewer than a fifth of those children who enroll in class I ever complete class VIII. The nominal literacy rate of women is around 13 percent, a third that of men's; effectively, the vast majority of women are illiterate. By the 1970s, it had become clear to many that a more explicit attack on the multifaceted nature of educational deprivation was required.

In 1986, India launched a new National Policy on Education, under the guidance of an exceptional Secretary for Education, Anil Bordia. He combined two rare qualities. First, he dared to dream of education as a revolutionary force for social change, and second, he had the administrative and political skill to turn dreams into realities.

The policy places "special emphasis on the removal of disparities and to equalize educational opportunities by attending to the specific needs of women." Chapter IV of the policy states:

> Education will be used as an agent of basic change in the status of women. In order to neutralize the accumulated distortions of the past, there will be a well-conceived edge in favor of women. The National Education System will play a positive, interventionist role in the empowerment of women.. . . . It will foster the development of new values. . . . The removal of women's illiteracy and obstacles inhibiting their access to and retention in elementary education will receive overriding priority through provision of support services. . . . The policy of nondiscrimination will be pursued to eliminate stereotyping.[2]

In July 1987 Mr. Bordia appointed two women from different parts of India to travel the length and breadth of the subcontinent. Their mandate was to talk with women and men at every level of society, educationists in government teaching and research centers, and nongovernmental activists and service providers, to discover what would make a difference to India's discouraging educational record for girls and women. He wanted system-scale experimentation, not another small project.

Outline of the Program

The program that was formulated on the basis of such discussions was unique in India at the time in bringing together in a tripartite management structure three different groups: women activists, nongovernmental agencies, and

Department of Education officials. The women activists provide the strategy and the vision, effected through carefully structured management systems. The nongovernmental organizations provide training support and field-level assistance to the women's group facilitators and other functionaries. The Department of Education makes available its services and personnel.

The program was launched in ten districts in three states, Gujarat, Karnataka, and Uttar Pradesh. In 1991, the first steps were taken to expand to another two districts in Karnataka and to initiate comparable programs in Andhra Pradesh and Bihar (see the accompanying map).

The program operates principally at the village and district levels. An important organizational innovation at the state level enables local activists to have a degree of autonomy unusual in India. At the state level, Mahila Samakhya societies are registered to receive funds and act as the fiscally and

Mahila Samakhya Program: Uttar Pradesh, Gujerat, Karnataka.

Table 7-1

Overview of Scope and Coverage of Mahila Samakhya Program, January 1992

State	No. of Villages	No. of Women's Group Leaders	No. of Group Facilitators
Uttar Pradesh	340	421	38
Karnataka	450	932	49
Gujarat	240	313	34
Total	1,030	1,666	121

financially responsible program authority, independent of the central or state government. The executive committee membership, under the chairmanship of the State Secretary of Education, reflects the tripartite representation. Nonetheless, the program is carefully structured so that there is a preponderance of local women program workers under the leadership of a female State Program Coordinator. The role of the committee is to facilitate, not to direct, plan for, or manage the work of the district and village level activists, to whom it remains accountable.

The program overall is supported by a national Coordinator and a National Advisory Committee. Their role is to be advocates and defenders of the program in the central policymaking circles and to unsnarl any administrative and financial matters that cannot be resolved by the state-level Mahila Samakhya societies.

In each district, a District Implementation Unit, staffed by women program functionaries, initially coordinates the work of the nongovernmental collaborators, the education officers, and the women's group facilitators. The women's group facilitators work with poor village and tribal women to develop their sense of self-worth, the basis of all that follows. The whole thrust of the continuous training is to empower the group facilitators, and in time the members of the women's groups themselves, to take control of their own activities. The program is not intended to be a permanent structure; it is conceived as a catalyst to bring about systemwide change.

By the end of 1992, there were more than 1600 groups and approximately 50,000 group members.

Distinctive Features

The Mahila Samakhya program itself provides few other inputs or services. Its task is to enable women to reach out to the services and facilities that already exist under other programs, to help them make the links with the male-dominated bureaucracy, and to support them as they develop strategies for dealing with the problems they face. The program is not designed to be a permanent structure or an alternative channel for the delivery of services. It features three characteristics that remain the hallmark of its work: dialogue, partnership, and process.

Dialogue. The Mahila Samakhya program design itself emerged from a process of lengthy dialogue. The experience convinced the key actors that continuing dialogue should be adopted as a core management principle, essential to bringing together disparate agencies with diverse traditions.

Many of the nongovernmental agencies that were interested in working with the program were suspicious of the government's intentions and capacity. They tended to see government officials as oppressors of the poor. In general, they considered neither the central nor the state governments to be willing in practice to support anything so radical as the Mahila Samakhya program. The nongovernmental organizations were often also wary of each other, jealous of their own expertise and achievement. Their charismatic leaders were not used to allowing others into their territory.

Department of Education officials in their turn often found it difficult to understand the women's point of view and felt threatened by the implication of past failures. Men at all levels found it hard to accept that the program would be, or could be, run by women and for women.

At the village level, dialogue is the key to liberating women's fears and building a sense of solidarity among them. As one group leader said:

> Before, no one listened to women; now we have the chance to tell what worries us. We learn by being together. Our life is so small; at first we couldn't see how we could get out of our situation. We felt so hopeless. All we could do was sit and cry. Now we have joy in our lives. We are no longer alone. We can write an application, protest when the officials exploit us.[3]

Dialogue is also the key to bringing poor women and government officials to a closer understanding of each others' roles and visions. It is not always an easy interaction. The relationship does not necessarily go smoothly. People hear things they would rather not hear or have to deal with. Yet the Mahila Samakhya program has found dialogue to be a powerful way of moderating the problems of government programs in India, which are hierarchy, regulatory control, and bureaucratic inertia. One woman scolded a local official in these terms:

> Now you are here, that is good, you can see how we live, hear our voices, but when you go back to your office your eyes are closed and your lips are sealed.[4]

Partnership. Few initially believed that the tripartite management of the Mahila Samakhya program would succeed. The views and values of the three groups seemed to be too divergent: "The most ignorant person in the whole program is the government servant"; "It is the government's role to deal with people's problems, not the voluntary organizations'. They are always stirring the people to accuse us unfairly"; "What are we to do with these men! It is 'Bhai' this, 'sahib' that, and always 'sir', 'sir': when do they ever show us respect?"[5]

Nonetheless, the partnership works. The people involved all ultimately recognize that service must be complemented by self-management. As a senior Administrative Service officer in New Delhi acknowledged, a poor country cannot develop into self-confident nationhood if the people are always being handed things or are always having to beg for things from others. An enabling process must be instituted that moves from an expectation of service to an awareness of self-empowerment. Not one of the three partners on its own can shift the inertia, at least not on a scale that makes a difference to the system as a whole.

The nongovernmental organizations have the experience and skills for intensive, micro-level action and the capacity for creative and flexible response. The government has the policy brief and power to mobilize and direct resources and services in support of development, but it is tangled in red tape, hierarchical relations, bureaucratic regulation, and time-bound planning to tight targets. The women in the program bring their commitment to changing the lives of women and, through that, the lives of children and men in the family as well.

In the end, the program works because the women in the program are determined to make it work. More than that, they are determined to make it work in ways that express the visions and aspirations of women.

Evolution, Not Replication

The initial design of the Mahila Samakhya program was unusual in that no blueprints for action were imposed from the center and no numerical targets were set. As Mr. Bordia remarked:

> The numbers game is where the government creates its own problems. In most programs, the whole thing becomes driven by the need to achieve the targets set out in the central plan; activities are no longer responsive to the actual situation and the only accountability lies in meeting the target. In the Mahila Samakhya program, we know what we are setting out to do. We do not know what will happen. We don't know what we can do until we start doing it.[6]

Process

The concept of process is clearly distinguished in the Mahila Samakhya program from that of planning. The emphasis on process is consistent with the emphasis on dialogue rather than hierarchical control as a managerial and supervisory tool and on partnership rather than contractual or bureaucratic relations. It implies an acceptance of ongoing collective reflection and analysis, evaluation, and learning, a willingness for things to evolve rather than simply grow in a linear fashion. It expresses a desire for expansion as creation, as reproduction, rather than mere replication. A distinctively feminine point of view, it contrasts sharply with notions of growth as mass production of goods and services.

Management Style

The use of a process approach has meant that new tools had to be developed for monitoring and evaluation and new accounting systems and budget planning cycles had to be created. It has shifted the emphasis from impersonally transmitted written records to highly interactive and frequent meetings during which information and experience are shared vertically and horizontally. A wide variety of media, including song, dance, and theater, are used. Through carefully ordered overlapping committee memberships, decision making is kept as close as possible to the point at which experience accumulates. As one woman trainer noted, "It is the analysis which is the process and the event which is the information."[7]

The implications are that the shape of the program emerges from the specific circumstances confronting women in each of its areas of implementation. The Mahila Samakhya creates its space among each state's educational and administrative traditions and the potentially crushing local social, economic, and political pressures. The resulting variation in structure and detail remains coherent and manageable, however, because the initial process of consultation and dialogue has created a set of guideline principles. These principles serve as the touchstone for all decision making.

The Nonnegotiable Principles

Flexibility and diversity are matched by nonnegotiable principles that define the parameters of empowerment. They are a constant reference against which decisions and actions are held accountable: "Women become empowered through collective reflection and decision making."

The parameters of empowerment are:

□ building a positive self-image and self-confidence;

□ developing the ability to think critically;

□ building group cohesion and fostering decision making and action;

□ ensuring equal participation in the process of bringing about social change;

□ encouraging group action in order to bring about change in society;

□ providing the wherewithal for economic independence.[8]

Experience during the initial phases has given rise to a further set of principles, governing the process of implementation:

1. The starting phases, when women are consolidating their independent claims on time and space, must not be hurried or short circuited.

2. Women participants in a village determine the form, nature, content, and timing of all the activities in their village.

3. The role of program functionaries, officials, and other agencies is facilitative and not directive.

4. Planning, decision making, and evaluation processes at all levels are accountable to village women acting together.

5. Education is understood as a process that enables women to question, conceptualize, seek answers, act, reflect on their actions, and raise new questions. Education is not to be confused with mere literacy.

6. It is accepted that as an "environment of learning" is created, what women decide to learn first may not be reading and writing. Women's priorities for learning must always be respected.

7. It is accepted that given the time, support, and catalysts for such reflection, women of their own volition will seek the knowledge they need to gain greater control over their lives.

8. The educational process and methodology must be based on respect for women's existing knowledge, experience, and skill.

9. Every intervention and action occurring in the program must be a microcosm of the larger process of change; the environment of learning, the respect and equality, the time and the space, the room for individuality and variation must be experienced in every component of the program.

10. Women's awareness and perception of their role in family and society, coupled with a determination to participate in the decision-making process, will always lead them to demand education for themselves and their children. This, in turn, will create an effective vocal demand for educational facilities in the concerned villages. In an environment where this demand is articulated in a structured manner, specific inputs can be designed and introduced to meet their educational needs.[9]

The following sections examine how these principles translate into practice, through a series of personal and social transformations. They illustrate how the contribution of women to the resolution of population control and environmental problems at the micro level offers hope of bringing about systemic change with an impact on a wider scale.

Personal Transformations

Nothing will change until poor women from the villages are able to shed the fears and insecurities that crush their talents and creativity. The Mahila Samakhya program provides a cocoon, a safe arena where the values that are a part of women's lives are no longer to be hidden away but shared and honored so that all can draw courage from them. The Mahila Samakhya program creates a supportive forum for discussing such hidden problems as reproductive health and rape and violence, which fill women with guilt, shame, and humiliation.

Women's Self-Image

The Mahila Samakhya program places great value on a particular kind of preparatory and ongoing training for the often barely literate group facilitators and for the illiterate group leaders. For women who pass from a childhood of hard work to a lifetime of hard work as wife, mother, and widow, constantly at the service of others, the training process aims to give back to them their sense of self-worth, their joy in play, and the freedom to laugh out loud.

Great value is placed, too, on breaking social and internalized barriers that lead to isolation and fear of others, which keep women apart from each other. The selection of women who come forward to train as facilitators is a sensitive matter because of deep-seated caste, class, religious, and other frictions. After the program experimented with various selection criteria, it was discovered that one of the most important turned out to be an individual's own attitude to the challenging work ahead. Initial interviews and training are held at a place that means all applicants must travel and stay a short time away from home. It is their first test of whether they have the courage to depart from the customs that circumscribe their lives.

Women of low caste and tribal status and women who are the wives and daughters of minor officials and higher caste families learn to sit together, to eat together, and to sleep and wash in the same place. Their differences are reviewed in reflective, analytic sessions, which also draw out the commonalities among the participants, as women.

The selection of trainers is an equally sensitive matter. The Mahila Samakhya program seeks out trainers who are able to show through their own behaviors and training approach that they share the program's goals. The chosen trainers make no distinctions of dress or behavior between themselves and the participants. The emphasis in training approaches is on collective learning, not on didactic modes of teaching. The development of personal and collective self-confidence is among the first learning objectives.

The women's group facilitators, the majority of whom live in villages themselves, reproduce the training process in the program areas, as they make contact with village women. The women in turn come to realize that their informal meetings create an awareness of themselves as a group, with the potential for taking the process of continuing learning into their own hands: "We are not friends for just a few days. We are organizing so to be together for many years"; "We see that it is not true that women together fight together; that is only a story put about by men to stop us becoming powerful. Now we can share what we feel, now for the first time we are no longer ashamed of telling our stories."[10]

The program provides a small stipend to the group facilitators and a compensatory sum to group leaders to make up for their loss of earnings from wage labor but makes no rules about how the groups should organize themselves or use the money or how frequently they should meet the facilitator or what services they ask of her. In some places, groups have decided that group leadership should revolve among the members; other groups decided that it should be shared among two or three members. The compensatory sum is sometimes taken by the leader; in other cases the group decides to use it to support the group's activities.

As the program has matured, the groups have met together in larger assemblies, called *melas* in Hindi. *Melas* are popular traditional forms of assembly that are open to women and are often a time of merrymaking. The *melas* further enlarge and extend opportunities for the development of a collective perception of women as having an active role in the larger world. As one woman said, "I used to think we had only two eyes. Now I understand women have a thousand eyes, to see around Karnataka and even into the world beyond."[11]

Values and Meanings

At many of the program's training courses and meetings, the women conduct sessions in which one participant chooses a text to stimulate reflection on the values that are important in women's lives. They understand that system change must be connected to change within oneself. A group leader during the all-Karnataka assembly in 1990 chose a well-known poem by Akkamahadevi:

> Without understanding yourself,
> What use your understanding the world?
> When you yourself possess awareness,
> Why seek answers from others?[12]

Discussion of the text in the context of the work of the Mahila Samakhya program led to the following ideas:

□ "Without looking into and understanding oneself, we cannot help others to understand themselves and change."

□ "Before thinking that I can do something for poor women, I must first understand what I, as a woman, want to be; only then will my actions or my work have real impact."

□ "If we don't know our own potential, we cannot identify or see the potential in others."

□ "When we can see ourselves clearly, the whole world also looks different."[13]

Metaphors of Time and Space

The program has given rise to powerful symbols of women's right to their own time and space. For the women themselves, meeting together is in itself a symbol of their collective strength and a chance to forge strong emotional bonds of togetherness. This was symbolized by the exchange of items of clothing among women attending the all-Karnataka *mela* in March 1990.

The women have also claimed their own space in the form of *sangha huts* (group meeting places). The program offers support for groups to acquire land and construct their own huts. In addition to being practical, the huts are a visible symbol to the whole village that women have a right to their own space.

In Rajkot District, Gujarat, as the groups began to develop their ideas for *sangha* huts, the District Implementation Unit sought the assistance of a woman architect who had experience in low-cost construction. With the aid of the group facilitators, she developed inventories of local materials and designs, priced them, and provided the group facilitators with sufficient information to stimulate the construction ideas of the group members. Members were encouraged to initiate the process of approaching the authorities for land, working out the implications for siting the hut in one or other part of the village, and acquiring title to the land.

The members were challenged to think through the concept of the huts as Mahila Samakhya program huts or as huts that truly belonged to the group members themselves. At first, some members wanted to work on the huts for labor wages, but they came to realize that, unless they donated their labor and became involved in the decision making, the hut would be just another construction job, and they thereby would have placed themselves in a dependent contractual relationship with the program.

Others became enthusiastic at the opportunity to train as masons, who are customarily men. Eventually, women from eight villages volunteered for training in masonry and low-cost construction. Their example had a great impact on other women and men in the surrounding communities. The women themselves realized that they could make a sound shelter out of few and cheap materials, rather than toiling for hours and scrimping to save over many years, to help their families build a "proper" house of concrete. From the information, skills, and experience they acquired in designing and building the huts, the women realized how they could save their own time and labor, yet create their own space.

Breaking with tradition, the Mahila Samakhya program rented residential bungalows, not office accommodations. Decorated with the bright and welcoming products of women's handicrafts, they offer a sanctuary for women victims of violence or sexual harassment and a safe place for women to meet for training and discussion. There is space to sleep, cook, and wash. The bungalows at the district and state level, and the huts at the village level, are perceived as powerful material expressions of women's right to their own space and time and a symbol of a woman's right to protect and guard her own person from violence and sexual harassment.

The bungalows provide neutral ground for government officers, members of voluntary agencies, and members of the Mahila Samakhya program to meet together. They encourage the administrative staff who work there to keep in touch with the field work and the issues and the aspirations of the program. As such, the bungalows assert the nonnegotiable principles of developing nonhierarchical relationships and collective strength, in stark contrast to office environments, which emphasise hierarchical status and social distance. As one woman expressed it, "I came to this place with two bags— one empty and one full. I spilled out all that I had brought . . . and I am still going back with two sacks filled to the brim with new ideas and insights."[14]

Women's Reproductive Health

Time and again, village women identify a host of problems associated with their sexuality and fertility as major concerns that they have never been able to talk about before: "We were told that if we were sterilized we would receive some land but we were deceived. Now I have no land, only constant pain"; "Our daughters in Bijapur, the unlucky ones are given to the temple: what kind of life is that?"; "When the landlord's sons come, what can we do? If we refuse them, our husbands won't get work"; "My husband comes home drunk and I refuse him because they told me I would die if I have another child. Then he beats me, as if I were a dog."[15]

In Bijapur, Karnataka, the problem of giving daughters to the temple to provide sexual services (the *Devadasi* system) is particularly acute. Members of the women's groups and their group facilitators are slowly developing strategies for confronting the practice and the negative attitudes toward women that accompany it. In one case, when the son of a *Devadasi* taunted the group facilitator with derogatory sexual comments for mixing with loose women, she berated him for his attitude, and challenged, "Instead of behaving so cheaply, you should see what you can do to change the situation of women like your mother, and the attitude of other men!" On her next visit, he apologized and asked her and the women's group to help him organize the young men into a support group for oppressed and powerless women.[16]

In a preparatory meeting in Tehri Garwhal, Uttar Pradesh, in February 1989, the women participants requested a special night session to discuss problems of menstruation, childbirth and abortion, the reproductive organs, and the infections that afflict them. Never before had they had a chance to speak openly about these matters. They were eager to learn a vocabulary for naming what troubled them. They wanted to understand the causes. They wanted to know what to do so they would no longer suffer pain, humiliation, and shame.

They discovered how each felt herself to be the victim, not the beneficiary, of the health and family planning programs that purported to address their needs. The women dared not or could not express their inner feelings to the health workers and doctors. The women often did not understand what they were told. When they tried to explain their problem in their own words, the doctors and nurses did not listen or did not understand.

At the request of village women, training in women's reproductive health (a much broader concept than family planning) has become an important component in all three states. Contact has been made with women doctors and nurses who are willing to provide information and treatment. By helping women to understand how their bodies work and providing advice on good practices and recipes for herbal remedies for common complaints, the program has given women the chance to take some control over the management of their own sexuality and fertility.

Social Transformations

Although the Mahila Samakhya program is women-centered, the importance of bringing about wider transformations in attitude and behavior is fully acknowledged. The program devotes considerable thought and energy to bringing men into the process, developing new social services in the village, and demonstrating alternative models of leadership and collaboration.

Co-opting Men

The program functionaries, and in turn the group facilitators, work hard to develop supportive relationships among the various male officials concerned with the program. Another aim is to enlarge the kindly but sometimes patronizing opinions of charismatic male leaders within the voluntary sector. A further tactic is to show how the empowerment of women leads to the betterment of family life and more effective village development.

The support of men and youths is enlisted in the running of the women's assemblies, for example. Men cook for the women, help organize the supply of tents and other facilities, and generally release women from the daily chores that otherwise tie them to their homes.

The Mahila Samakhya functionaries also organize workshops for men and young people, partly to share with them the work of the program and partly to provide opportunities for men to reflect on how the participation of their wives, sisters, and daughters brings benefits to all. They are confronted at the workshops with their own gender biases—a particularly difficult but necessary moment, then helped to develop their ideas about how to bring about a better balance between men and women within the family and village society.

Another important task that group members have identified for themselves is to restore the self-confidence and dignity of their menfolk. Men's experience of poverty and dependence often leads them into wife-beating, drunkenness, or desertion. Particularly in the tribal areas of Uttar Pradesh, where desperate inequality, lawlessness, and religious and cultural conservatism make life unbearable for many of the poor, women see that their menfolk are utterly demoralized. The group members also willingly defy tradition and join with the men in their wage struggles, for instance, thousands of them daring to march to protest the illegal exploitation of labor.

Educating Children

Mahila Samakhya women realize that the education of children is central to the continuation of systemic change. Creative experiments to overcome negative views of education fostered by the government's schools, nursery schools, and creches occur throughout the Mahila Samakhya program areas. One such experiment, in Varanasi District, Uttar Pradesh, has led to the opening of "Flying Magic Carpets" (*Udan Khatolas*).

At an internal evaluation session in January 1990, some of the higher caste group leaders who were already literate expressed the feeling that they still had not been able to break all the barriers that would enable them to work comfortably with the poorest women. They also noted that one of the most important visions such women expressed was to be able to send their children, especially their daughters, to school.

With further discussion, the idea of *Udan Khatolas* emerged— community centers that provide attractive, safe venues for relevant learning for the children of poor families. A children's education worker from another state helped the Mahila Samakhya program to develop the idea.

A children's *mela* was held. Puppetry, theater, and music were used to develop children's creative skills, help them express their own experiences, and interest them in learning. The things the children produced at the *mela* subsequently were used as teaching aids. Mahila Samakhya group facilitators and literate group leaders (who have become the *Udan Khatolas*'s female teachers) were so inspired by the assembly that a series of assemblies were held throughout the district, culminating in a *mela* for the entire district.

Although quite a number of problems remain, more than half the participants are girls, and the classes successfully mix pupils from different social and economic backgrounds. The Mahila Samakhya program provides roll-up portable blackboards and helps the movement make contact with sources of information, materials, and expertise. Mothers and older children are encouraged to sit in and assist. The pupils' parents and the female teachers together identify when, where, and for how long classes should be held. As the pupils progress, parents are encouraged to enroll their children in the formal school system.

The Development of Creches

The program also links poor women to the government's creche program. Alternatively, training support is provided for those women's groups that want to establish and manage their own creche. The village women are quite hard-headed about the need for such a facility. They identify the care of younger children as a major reason why their older daughters are prevented from attending school or staying in the school system.

During the Mahila Samakhya training, the women are assisted to think through the steps needed to set up a creche, the resources available, the organization and management, its location, who can make use of the service, and so on. They also are helped to explore their own perceptions of childhood and the value of children. They identify clearly how girls in particular suffer from having no adolescence, no time to find themselves between childhood and early marriage. They analyze how the lives of both boys and girls are permanently blighted by never having a chance to acquire the tools for learning. They are determined to prevent the pattern of deprivation being replicated in the next generation.

Changing the Quality of Roles and Relationships

Women in the Mahila Samakhya program from the start have been acutely aware that if, as the program grew, the traditional forms of hierarchical authority, accountability, leadership, and decision making were replicated, the goals of the program could not be achieved. Space and time, therefore, are deliberately provided for collective reflection and analysis of everyone's behavior, for reaffirmation of the ways in which new roles and relationships might be created, and for the celebration and reinforcement of the collective esprit de corps.

One such occasion was the first all-Karnataka assembly held in Kowlagi village, Bijapur, March 2–7, 1990. It brought together the State Program Coordinator, district level functionaries, including the office staff, trainers and resource people from voluntary organizations and women's research centers, and group leaders and facilitators from more than 200 villages in the three districts of Mysore, Bidar, and Bijapur.

One exercise conducted during the assembly focused on the way in which women's *melas* had been organized in each of the districts and on how the all-Karnataka assembly itself had been organized. In one case, all the administrative staff, and not just the program functionaries connected to the field work, had joined in the effort. By sharing organizational responsibility widely, while identifying and respecting each person's role, everyone came to have a stake in the *mela*'s success. In another case, everyone had waited to be allotted a task by the coordinator, leading to confusion, resentment, and an unfair burden on the shoulders of one person.

This exercise led to another, in which everyone was asked to define the role and responsibilities, as he or she saw them, of the district level team. It became clear that many of the group facilitators were inclined to transfer responsibility to the District Coordinator and her team and to look to them for emotional support as "mothers." Further discussion clarified the strengths and weaknesses of the group facilitators leaning on the District team as mother-surrogates. They realized the danger of dependency if members of the women's groups came to lean on the group facilitators.

Later, the participants worked in small groups to analyze the way that accountability, collective responsibility, and delegation were being carried out in their work. Three important clarifications emerged:

□ When we work with a sense of personal authority, our work is more effective, enjoyable, and energetic than when we work under the directives of others or out of fear of other people's authority.

□ When we are able to take timely decisions and respond to the demands of the given situation clearly and authoritatively, we develop a sense of ownership and belonging over the process; otherwise, it is always as if we are doing someone else's work, or carrying out someone else's orders.

□ Sometimes, however, we need the guidance of others in making decisions, to enhance the quality of our work. For instance, if we are not able to exercise our personal authority in a certain situation, if we are wavering and uncertain when the need is for clarity and decisiveness, then the exercise of authority by others becomes important for achieving the larger objectives.[17]

Another important dimension of the Mahila Samakhya experience and training is the emphasis on understanding and breaking free of the pressures that lead women to oppress other women—mothers-in-law the newly wedded wife, mothers their daughters, keeping them home from school to help with the chores, or wives reinforcing their husbands' disappointment when the newborn child is a girl. They analyze how women's status is defined always in reference to their male relations and how, lacking any control over their menfolk, older women try to control women or girls who are weaker than themselves.

Many of the women who have taken the step of becoming group facilitators themselves had experienced these pressures when they first came forward for training. They were told that by moving around with strangers they would be shamed in the eyes of the world. They were told that they would no longer be suitable marriage partners. They were told they would disgrace the family if they mixed with women of other castes or religions. In finding the courage to deflect or defeat these views within their own families, they give strength to all women.

Group members and facilitators also take every opportunity to explore and celebrate the positive aspects of womanhood and femaleness. In Varanasi in Uttar Pradesh, the women's group members publicly celebrate the birth of a girl in the village with a song that tells of the joy a daughter brings to the home and the equality of boys and girls.

Relationships with officials and other authority figures also figure largely in the training sessions. Women create role-playing sessions about what usually happens, then construct creative strategies for a more self-confident, well-informed approach. The groups identify a case that concerns one of their members, such as cheating over distribution of the food ration, and determine ways in which they can use their collective strength to confront the corrupt official. At meetings such as the women's assembly in Bijapur or other occasions when officials are invited to be present, the officers, however prestigious, are invited to sit with the women in a circle on the ground. The dias, the red carpet, the chair, symbols of power and dominance, are done away with.

Learning and Applying New Skills

It is not enough for the Mahila Samakhya program simply to place the tools of learning in the hands of women. Opportunities for women to practice their new skills and derive more than psychic and emotional benefit are also important.

Women's Literacy and Education

Women and young girls in the Mahila Samakhya program reach out to literacy and school enrollment in many different ways. The program responds by encouraging and supporting the widest possible degree of experimentation and creativity. In some cases, the group decides the priority is to badger the Adult Education department to hold literacy classes. They choose a time and place to suit their convenience rather than, as more usually happens, that of the instructor. Subtle social pressures are applied to ensure that the instructor turns up regularly and on time.

In other cases, the women develop their own materials to assist their first steps in reading and writing. In Bidar District, Karnataka, at the request of the women's groups, a small news and views magazine, *Namma Nimma Matu* (Your Words, Our Words) was started in the first half of 1990. It provides materials in the women's own words, in the form of their contributed songs, poems, stories, and opinions, to encourage them along the path to literacy.

In Mysore, they have started "Sollu" (the chorus line in traditional songs), and other districts have developed similar magazines. The impact within the villages is enormous as the women begin to recognize their own words and the men begin to marvel that a laboring woman can sign her own name and read simple poems to her children.

In Karnataka, the group facilitators actively participated in 1990 in the Department of Adult Education's motivational campaign for mass literacy. They aided and participated in folk dramas and village plays that emphasized the benefits of the education of women and girls. One of the key themes focused on education as a means for overcoming dependence on others for information.

In other areas, the women's group or the group facilitators have approached a literate woman in the village to help the group get started or have co-opted their own school-going children to help them. They arrange the time and place, determine how fast they want to go, and seek out materials in their local dialect or start developing their own. In Sabarkantha District in Gujerat, a local dialect primer has been developed with support from women in the Gujarat State University, based on group members' experience of the life cycle of women.

Women and Environmental Problems

Group members encounter a wide range of environmental problems. In Manikpur Banda, in Uttar Pradesh, the main problem the women have identified is access to drinking water. Because they spend 4 to 6 hours collecting water, girls older than 8 years old are not able to attend any school or training classes. The group facilitators, the nongovernmental organizations involved, and the District Implementation Unit work together to get the provision of drinking water into the district development plan. They also investigate measures they could take themselves to ease the problem.

In all districts, especially in the tribal areas, the women's groups organize themselves to acquire land and forest areas registered jointly in their husbands' and their own names or, if a woman lives alone, in her own name.

They also organize to control the cheating and exploitation of the forest officials and big contractors. In many areas these two interests work hand in hand to cut out the big trees in what is legally protected forest. The officials and businessmen collude in paying the collectors of forest products less than the official prices. Forest guards may even arrest women for collecting brushwood and hold them until their families pay a large fine to secure their release.

In Baroda District, in Karnataka, the Mahila Samakhya program is working with BAIF, a voluntary agency focusing on agro-industry development and natural resource management. Members of the District Implementation Unit and group facilitators together reviewed women's involvement in the 850 dairy centers that had been established. They found that whereas men received the training, the inputs, and the cash returns, it was the women who did most of the work of cutting and carrying fodder for stall-feeding the buffaloes and cows, fetching water for the animals to drink and their udders to be washed, keeping the stalls clean, and milking the animals.

BAIF realized that the women had a great deal of knowledge about where to find the right kind of fodder, how to keep the animals healthy, and the problems of fetching sufficient water. For their part, the women had many questions, many things they wanted to know about dairying from BAIF. Subsequently, BAIF modified its activities to ensure that women were included in its technical training sessions and in training on keeping proper milk accounts. The women, seeing the need, reached out for the first time for classes in literacy and number skills.

Making Things Visible: The ASTRA Ole

The Mahila Samakhya program helps women to deal with the environmental problems that concern them in various ways. The case of the ASTRA Ole cook stove provides further insight into the strengths of treating environmental issues not merely, or primarily, as biological and physical problems. They are opportunities for people to learn how to better their lives and withstand the pressures to overexploit natural resources.

Group members in Karnataka identified the problem of lack of fuel and the health hazards and other problems connected with existing cooking technology. The Mahila Samakhya functionaries contacted Application of Science and Technology to Rural Areas (ASTRA), a unit of the Indian Institute of Science in Bangalore. ASTRA had developed a cheap, smokeless cook stove.

ASTRA's previous attempts to introduce its stoves through the village councils had not been successful. Somehow, the way ASTRA had gone about it had given rise to the idea that the stoves were not efficient and still smoked a lot. Because ASTRA's own staff were convinced the stoves offered real and substantial savings in money, time, and energy, they tried various ways to overcome these negative views.

In Bidar District the group facilitators and ASTRA field workers helped train women artisans, together with members of the women's groups, in the construction and use of the stoves. The training at first was rather mechanical, showing how but not why such and such a thing was done. Without complete information, the group members felt they did not have the information necessary to allow them to adapt the design and make innovations suited to their own circumstances and houses.

In Mysore, the District Implementation Unit and group facilitators surveyed their members to identify in detail the reasons for their apparent dislike of the stove. In the tribal areas, for example, the women did not like not being able to see the flame because they felt they could not then control the fierceness of the fire. They believed that food not cooked by a naked flame was unhealthy.

A concerted effort was made to get to the heart of the matter during a special session at the all-Karnataka women's assembly in Bijapur in March 1990. The session is described here in some detail because so often those who have no contact with the reality of poor women find it almost impossible to accept that such disadvantaged women can ever handle "difficult" environmental concepts, or analyze their own situation in a sophisticated way, or determine appropriate strategies for attacking their problems.

Participants first explored and analyzed the concept of *energy*. They worked in small discussion groups to identify all the forms of energy known to them, both spiritual and physical. They developed an inventory of the three main types of physical energy used in the village: human, biomass, and animal. Then the concept of the *calorie* was introduced as a measure of energy consumption. Various visual means were used to present the data collected during the ASTRA survey in Mysore. The women were stunned to realize that human energy was the second most important source of energy used and that more than half was contributed by women. They knew this in their hearts but never before had the means or the tools to see the matter so clearly.

They went on to analyze the implications for the productivity of labor and the exploitation of the village ecosystem. They paid special attention to the impact on women's health and nutrition. By analyzing their own experience in light of the survey data, they saw the great imbalance between women's food intake and their work output. They saw further how this led to low birth weight babies, difficult pregnancies and problems with lactation, the death of infants, and their own constant fatigue and illnesses. They realized how the imbalance came to be perpetuated in the treatment of daughters. The session concluded with the identification of a range of work-relieving technologies, including solar water pumping and water heating, and a plan to make contact with potential sources of information and assistance.

The Importance to Program Success of a Sense of Mission

The Mahila Samakhya program was established with the conviction that mere expansion of the number of school facilities or teachers and adult educators does not translate into effective access to education for girls and women. Yet without a significant and rapid increase in the education of girls and women, India cannot achieve its population, health, environmental, and economic goals.

The Mahila Samakhya program provides four things:

1. A safe place and time for women to express their energy and creativity

2. A forum in which women can reflect critically on their predicament, analyze their position in relation to the wider society, and develop their own ideas and priorities

3. A mechanism through which they can exercise collective pressure on the family and society to transform the situation

4. The opportunity to articulate their demands and needs in an effective and structured way

The mission of the Mahila Samakhya program drives its progress. Personal, even emotional, commitment is essential to overcome the inertia of large, male-dominated, bureaucratic, and supply-oriented educational and developmental services. With the best will and the deepest understanding in the world, it is unlikely that men alone can ever or would ever commit themselves so fully to the cause of women's education. Fortunately, men such as Anil Bordia have the judgment and generosity of spirit to see that women's leadership and power to act are critical to getting the breakthrough initiatives off the ground.

The mission of the Mahila Samakhya program also drives its management. Decentralized, participatory, flexible, and innovative planning and decision making are essential if the larger outcomes are to be driven by, and remain accountable to, the needs and priorities of women themselves.

If the program were to become driven by targets, by numbers, by the large policy picture, it would no longer connect with women's lives. If the Mahila Samakhya and similar programs failed to liberate women's own energy and the courage to transform family and society at the local level, the larger society would not be able to achieve the transformations it desires in the name of development, economic growth, and environmental sustainability.

PART

IV

An Exploration of
Reproductive Health

The Shrieking Sisterhood

The expansion of family planning services is as much in the interest of the environment as is the education of women and girls. Calculations based on survey data from around the world show that if the expressed needs of all men and women who want but do not yet have access to information, services, and contraception were to be met, then the rate of continuing contraceptive use would be sufficient to achieve the United Nations' medium range population projection.[1]

Education alone is not sufficient to achieve this goal. Neither women nor men can manage contraception effectively and safely without access to information and services. If women do not have rights of access to information, services, and reproductive choice, then their exercise of all other human and civil rights, including their right to education, is compromised. There is no either–or policy choice: education, family planning services, and reproductive rights are all essential components of the agenda.

The history of the attempted implementation of contraceptive-led, target-driven population control nonetheless has sharpened understanding that critical choices are to be made in the formulation of population and health policy. Choices that initially seem right, even humane in terms of the large picture, can lead to authoritarian, coercive outcomes. The degree and scale of distress that result, as in India under Indira Gandhi's emergency rule, when poor men and women were induced, for example, to undergo sterilization at sterilization camps run by army doctors in return for gifts of clothes or the promise of land, undermine the achievement of the initial policy goal.

Advocates of control must understand why providing more of what women want, in the way they want it, is more likely to bring about a sustained decline in fertility than a contraceptive-led, target-driven approach to family planning. The remainder of this chapter shows why this is so.

In the Way That Women Want

Too often, the phrase "in the way women want" is taken as special pleading on the part of a handful of embittered Western feminists. Their voices are discounted in the face of the seeming urgency of simply expanding the provision of service and contraceptive use. In fact, there is a growing, worldwide movement of women's health advocates, a movement that includes both women and men, backed by an unparalleled breadth and depth of experience in trying to design and implement appropriate, effective, user-oriented services.

In trying to make clear, however, what women want, women's health care advocates find themselves awkwardly placed in the present debates on population control. They recognize that, over the past several decades, the perception of an impending demographic disaster has driven much of the investment in family planning provision and contraceptive research. Women welcome the investment and, in fact, argue for greatly increased provision. They want expanded access to the means to manage and protect their reproductive health, even if the quality and type of service does not yet match the ideal.

Nonetheless, many women's health advocates criticize the way that resources have been spent in the past and reject the demographic justification. In practice, controlling births under the demographic imperative too often has come to mean controlling women's fertility. Women do not want their bodies and emotions to be the targets or the means of fulfilling other people's agendas, regardless of whether these agendas are pronatalist or antinatalist.

A Necessary Component: Safe Management of Sexuality

Intervention in fertility outcomes necessarily implies intervention in sexual behavior, possibly an even more sensitive issue than fertility itself. The expression of sexuality is woven into the power dimensions of gender relations. The consuming interest of population control advocates in controlling fertility, however, has blinded them to the importance of sexuality and the power relationship between men and women.

Men often feel ambivalent about allowing their wives and girlfriends to use contraception lest they thereby lose control over the women's sexual behavior. On the other hand, the main contraceptives that afford women some protection against the health risks of male sexual activity (the condom and, more recently, the female condom) are dependent on male consent and cooperation:

> For those choosing to be sexually active, contraception reduces, but does not eliminate, the risk of either pregnancy or RTIs [reproductive tract infections]. Unfortunately, the contraceptives with the best record for pregnancy prevention provide minimal RTI protection. Some contraceptives may even raise the risk of certain infections. Thus, decisions about contraception by individuals, communities, and policymakers should involve balancing the relative need to prevent RTIs and unplanned pregnancy.[2]

Better management of fertility thus does not necessarily entail for women themselves safe management of their sexuality. Yet, because of the links to reproductive health and contraceptive use, neglect of sexuality may undermine the achievement of fertility goals.

Reshaping the Population Agenda

Women's health advocates are building on the experience of the past several decades of family planning to formulate a new population agenda. The agenda builds on the guidelines of the World Population Plan of Action (WPPA). The WPPA was articulated first at the 1974 United Nations Bucharest Conference on Population and Development. Although it has been revised at subsequent population conferences, its key recommendation to governments remains "to respect and ensure, regardless of their demographic goals, the right of persons to determine, in a free, informed and responsible manner, the number and spacing of their children."

Women health advocates from diverse backgrounds and geographic regions met in London in September 1992 to discuss how women's perspectives on reproductive health and rights might influence the preparation and deliberations of the 1994 United Nations Cairo Conference of Population and Development. Each individual is a member of larger national and regional women's health movements and networks. Their closing statement has been widely circulated as representing the views of an influential female leadership that can no longer be ignored.

The framework for the new agenda includes the recommendations that:

□ Ethnic, racial, class, and other particularities of place and time be recognized in the way that reproductive health services are provided

□ The gender dimensions of women's social and economic vulnerability to infection, unwanted pregnancy, genital mutilation, rape, and other forms of sexual violence, be recognized and specifically addressed as necessary complements to family planning services

□ Objectives be expressed in terms of well-being and not population control

The Ethical Dimension

Fundamental ethical and human rights principles underlie what women seek, including:

□ Women, no less than men, are the subjects, not the objects, of developmental policy.

□ Women have the right, no less than men, to determine when, whether, why, with whom, and how they express their sexuality and manage their fertility.

□ Men, no less than women, are responsible for the effects of their sexual behavior and fertility on their partners' health and well-being.

□ Practices and attitudes that violate basic human rights and the principles of equity, noncoercion, mutual respect, and responsibility are not acceptable.

□ Women's reproductive rights are not to be subordinated, against their will, to the interests of others or to interests formulated in the name of the public, a religion, an ideology, the state, or the world at large.

Women-Centered Reproductive Health Services

As part of the new agenda, women's health advocates argue persuasively that the interdependence of fertility, sexuality, and gender power mean that what is provided under the rubric of family planning and how it is delivered need to change.

Women want to be able to regulate their own fertility safely and effectively, conceiving when desired, terminating unwanted pregnancies, and carrying desired pregnancies to term. They want to remain free of disease, disability, and danger of death due to reproduction and sexuality. They want to bear and raise healthy children.

Components of women-centered reproductive care thus include:

□ Education on sexuality and hygiene

□ Education, screening, and treatment for reproductive tract infections and gynecological problems resulting from sexuality, age, circumcision, multiple births, and birth trauma

□ Counseling about sexuality, contraception, abortion, infertility, infection, and disease

□ Prevention and treatment of infertility

□ Safe menstrual regulation and abortion when contraception fails or was not used

□ Prenatal and postpartum care and supervised delivery

□ Infant and child health services[3]

Women's Perspectives on Contraceptive Technology

Contraceptive technology typically is promoted under policies of population control on the basis of its effectiveness in preventing births. Women are at least as concerned with contraceptive efficacy in terms of protecting their

health and the degree to which a technology is dependent on the cooperation of men. Unless such concerns are addressed, contraceptives increasingly
will become the focus of growing tension between women's reproductive
freedom and the manipulation of women's fertility to achieve public-interest
goals. At the heart of the tension lies the desire of many women to increase
control over their own fertility and sexuality as a means of increasing their
control over the management of their own health and lives.

Challenge to Traditional Beliefs

Women's perspectives on contraceptive technology challenge the belief,
deeply embedded in religious and cultural convictions, that men have the
right to control women's fertility and sexuality. An age-old fear of unbridled
female sexuality not directed toward procreation haunts the debate. The rejection by women of the view that the purpose of their sexuality is to satisfy
the sexual needs of men is profoundly threatening to existing patterns of
male dominance. Women, however, do not or cannot trust men to take responsibility for protecting them from infection and unwanted pregnancy.

Women thus are prepared to accept the biological risks of contraception, but
often they do so with mixed emotions. Women recognize and appreciate that
in general the result of the increasingly widespread use of modern contraceptives has been beneficial to women's health. The benefits have been won largely
through the direct effect of preventing pregnancy and the mortality and illness
associated with pregnancy and childbirth. Nonetheless, many women, at one
time or another, have had negative experiences using modern contraceptives.

The reasons often have as much to do with the conditions in which contraceptives are made available as with the technology itself. Some of the reasons are dislike of the physical intrusion required for the insertion of some
methods, difficulty of use in actual home conditions, cost, inconvenience,
dislike of the medicalization of intimate and private acts and of dependence
on the provider or partner, mistrust of the longer-term consequences and
risks of using a method, and lack of follow-up and lack of concern about side
effects on the part of service providers. In short, women take into account a
range of concerns, such as safety, privacy, and their ability to control their use
of the method, and not just the method's effectiveness as a contraceptive.

It is these three factors, the balance of gender power, the ambiguities of
women's approach to contraception, and their desire to balance a number
of concerns when choosing a method, that challenge existing processes of
technology development and service provision.

The Safety of Contraceptives

Scientists and medical practitioners have been concerned about the biomedical aspects of safety in the development and introduction of new methods.

Much of what is known of the *noncontraceptive* health effects (negative and positive) of contraceptives, however, is derived from research in North America and Western Europe. Direct extrapolation from experience in industrialized countries to other settings might well prove inappropriate. Research in developing countries on the contraceptive-related safety effects initially focused on getting as many men and women as possible to use effective contraception for as long as possible. WHO subsequently led the investigation of a broader set of safety issues, including the degree to which social factors might affect contraceptive practice.

Further, the definition of safety has been left almost exclusively in the scientific domain. The views of users have neither been solicited nor considered in the design process. Much of what is known about safety has been prompted by the spontaneous reporting of adverse effects after a method has been introduced.

Nonetheless, much is still unknown about the noncontraceptive health effects of contraceptives in conditions of acute poverty and disease and about possibly variant effects among women of different communities. Nor is it known which effects are generalizable to women throughout the world and which are specific to a community, class, or age group in a particular context. Some effects are known to be specific, such as the high rates of amenorrhea among Pakistani Norplant users compared with the low rates among Swedish women.[4] The degree to which women in either country might regard these patterns as problematic is simply not known.

Women's health advocates point out that the implications of such effects cannot be determined by doctors and scientists alone. Users make their own assessments of what is tolerable. Menstrual disturbances, for instance, which scientists might consider medically unimportant might be viewed by women, or a particular group of women, as inconvenient, disruptive, frightening, or an indication of poor health. The judgments they make on these points, in turn, affect their assessment of the overall safety of the contraceptive method.

Women's views on the safety of the IUD and sterilization in particular are affected by the care with which these methods are delivered, irrespective of their inherent safety. Women's views are affected, too, by the ease with which they can secure immediate and effective reversal of the method if their life circumstances should change. Further, their views on the safety of a method are affected by factors that might have nothing to do with the safety of the method as a *contraceptive* but which the method exacerbates or leaves them vulnerable to, such as a sexually transmitted infection. Women's concept of safety tends to be conditional and relative, not absolute.

In brief, women's health advocates stress that the issue of contraceptive safety must be viewed in the light of a mix of women-specific concerns, including women's personal and social circumstances, the availability of health and family planning services, the quality of care, women's access to care, the mix of methods actually available, and the availability of safe abortion in the event of method failure or improper use.

All these considerations, in their view, should guide the contraceptive research and development process and the selection and promotion of methods. In practice, however, contraceptive research is driven by discoveries in the biological sciences. As Dr. Faundes, then working with the Population Council in Brazil, commented, "I don't know of a time that the development of a new contraceptive was started by saying, what women need is this, so let's try to study a method that responds to this need."[5]

Efficacy of a Contraceptive Method

Scientists and other researchers have tended to concentrate on efficacy in terms of method failure and user failure. The concren of women is a more pragmatic test of quality: fitness for function, that is, how a method works for them in their lives.

From a woman's point of view, a method's efficacy is assessed in such terms as whether concern for her sexuality or her fertility is uppermost in her mind at the time of use; if the method involves a partner's cooperation, then her view of her partner's reliability and care; if it involves a provider, then considerations of whether she can easily get the method changed or its effect reversed on demand; and, if the method fails, whether her options realistically include acceptance of the child by both partners, marriage, adoption, or access to safe and affordable abortion services. That is to say, a woman's assessments of efficacy involves trade-offs.

Women's health advocates make a strong connection between efficacy and abortion services. Many people find the whole matter of abortion a particularly troublesome issue, not just in its practical implications but also on ethical and religious grounds. Yet the issue cannot be avoided.

Contraceptive technologies are imperfect, and failure rates can be high.[6] Additionally, safe, legal abortion services allow women greater freedom to choose the contraceptive method that best suits their needs, even if their preferred method provides less certain contraceptive protection. As it is, an estimated 40–60 million women seek abortions every year, many as a last resort in the event of contraceptive failure. Around 200,000 women die as a result of unsafe procedures, while the consequences for many thousands of other women are calamitous. Ninety-eight percent of those who die are from developing countries. Treatment of incomplete and septic abortions also imposes high costs on hospital emergency services, perhaps an insupportable burden wherever public health services are already under pressure. These deaths, complications, and costs are avoidable.[7] Population control advocates need to consider whether it is acceptable to promote contraception without also supporting safe legal abortion services, given the consequences for women, families, and health services of managing unwanted pregnancy through unsafe procedures.

Reproductive Tract Infections: A Neglected Problem

Reproductive tract infections are another dimension of sexual and fertility behavior that have been neglected by population-driven services. Women's social and biological vulnerability to such infections, including HIV infection, has unacceptably costly and tragic consequences for individuals and society.

In an authoritative review of the evidence of the effectiveness of antenatal and maternal health care, the World Health Organization recently concluded "the potential for improving maternal and child health through detection and treatment of sexually transmitted or genito-urinary tract infections is high."[8] However, the demographic effects of reproductive tract infections, and their consequences for family planning programs, are still not generally appreciated.

Reproductive tract infections encompass three types of infection: sexually transmitted diseases (STDs), including HIV; overgrowths of organisms normally present in the reproductive tract; and infections caused by improperly performed procedures such as IUD insertion or abortion. Whereas it is obvious that the biological burden of unplanned pregnancy, whether carried to term or terminated, falls entirely on women, the gender bias in the biological burden of reproductive tract infections is less widely perceived. Their disproportionate effect on women arises from (a) anatomic differences between men and women that make reproductive tract infections more transmissible to, yet harder to diagnose in, women than men; (b) the fact that STDs are more often asymptomatic in women than in men; and (c) long-term consequences, which are more common and more harmful for women than men and more often lead to death.

The social and economic consequences are also disproportionately severe. In many cultures women are blamed as the prime sources of infection. A woman may be chased away from her children, family, and community if infection is detected. She may be divorced or forced to accept second or additional co-wives if she fails to bear a child or the number of children her husband demands, even when the cause is her husband's infertility resulting from infections acquired from relationships outside the marriage. She may have no access to the means to protect herself from an infection her partner brings into the relationship or no right to use those means or to insist that her partner take protective measures.

Unfortunately, the diagnosis and treatment of reproductive tract infections have tended to fall between STD programs on the one hand and ma-

ternal and child health programs on the other. STD control programs typically serve men and high-risk groups: such programs have no contact with
the majority of women. They emphasize after-the-fact curative intervention
in sexual behavior and directive counseling to prevent further spread of infection. Maternal and child health programs typically serve women and have
little or no contact with male clients or with young girls; they typically offer
little or nothing in the way of counseling about reproductive tract infection,
diagnosis, or treatment; they emphasize before-the-fact, nondirective counseling and preventive intervention in sexual and reproductive behavior.

Data from numerous countries indicate that STDs are major determinants
of perinatal, neonatal, and maternal morbidity rates. In Kenya for example,
some 10 percent of all births in 1987 were adversely affected by maternal
STDs; more than 22,000 infants died or sustained permanent disabling consequences.[9] Population control advocates must be concerned by such figures,
for high rates of infant death sustain a preference for high fertility.

In addition, as already noted, problems arising from infection, including
infertility, may be attributed to the use of contraception and lead to an un-
willingness to use the more effective pregnancy-prevention methods or any
at all. Further, the impact of reproductive tract infections on a community
may diminish the willingness to delay the conception of a first child or to
space subsequent births.[10]

The severity and spread of STDs also may affect demographic outcomes by
bringing about premature death before reproduction occurs, by reducing reproductive competitiveness, that is, the success of couples in producing children, or by directly diminishing reproductive capacity. Both empirical data
and mathematical models indicate that, in an increasing number of countries,
the incidence of HIV infection in particular may reduce rates of population
growth significantly over the next several decades.[11]

In private conversations, a number of population control advocates appear
to view the demographic effect of reproductive tract infections with some
complacency as the alternative to contraceptive-led fertility control. This
view reverses the chain of causes and effect. Effective contraceptive-led fertility control must include diagnosis and treatment of reproductive tract infections as routine components of health services.

Socioeconomic Dimensions

Measures to reduce women's social and economic vulnerability to infection
have been identified by the Eighth International Conference on AIDS as one
of the six priorities for global action to halt the spread of the disease. The task
is made more challenging by the rapidly changing nature of the family and
the household.

The Changing Nature of the Family and the Household

Rapid socioeconomic change is transforming the ways in which families are made, households established, and marriages occur. Both men and women in these changing conditions face difficult challenges to manage their sexuality and fertility in ways that do not impair their health or compromise their fertility.

Much social policymaking and legislation continue to be founded on the belief that the most frequently occurring type of household is an acknowledged family unit, whose core members are a male head of household and his wife in a registered and stable union, who conceive children only within marriage and jointly care for the children until their maturity. More and more, the reality is something else. In an increasing number of countries, in more than a third of cases overall and among poor households in more than half of all cases:

□ Households comprise women and their children.

□ Children are dependent on the economic resources of a single parent, most often their mother.

□ One spouse is absent for extended periods of time.

□ Children no longer grow up with both their natural parents.

□ The birth of a woman's first child precedes her marriage.

Marriage is now only one way in which households are formed, and the biological family is no longer automatically synonymous with a residential unit or a stable union. The management of sexuality is no longer subsumed within the management of fertility within marriage. Both men and women are learning to manage their sexuality and fertility and to protect their health in new ways.

Contraceptive technologies and services form part, but only a part, of the solution. The challenge is especially problematic for women because[12]:

□ Their access to resources for survival, and adult status, typically is conditional on childbearing, within or without marriage.

□ Short of abstinence or male condom use, the technologies that best protect women from conception offer no or unreliable protection from reproductive tract infection. The female condom, often cited as the solution, has severe limitations in respect to both contraception and protection; it can, for example, be removed easily by an unwilling partner and allows penile entry alongside the sheath.

□ Women must bear the biological burden of contraceptive use in order to avoid the risks of pregnancy.

□ The risks of infection for men and women are not equal; a woman faces a higher risk of receiving an infection from an infected man than a man does from an infected woman.

□ Young girls and women typically lack the power or the self-confidence to insist that their partners take responsibility to protect them from infection or conception, yet their partners, society, and contraceptive services often deny young girls especially the right or the means to protect themselves.

Increasing Numbers of Households Headed by Women

The percentage of women classified as heads of households in official, and thus conservatively estimated or measured, figures is high. In 45 countries, including the United States, more than 20 percent of households are headed by women; overall, up to 30 percent of households throughout the world are now headed by women.[13] Women-headed households typically are poorer than households headed by men and often are composed of several female generations with high rates of dependency. Poverty is both a cause and a consequence of such household formations. The phenomenon of female-headed households is likely to persist as long as the forces of economic instability and impoverishment persist.

The rate of growth in households headed by women is rapid everywhere and, in some cases, quite startlingly so. There has been a 70 percent increase in the United States over the past 29 years, for example, a 32 percent increase in Ghana over 27 years, and a 57 percent increase in Peru over 11 years.[14] The increase challenges family planning and reproductive health services to make assistance available to women in their own right without requiring spousal or parental consent, at times that do not threaten loss of earnings or child care, and at a cost that is affordable to women.

The Demographic Causes of Marital Instability

In demographic terms, the causes of marital instability include differences in age between spouses, divorce, separation, or death of a spouse, multiple partners, adolescent fertility, migration, and unpartnered childbearing. The mix of demographic causes and the point at which poverty, disruption of civilian life, epidemics, and other socioeconomic factors trigger one or the other vary from place to place.

In Bangladesh, for example, the age difference between girls and their husbands at first marriage is more than 9 years. A woman has a one in three chance of being a head of household by the time she is 40–49 years old, primarily as a result of widowhood. Divorce, however, is also a major cause of marital breakdown. As poverty bites deeper, the pressure increases on families to marry off girls as soon as possible (girls being regarded as a consumer burden on the parental household), while the chance of parents completing promised dowry payments decreases. Around 11 percent of girls contracting marriage as teenagers experience a breakdown in their marriage within 5 years. In conditions of acute poverty, parents and brothers are increasingly reluctant or unable to take the girl back; a substantial proportion of female heads of households in Bangladesh are still young women.

The immediate reasons cited by Bangladeshis experiencing a marital break-down typically include failure to produce a child or, in particular, a male child, and failure to keep up with dowry payments. For women, the final consequences of reproductive failure are increasing economic marginalization and an early death; a disproportionate number of women in Bangladesh who are either childless or without living sons die before they reach the age of sixty.[15]

Marital instability reduces the number of years in which women in their reproductive phase (15–44 years) reside with their spouses. A number of African surveys allow the proportion spent not in residence to be measured: for Kenya the proportion is 43.1 percent (1988 data), in Ghana 50.1 percent (1988), and in Mali 19.5 percent (1987).[16] It makes no sense to make family planning services and contraceptive availability dependent on spousal consent if a significant and increasing proportion of spouses are not living together, and men and women in their reproductive and sexually active years spend long periods apart from their official partners.

Nor does it make sense to tie family planning services exclusively to maternal and child health services. First, the maternal and child health setting typically does not attract or serve adolescents (male and female) or older men and women. Second, the proportion of a woman's life physically devoted to child-rearing declines as fertility declines; it now occupies only about seven years of a woman's life in an industrialized country and about 16–17 years in a developing country.[17]

Whereas child-bearing and nurturing continue to impose a distinct pattern on women's lives, a woman may be vulnerable to sexual experience and unwanted pregnancy for at least as many years as those spent in maternity. Increasingly, a woman's lifetime experience is conditioned by profound economic and social transformations that tend to separate men's and women's responsibilities and obligations with respect to reproduction, production, and consumption. The implications need to be recognized in policy, service provision, and technology design.

The Shrieking Sisterhood: An Example from History

A largely forgotten historical episode in late nineteenth century England provides a vivid illustration of the themes so far discussed in this chapter. It involves the passing of the Contagious Diseases Acts, one of the first serious attempts in modern times to manipulate and control the sexual behavior of women and reproductive health through government intervention. Many of the concerns that still vex the formulation of population policy, contraceptive technology, and reproductive health services, surfaced then.

The gender dimensions of sexuality and reproductive health subvert apparently simple technical interventions. An elite circle of male politicians and the medical establishment formulated legislation that melded the male point of view with the public interest. The legislation created more problems than it solved, and the cost was borne mainly by women.

The Contagious Diseases Acts

The Contagious Diseases Acts of 1864, 1866, 1868 (in Ireland), and 1869 were introduced initially to control the spread of venereal diseases in garrison towns and ports. Thereafter they were defended on the broader grounds of public health and the defense of the social and moral order. The Acts can be seen as explicit policy expressions of an elite male sexual ideology, which enshrined the double standard of men's right of access to sexual services while punishing those women who provided them.

Women who provided sexual services were considered by the Acts' parliamentary and medical protagonists to have entered prostitution as a result of their own unrestrained sexual appetites and thereby to have forfeited their claim to womanhood. Thus, they were held to be deserving of the harshest penalties. Women who sold sexual services were identified as the instruments of moral corruption as well as the prime source of sexual infection, who, simply by their existence, compromised the purity, fertility, and feminine mystery of well-brought up girls and married women.

The attitudes identified here are precisely those that women may meet today if they seek treatment from a male doctor for a sexual or gynecological infection.

Draconian Measures

The new science of statistics, which yielded alarming evidence of the incidence of sexual infection among serving naval and army men, lent authority to the promulgation of draconian sanitary measures against women. Under the Acts, a woman could be identified as a common prostitute by special plainclothes policemen and subjected to a compulsory, fortnightly internal examination. If found to be infected, women could be shut away in closed wards in "lock hospitals" for compulsory treatment for up to nine months.

The term *common prostitute* was never precisely defined, and the authorities were given wide discretionary powers of arrest under the Acts. If brought to trial for refusing to comply with the medical authorities and the police, a woman had to prove her virtue, that is, that she did not sleep with men, whether for money or not.

The policy was backed by a medical technology, a pharmacopeia, and a body of professional opinion that in general claimed far greater understanding of the cause and course of syphilis in men and women than was in fact the case. Gonorrhea was regarded as trivial in its consequences as far as women were concerned. In general, no distinction was made between gonorrhea and infections of the vagina. The treatment of syphilis focused on the administration of mercury, at therapeutic doses close to lethal. Purulent discharge and chancroid sores typically were treated by caustic ointments and cauterization of the womb.

By the end of the 1870s, gonorrhea as a cause of female infertility and pelvic inflammation had been medically established. The uselessness, even harmfulness, of the standard medical treatments of sexual infection were more widely acknowledged and the role of everyday liaisons in the transmission of infection more broadly recognized. The Acts' failure to meet their objectives gradually became apparent to all, and in 1883 the Acts were suspended.

The Ladies National Association

Under the leadership of the Ladies National Association (LNA), women activists played a large role in getting the Acts suspended. In a long process of parliamentary lobbying and public campaigning, they won the support of a number of more enlightened male medical practitioners, parliamentarians, and husbands.[18]

Intemperate vilification was a more common male response. The LNA's members were dubbed "the shrieking sisterhood" by the *Saturday Review* for their public campaigns against the Acts. The LNA lambasted the Acts as the embodiment of state sanction to "torture and corrupt" working women. They forced public discussion of topics considered unsuitable for "pure" women.

The LNA opposed a medical establishment that condoned male promiscuity as a physiological necessity. They protested the male medical usurpation of traditionally female roles as midwives and family health care providers. They refused to accept that cold numbers alone should determine policy and drew attention to the human consequences of infection for both men and women. Worst of all in the eyes of their detractors, they challenged male sexual supremacy in marriage and espoused the cause of voluntary motherhood.

Women's Rights and Status

Many of the LNA leaders had participated in earlier struggles against slavery and the Corn Laws before transferring their attention to women's rights.

Drawing on their earlier experience, they defined women's rights broadly in terms of a struggle for women's emancipation. Women's rights to higher education, medical education, the vote, and the necessity for reform of marriage, inheritance, and property laws all formed part of the broader agenda. The LNA also promoted a range of medical and health reforms and honored women's traditional knowledge of healing and the safe management of menstruation, pregnancy, and delivery. Further, as many of today's feminists and environmentalists do, they rejected the growing practice of experimentation on animals in the name of medical progress.

In addition, the LNA challenged the prevailing views of women's status as dependent on and defined by their familial relationship to men. They sought to expand the limits of female identity beyond those of mother and spouse. They proposed an ideal of companionate marriage on terms of equality and shared responsibility, rejecting the norm of submissive, dependent, and passive subordination to the male will.

The leaders of the LNA viewed their repeal campaign against the Acts as part of a larger program of struggle for human dignity in the context of rapid social and economic change. They drew attention to the inadequacy of women's wages, which forced many poor women in crisis onto the streets, and to the gender-defined labor markets that kept women out of the better-paid industrial jobs.

They also drew attention to economic policies that kept many men unemployed or employed at subsistence wages and that contributed to the break-up of marriages and otherwise stable informal unions. In placing casual sexual relations in the context of changes in family formation, marriage, and employment as a consequence of rapid economic change, the LNA also challenged the idea of prostitution as the occupation of a depraved female underclass.

The LNA's campaigns were driven, too, by an underlying anger and bitterness against the irresponsible abuse of the power men held over women:

> It is *men*, only *men*, from the first to last, that we have to do with! To please a man I did wrong at first, then I was flung about from man to man. Men police lay hand on us. By men we are examined, handled, doctored and messed on with. In the hospital it is a man again who makes prayers and reads the Bible for us. We are up before magistrates who are men, and we never get out of the hands of men.[19]

The Sisterhood Today

Many of the points made by the Sisterhood of mid-Victorian England rank high on the list of today's women's health advocates:

□ A pragmatic and humanitarian desire to address the needs of individual men and women at a time when rapid social and economic change is transforming the nature of sexual partnerships, the household, and the family

□ Rejection of the "tyranny of numbers" as the basis of policymaking

□ Rejection of exclusive male medical control of fertility, contraception, and sexual health

□ Rejection of male views of the risks of motherhood; the risks, safety, and appropriateness of contraceptive technology; and the diagnosis and treatment of infection

□ Assertion of women's reproductive rights as an indivisible component of human rights

□ A view of reproductive health services as forming part of a broader agenda of women's emancipation and socioeconomic change

□ A vision of women's autonomy that challenges male supremacy and the limits set by the roles of wife, mother, and familial relations mediated by men

□ An explicit linking of structural economic change, poverty, and the management of sexuality and fertility

The Tyranny of Numbers: The Bangladesh Case

The population policies of Bangladesh and the way they have been implemented are an abiding topic of conversation among women's health advocates and developmental assistance agencies. For some women, the case exemplifies the unacceptable costs of population-driven policy. For other observers, the case exemplifies the vulnerability of the South to policy prescriptions unacceptable elsewhere. Still others see it as a complex mix of too much of the wrong kind of family planning intervention and too little, too late of the right kind. Some in the population control community regard the returns to the huge investments that have been made as a success story, claiming that the prevalence of contraceptive use has reached 40 percent. Others believe a more realistic figure for the overall prevalence of contraceptive use (even stretching the definition to include abstinence, withdrawal, and rhythm methods) is on the order of 28 percent.

The purpose of retelling the story here is not to come to some final assessment among these competing views. The aim is to enrich understanding among nonspecialists of how seemingly obvious and necessary population policies and interventions can come to grief.[20]

Early Initiatives

When the East Pakistan Family Planning Association was founded in 1952 (some 20 years before Bangladesh gained its independence), its program outline made explicit reference to the need to slow the growth in population. The need for family planning in relation to problems of food supply and national development was stated as an explicit justification.[21]

On the basis of a report issued by the Population Council in 1960, the government began offering family planning through the health services and gave its blessing to a number of experiments in the delivery of service. The link to health-based rationales for family planning, however, did not become firmly established, either conceptually or operationally. Analysis of rates of population growth, economic growth, employment prospects, and the limited land availability together gave rise to increasing anxiety within government and assistance agencies alike. More urgent, more forceful, and more specifically control-oriented interventions seemed justified as a developmental necessity and as the humane alternative to the increasing misery of the poor.

The New Urgency

A period of expansion and intensification of contraceptive-led family planning began in 1965. A Family Planning Board with considerable financial and administrative autonomy was set up, targets were established in terms of numbers of contraceptive acceptors, and women were hired to work in the villages, motivating women to accept contraception. Analysts in particular commended the effort to communicate with and inform village women about matters still considered in conservative Bangladeshi circles as highly sensitive and that involved women motivators in moving around the rural areas, defying the norms of female seclusion.

The intrauterine device (IUD) was the main contraceptive method initially given priority, requiring insertion in a clinical setting by trained staff. This method was supplemented by female sterilization (which was limited by poor access to surgical facilities) and by the condom. Shortly afterwards, male sterilization was added to the list. The decision to emphasize methods that could be medically supervised and that offer semipermanent or permanent contraceptive benefits was widely considered to be responsible, appropriate to the policy goal.

The dynamics changed, however, when a set of financial incentives was introduced for doctors, paramedics, and recruiters who brought in volunteers for service. The incentives were based, respectively, on the number of operations, insertions, or acceptors. Acceptors were offered cash compensation for loss of earnings and saris or lungis (designated "surgical apparel") if they opted for sterilization. The incentives were developed under pressure to make a decisive intervention on a scale that might make a difference, to keep an already huge problem from becoming unmanageably large. There was also, in part, a genuine recognition that time lost from work imposed survival costs on the very poor.

The combination of numerical acceptor targets and financial and other incentives gave rise to widespread abuse. Although a few had signaled in advance their disquiet at the possible consequences in conditions of acute poverty and weak controls, the scale of abuse and the rapidity with which abusive practices became entrenched had not been foreseen.

Records were falsified in order to claim incentive fees. Information, counseling, and follow-up of clients were neglected. Speed rather than care became the watchword of all but the most scrupulous doctors offering services under the incentive program. Little effort was made in the case of IUD insertion to diagnose infections that might be transmitted into the upper reproductive tract. Far from being supported to make informed and voluntary choices, poor men and women were encouraged to offer themselves for sterilization in order to receive the cash and clothing compensation.

A Fresh Look

The liberation war of 1971 disrupted services and thereby allowed opportunity for a fresh look at policy and operations. Delegates to a national seminar recommended the suspension of the incentives, the introduction of hormonal oral contraception (birth control pills) for door-to-door distribution, relaxation of the abortion law, and the integration of the antimalaria campaign with the health and family planning services. These recommendations were largely accepted. Family welfare workers, previously responsible for antimalaria activities, took on community-based contraceptive motivation activities and the distribution of hormonal contraceptive pills.

The First Population Policy

The extraordinary demographic pressures facing the new country and the desperation of women's need for family planning as an alternative to unsafe abortion convinced the new government that a more vigorous approach was necessary. Many Bangladeshis, including women, approved the government's commitment to the expansion of services.

The First Five-Year Plan, 1973–1978, expressed the new government's commitment in terms of safeguarding the country's ecological viability. It stated that "no civilized measure would be too drastic" in pursuit of a reduction in population growth. In 1976, the government formally adopted a national population policy with explicit control objectives.

Remuneration for physicians was reintroduced to increase IUD acceptance and the uptake of a new and controversial female contraceptive, the long-acting injectable, Depo-Provera. At that time, the U.S. Food and Drug Administration had called a halt to clinical trials of Depo-Provera in the United States, and questions were raised about its appropriateness as a contraceptive in the poorer and less hygienic conditions of Bangladesh. A number of nongovernmental agencies that were collaborating in the government's family planning efforts criticized the method as its side-effects became more generally known. The government continued to recommend its use under clinical supervision, however, as a useful and possibly beneficial method for some women.

The effect of incentives on the use of IUDs and Depo-Provera was muted. Women's early experience of both methods was poor. Rumor of side-effects spread, and women generally refused to use either method as long as alternatives were available, a reluctance that persists to this day. In light of the overall program, however, it was reasonable to assume that the demographic and health consequences of low use would be slight, and little effort was made to address women's concerns.

The U.S. Agency for International Development (USAID) launched an inundation program to flood Bangladesh with pills as a solution to the continuing scarcity and inadequacies of clinic facilities and trained personnel. The pills were issued free through the existing community-based distribution program. Commercial retail outlets were allowed to sell pills and condoms for nominal sums to anyone who asked for them.

The risks of the pills being misused, or used by women who on health grounds should have used another method, were considered before the program was launched. Numerous health, family planning, and population control experts concluded that, compared with the public and private costs of repeated pregnancy, unsafe abortion, and continuing lack of access to any reliable method, the level of risk was acceptable.

The Family Planning Board was abolished, and in 1975 a Division of Population Control and Family Planning was set up within the Ministry of Health and Population Control. Population control activities were initiated through eight other ministries, and the collaboration of nongovernmental agencies was encouraged. After the International Year of Women in 1975, targeted "women in development" activities were launched with the purpose, among others, of increasing women's authority to make their own family planning decisions. At the time, these initiatives were praised as examples of the best practices known to the international population control community.

Exaggerated Expectations

Modest successes in limited areas gave rise to exaggerated expectations. Five areas were identified for intensive family planning campaigns with the aim of showing that zero population growth could be achieved, even in the difficult conditions of Bangladesh. An impossibly short time of 4 years was set within which to accomplish this. Drastic targets were set for a reduction in the total fertility rate (the number of children born to a woman if she lived to the end of her child-bearing years), net reproduction rate (the number of daughters a newborn girl will bear during her lifetime, that is, the extent to which a cohort of newborn girls will reproduce themselves), and contraceptive prevalence (rates of contraceptive use, excluding withdrawal, rhythm, or abstinence).

Widely circulated policy documents identified the target population as the unemployed, low-income poor, and the destitute. No doubt, people with the most insecure livelihoods and weakest claim on housing deserved as much as anyone better access to the means to manage their sexuality and fertility safely. But the way the policy was implemented in practice soon gave rise to suspicion of the government's intentions.

Adjustment and Reflection

By 1980, a marked shift had occurred toward promotion of the semipermanent (IUD) and permanent methods (sterilization), as service providers sought to meet the targets. At the same time, organizational adjustments integrated the family planning, maternal and child health, and health services. The effect was to make a greater number of clinical and surgical facilities available to the family planning program for the insertion of IUDs and the performance of sterilizations. The adjustment also in theory, however, shifted the policy rationale once again closer to health objectives.

The government recognized that cases of abuse continued. Regulators sought to curb malpractice by intensifying and expanding the training of private- and public-sector service providers. They tightened the registration of private physicians performing sterilizations. In addition, the government introduced a range of socio-legal measures to encourage smaller families and later marriage.

None of these measures had as great an impact as intended. Neither training nor registration addressed the wider structural conditions that fed abusive practice in conditions of poverty. Where they had a choice, women continued to prefer methods other than the IUD and sterilization. Maternal and child health clinics and health centers were still too few in relation to the scale of need, and performance standards were too low to make any dramatic impact on the health of the majority of women and children. The social and legal measures, though well-framed and in some respects even imaginative, were of little consequence except where they were tied, as in some non-governmental organizations' programs, to community-based legal information and education services and locally acceptable mechanisms for enforcing compliance.

The Crash Program

A mid-term evaluation of achievement under the Second Five Year Plan, 1980–1985, led to a period of further intensification. The military government then in power launched a crash program. Midwives and field-level health and family planning workers set targets for the number of village and ward level acceptors, by method, that they were supposed to recruit. Those who failed to meet their targets were threatened with punitive sanctions. District and subdistrict administrations turning in "best performances" in terms of IUD insertions, injectable doses administered, and sterilizations accomplished were rewarded. The government also reintroduced incentives for sterilization acceptors, as well as sterilization and IUD referral fees for health and family planning field workers. In the district of Mymensingh, the Army began a campaign of compulsory male and female sterilization.

The implementation of these measures raised a storm of protest. Survey after survey, backed by increasingly vociferous critiques by the community of nongovernmental organizations, showed that the abuses of the previous era of targets and incentives had returned in force. Voluntary, informed consent and client choice of method were revealed as largely a fiction. Many individual cases were documented of clients' use of methods that were medically counterindicated or, in the case of sterilization, ineffective in population control terms because clients had already completed their families. District and subdistrict administrations were found to be withholding the wheat ration from destitute women unless they accepted sterilization.

By early 1985, the international donor community of bilateral and multilateral agencies that had been supporting Bangladesh's population policies had become alarmed at the increasingly negative reports of the consequences of the crash program. The World Bank drafted a (third) program of support for population and family health activities for presentation at the annual donor aid pledging meeting, but it failed to win acceptance. Eventually, a number of donors withdrew their support for the population policy altogether or demanded substantial revisions and assurances that the worst features of the existing program would be abandoned.

Feminist Critiques

Bangladeshi feminists began to offer increasingly forceful commentary on the population policy and its implementation. They developed a highly critical analysis of government performance and donor support. They challenged the view that contraceptive-led family planning is the one, big, easy option for resolving population control and environmental problems in conditions of poverty and structural exploitation.

USAID became a special target of their criticism for appearing to force upon Bangladesh population policies, services, and methods that the U.S. government did not support domestically. They pointed to the U.S. delegation's strongly stated position at the 1984 World Population Conference in Mexico that more people do not mean less economic growth; indeed, the delegation had argued, population growth had been an essential element in American progress and that of other advanced nations. Further, the delegates had stated that if poor nations had a population problem, it was the result of the humanitarian efforts of the United States and other countries that had led to a lowering of death rates.

A number of Bangladehsi feminists argued that the disguised purpose of USAID's programs in Bangladesh was to provide markets for American pharmaceutical companies. They argued that American businesses, blocked from expanding at home by restrictive attitudes toward family planning and contraceptive availability, were seeking new markets under the cover of American aid.

Women formed a more united front when they accused the donor community of naiveté for failing to understand the temptations to corruption and abuse in a desperately poor society. They accused the population economists of failing to appreciate the consequences for the powerless of numerical targets administered by an insensitive but powerful bureaucracy.

They pointed out that in reality women had not had access to anything like the range of choice implied by the nominal list of methods available (sterilization, IUD, pills, condoms, vaginal foam tablets, two- and three-month injectables, Norplant subdermal implants, withdrawal, natural family planning, breastfeeding, homeopathic, and ayurvedic methods). As far as poor women in the slums and villages were concerned, information about the options was poor, services often inaccessible, or specific contraceptives unavailable.

Women researchers stressed that methods requiring male cooperation were difficult or impossible for women to initiate. In-laws often interfered in the adoption of other methods in their desire to see a male grandchild. They pointed out that methods that required privacy are problematic in the crowded conditions in which most Bangladeshis live, while those that give rise to disruption of menstrual bleeding interfered with sexual and religious duties and created anxiety. Others were problematic because of the high incidence of anemia among women or, if they were dependent on clinical facilities, because many of the local facilities could not maintain adequate standards of hygiene and care.

They further challenged the view that contraception alone was the best guarantor of maternal health. They accepted that in the prevailing conditions of acute poverty, by preventing pregnancies from occurring too early, too frequently, or too late in a women's reproductive years, many maternal deaths and the costs and complications of pregnancy and delivery might be avoided. But they pointed out that the experience of such countries as South Korea, Singapore, and Hong Kong indicated that safe motherhood as a universal expectation could not be achieved until contraceptive prevalence reached more than 70 percent and safe delivery became available to more than 90 percent of pregnant women. They argued that it was unlikely that such a high percentage could be obtained until major improvements occurred in other aspects of women's health and nutrition.

Women researchers argued that contraceptive use needed to be complemented by measures for the safe management of unwanted pregnancy, not the least in the case of contraceptive failure. Further, they argued that the contrasting experience of such countries as the Netherlands and England showed that, even with near universal use of contraception for planning and spacing children in both countries, there might remain significant differences in maternal and child mortality and morbidity. These differences depended, they pointed out, not on contraceptive use but on differences in the way that maternity and child health services were provided and the effective scope and reach of reproductive health services. One women's health advocate concluded:

> Given all these limitations, along with problems of service delivery, it is estimated that every year 750,000 women in Bangladesh have an abortion. Perhaps one-fifth of these have access to safe menstrual regulation through Government clinics; the rest risk their lives in clandestine procedures. For many women, a vasectomy for their partner is the ideal choice, but most men reject it. Most sterilization in Bangladesh is therefore undertaken by women, even though vasectomy is easier, safer and less expensive than tubal ligation." [22]

Differences of Judgment

At the heart of the debates that raged in the late 1980s in Bangladesh and that continue today over population policy, family planning services, and contraceptive choice throughout the world lie the deep differences in judgment about what is the most effective route to achievement of population policy objectives. The main polarities are:

□ A population control agenda that justifies services in terms of fertility reduction, opposed to a health agenda in which contraceptives and reproductive health services are seen as supportive of broader health goals

□ A population crisis approach that is prepared to sacrifice men's and women's rights, and funding for other programs, in order to concentrate on what is considered to be the prime task of boosting contraceptive acceptance, opposed to a developmental approach respectful of the principles of voluntary, informed choice, inclusive of maternal and child health services and measures to improve the sexual health, education, and status of women

□ A dedicated service approach that insists on focused delivery of contraceptive-led services, opposed to a client-centered approach that provides access to the range of services that men and women need to manage and protect their health, sexuality, and fertility, delivered in ways and at times and places that match the diversity of client categories and the different phases of men's and women's lives

□ A contraceptive-led approach that proposes that contraception is the best guarantor of safe and voluntary motherhood, opposed to a reproductive health approach that recognizes that the safe management of sexuality and fertility requires a range of services beyond contraception and maternity services

□ A coercive approach that assumes poor, illiterate men and women cannot be trusted to make those decisions in their own interest that would satisfy the public interest, opposed to a facilitative approach that supports and encourages individual men and women to make their own decisions, while shaping a context in which it is rational and possible for men and women to achieve smaller families and safe and responsible sexual relationships

Conclusions

Narrowly conceived, target-driven policies that seek to bring about population control through technical fixes lend themselves to coercive, authoritarian applications that are disrespectful of human rights and of the principles of voluntarism and informed choice that lie at the heart of the family planning movement. They are also ultimately ineffective, on four counts:

1. Increased rates of contraceptive acceptance do not guarantee high rates of effective and continuing use.

2. Target-driven policies give rise to a backlash or clandestine avoidance that in the end makes coercive population control inoperable.

3. Contraceptive services do little in themselves to change the context in which men and women make decisions about their fertility and sexuality: they simply augment the means available for their management.

4. By targeting women as the instrument for the achievement of state policy, target-driven policies diminish rather than augment women's capacity to make decisions in their own interest.

The alternate options are a health-based approach linked to democratic principles of development, incorporating client-centered reproductive health care that supports and promotes both women's and men's capacity to manage their own sexuality and fertility safely and responsibly. The broader agenda reconciles individual and public policy interests in ways that enhance and support the development of civil society.

Population control policies and environmental education share many of the same target clients, and both seek profound change in attitudes and behaviors. The past several decades of trying to establish and implement population policies and services carry important lessons for how population issues are handled in environmental education.

The three most important lessons might be:

☐ It is people not technology that count.

☐ Population control is a process, not an end.

☐ Those who are most affected must participate in the design of the means and the specification of the ends of policy.

To these might be added a fourth: the process must be accompanied by positive and creative initiatives. Constant harping on controls, regulation, sanctions, and coercion are demotivating. They tie up energy and commitment in confrontation and noncooperation, energy that is sorely needed for the pursuit of more creative activities.

9

Reproductive Health Initiatives in Bangladesh and Nigeria

It is in the intimate sphere of private decision making that population policies ultimately succeed or fail. As women begin to manage their own fertility and sexuality, they find it is not enough to transform the services available in the world at large: they must also respond to the unspoken realities of sexual relationships.

One of the most important of the hidden realities is women's experience of male sexual power as an aspect of men's physical and economic control over the lives of women. Violence within marriage, rape and mental abuse, incest and child prostitution are, if not typical, at least common. Many women accept violence and repeated pregnancy through fear of the economic insecurity that would follow on the loss of their partner's affection, or the threat of it. Thousands of women every year risk the costs, the pain, and the shame, associated with clandestine abortion, a trauma that could be minimized if men were more ready to take responsibility for contraception.

Poverty makes the achievement of loving, responsible relationships and the maintenance of stable families in which children can grow up all the more difficult. Poverty as much as fecklessness may turn men and women aside from fulfillment of their parenting roles. According to U.S. government data, the proportion of children born outside marriage has risen by a factor of four within a generation, as male unemployment has increased, bringing a corresponding rise in poor single-parent families, the majority headed by women. Nearly half of all families headed by single mothers live in poverty; 26 percent of all babies in the United States are born to an unmarried mother.

Contraceptive services can address only a small part of the problems caused by the underlying tensions in relations between the sexes reflected in such statistics. Reproductive health services and the three innovative community action programs described in this chapter take a bolder, more creative approach that goes beyond mere coping. In as yet modest ways, they show the potential for transforming the nature of gender relations, the foundation on which ultimately rests the achievement of desired population outcomes.

The cases are taken from the widely differing societies of Bangladesh and Nigeria. In their sensitive responsiveness to women's needs and gender relations in difficult, low-income environments, they hold the promise of safer, more humane and effective policies and services for women everywhere.

The Bangladesh Women's Health Coalition

Eleven years after the Bangladesh Women's Health Coalition (BWHC) opened its first clinic, it was supporting nine free-standing, rural and urban clinics, developed by women, primarily for women.[1] These clinics are the physical embodiment of a quality of care that satisfies both individual and societal goals. As with so many of the initiatives presented in this book, the clinics would not exist without the determination of women to prove that it is possible to transform circumstances by reformulating the basic concepts that shape the design of services.

Background

Despite the considerable investments that have been made in family planning and maternal and child health care services by both the government and nongovernmental organizations, the majority of women in Bangladesh still do not have access to family planning and maternal and child health care services. Without any question, the scale of need is almost unimaginably vast. More than 45 million women live in rural areas and more than 3 million in urban areas who are in their reproductive years, between 15 and 49 years old.

Around 40 percent of deaths among women in the reproductive age group are related to pregnancy, delivery, abortion, and other reproductive factors. Around 32,000 women die each year in childbirth. Where there is a surviving newborn, more than 95 percent die within one year of the mother's death. Between a quarter and a third of all maternal deaths are due to abortion, largely to induced abortion. Every year, between seven and eight hundred thousand women are estimated to resort to a clandestine abortion. Many of those who do not die suffer debilitating illness, infection, or sterility as a result of unsafe and unhygienic procedures. Medically induced abortion of pregnancies of 10 weeks or less is not wholly banned in Bangladesh, but it is legally restricted and in practice available primarily at the major teaching hospitals.

The evidence perhaps runs counter to the expectations of those who believe that women in Islamic societies are so protected that sexual relations do not occur outside marriage, that once pregnant, women always want to carry a child to term, that lifetime marriage is the normal lot of women, or that the chief dangers of maternity are experienced by older women or the frequently pregnant. Small sample surveys, however, indicate that more than 40 percent of the deaths from induced abortion are to women who claim to be married. More than 13 percent of all women of reproductive age are widowed or divorced, and many thousands more are separated from their husbands for prolonged periods; most have children to look after and provide for. Women in the age groups 15–19 years old and 20–24 years old each account for more than a fifth of all maternal deaths, with the highest absolute totals in the 20- to 24-year-old age group. Nearly a third of all maternal deaths occur among women who have not experienced a previous pregnancy or birth.

None of the women in these categories are well served by mainstream services, even if they had access to them, for a variety of reasons, including inconvenient service hours, lack of privacy, inadequate choice, lack of information, moral censure, rudeness and even abuse, apparatus that is frightening, particularly to first-time attenders, long waiting periods, and the need to visit different clinics for different services.

The Bangladesh Women's Health Coalition was set up to show how women's health clinics, even in one of the most impoverished countries in the world, can provide quality care to women who are in need, serve them with dignity, respect, and without censure, and together with their clients, develop the competence and courage among poor women to better manage their own reproductive health and the health of their children.

First Steps

The BWHC was established in 1980 by Sandra Kabir. She had been working in the regional office of Family Planning International Assistance (FPIA), an agency disbursing U.S. Agency for International Development (USAID) funds to nongovernmental agencies providing family planning services. After the Reagan administration decided to withhold funding for abortion and abortion-related services, USAID began to exert pressure on Bangladeshi and international organizations receiving USAID funds to segregate menstrual regulation and medically induced abortion from other services. (Menstrual regulation is a simple, low cost, safe, and in Bangladesh legal procedure for vacuum aspiration of the uterus.) Kabir joined a Bangladeshi organization, Concerned Women for Family Planning, but as it was receiving funding from FPIA, it also eventually came under pressure from USAID.

Sandra Kabir decided to establish a separate clinic for women requesting menstrual regulation services in a low-income urban area of the capital city, Dhaka. Initial support was provided by the International Women's Health Coalition, the Ford Foundation, and the Population Crisis Committee. She was inspired by three principles: clients must be treated with respect; individual needs must be met; and information and counseling must be provided to allow every client to make her own choices.

Openness to Client Needs

The three principles have shaped the development of the BWHC. They have led through experience to conclusions not usually considered important by family planning services, such as:

□ A mix of services is required, including menstrual regulation, children's health services, contraception, and women's health needs. In 1990–1991, 23 percent of the services dealt with family planning (including menstrual regulation), 39 percent with women's gynecological, obstetric, and health problems, and 38 percent with children's health and immunization. These proportions have been roughly constant over the lifetime of the BWHC.

□ Religious holidays and, in the four rural areas, the seasonality of harvest regulate the flow of clients to the clinics; staff, management, and administrative practices must be sensitive to these patterns.

□ Clients of urban and suburban clinics have a different pattern of need from those attending rural clinics, reflecting the relative instability and insecurities of life in urban slums; rural clients more often request general health and immunization services.

□ Many clients want to improve their overall capacity to deal with life through improved literacy skills. They exhibit a desire to learn that is stimulated and strengthened when clinic staff explain how women's bodies function and how contraceptive technologies work, as well as by the example of the staff themselves. By 1990, adult literacy classes were provided daily in all nine areas to groups of up to 15 women per group over a period of 6 months, taught by BWHC's community development staff.

In 1990–1991, the BWHC's nine clinics received 100,114 clients and provided 152,336 services, yielding a ratio of 1.52 services per client. The services included counseling, contraception, menstrual regulation, basic child and women's health care, prenatal care, immunization, and referral for other gynecological and obstetric care and sterilization. Whatever the reason for the visit, a client has access to all the services, 5 days a week, between 8 in the morning and 3:30 in the afternoon. Clinic hours have been adjusted several times to achieve the optimum match with women's working day.

Typically, a client spends about one and a half hours at the clinic. No appointments are made because telephones are not available to most clients and the phone system works poorly. Clinics are located in simple buildings in low-income areas. Locally made furniture, bright curtains, spotless cleanliness, and decorative posters and other simple displays create a welcoming atmosphere. The physical layout is carefully planned to ensure as much privacy to individual clients as possible and that adequate washing and toilet facilities are available, although the clinics are often crowded.

Nearly all the clinic staff are women. In light of cultural norms of modesty and a history of abusive male practitioners, clients generally prefer and feel safer with other women. Each clinic has two or three female paramedics, a program coordinator or administrator (typically with a Masters degree), a counsellor (a university graduate), a nurse's aide who dispenses medicines, two attendants, and two male guards. The staff are supervised by full-time physicians who also provide all medical and children's health services except immunization. In 1990, in three clinics the physicians were women, and in four they were men.

Against all traditions of government service, staff promotion and salary are strictly on merit, with equal emphasis given to technical and interpersonal skills and performance. The clinics are in turn supported by a small central office and board of directors, who also take advice from a core group of Bangladeshi women from various professional fields.

The paramedical staff are women from the clinic community. Selection criteria include a woman's attitude and skills, a minimum of 10 years' formal schooling, 18 months of government training as a family welfare visitor, and, typically, a number of years' experience as a family welfare visitor. Whatever their specific function, all staff are trained to provide basic health and family planning information. This not only provides more opportunities to answer clients' questions but extends the BWHC's impact out to the families and communities of the staff themselves.

Quality of Reproductive Care

The BWHC has pioneered discovery of what quality of reproductive care can mean in a low-income setting. Its record in providing quality care, sustained for more than 12 years across the range of its services, has pushed forward the boundaries to the point where what were once considered luxuries are becoming the standard for other nongovernmental organizations and government services in Bangladesh. Two services exemplify the case—client counseling and menstrual regulation.

Client Counseling

When the first clinic was opened, client counseling was hardly practiced and scarcely understood in Bangladesh. The BWHC believed that it is the client's right to know all she wants to know about her own body. The history of Bangladesh's population policy convinced the staff that the principles of voluntary, informed choice in family planning have no meaning unless counseling is valued, and that counseling makes an important contribution to strengthening women's capacity to manage their own sexuality and fertility.

Further, the BWHC recognized that deep-seated class and other attitudes meant that, in other clinics, providers had not provided and clients had not sought information about their problems, the way their bodies worked, why a particular treatment was being recommended, why the remedy should be used in the way specified, or the possible effects of treatment and what to do about them. One of the results has been the spread of major misconceptions and distortions among ordinary men and women concerning women's health, contraception, and related matters. (It is not strongly recognized enough in other settings, too, the extent to which past neglect of such services as counseling has created barriers to the further acceptance and use of contraceptive technologies.)

The BWHC's records illustrate time and again the pervasiveness of misunderstanding and false information. One client, when asked about her current contraceptive practice, said that everything was okay because she always took an oral contraceptive pill if she had had intercourse the night before. Another client in need of a menstrual regulation procedure was puzzled because her husband almost always remembered to use a condom and she thought she was safe from pregnancy. Another woman requested an injectable contraceptive because she had heard that if you take it two or three times, you never need to bother about getting pregnant again. Another woman, desperate to become pregnant by her second husband, associated her lack of success with the oral contraceptives she took when her first husband decided their three sons were sufficient.

Counseling sessions might work out to only 15 minutes each time the client visits a clinic, but counsellors stress to the client that she is welcome to return, welcome to request a change of treatment or contraceptive method, and welcome to seek more information. If a client brings her husband or partner, he is encouraged to join in the counseling session.

Clients seeking family planning advice receive information about a range of contraceptives. The pill is the most popular choice, followed by injectables. The IUD is the least favored, ranking lower even than the condom.

The Menstrual Regulation Procedure

Many clients arrive in a state of anxiety because they have had intercourse but used no contraceptive or have had no regular period since their last delivery or because they fear they or their partners have used a contraceptive incorrectly or that it did not work. A mother might bring her daughter, fearing that she has had intercourse against her will with someone from her own family or with a near neighbor, a not uncommon occurrence in the densely crowded housing conditions.

In cases such as these, clients are given careful counseling concerning the menstrual regulation procedure. No procedure is carried out unless the client herself gives full and informed consent. Clients are mostly married women of various ages, income status, and pregnancy histories. They typically are first-time clients who have never used a contraceptive and never had an abortion. The majority choose to use contraception after the procedure.

If consent to menstrual regulation is given, a careful bimanual pelvic examination is made and the client is checked for significant gynecological infection and medical or other counterindications. In about a quarter of the cases, clients are not eligible because they have waited too long. In that case, the client is urged not to resort to clandestine abortion and is given as much information as possible to support her in her difficulty. She is encouraged to share with her friends and neighbors the need to seek help early. In 14 percent of cases, clients have a medical problem that needs treatment before menstrual regulation can be performed. For those who prove to be eligible, the method and process is explained and clients are allowed, if they wish, to examine the apparatus. The procedure takes about 3–4 minutes. The BWHC, along with other practitioners, has demonstrated that fear, pain, and trauma can be eliminated or significantly reduced by the investment in counseling and the sharing of information and experience. The BWHC is convinced that menstrual regulation is an essential part of quality of reproductive care. Most clients do not regard menstrual regulation as a contraceptive but literally as a lifeline. By helping women to manage the risk of an unwanted pregnancy safely, the BWHC builds a new contraceptive-using clientele and reduces the tragic and preventable deaths and trauma of clandestine abortion.

The Community Development Program

The community development or clinic outreach program emerged in response to clients' and the staff's concern to bring those needing help in touch with the clinic services before major problems occurred. The financial sponsors of the BWHC were interested also in reducing unit costs by increasing the client load.

By June 1991, the community development program was reaching 9244 households. Households in the community development areas are registered by social workers using household registration forms. A community supervisor assigns each social worker a total of 250 households to work with: The social worker's role is basically threefold: to inform and motivate her clients concerning maternal and child health, gynecological, and contraceptive services, answer basic questions and clarify misunderstandings, and introduce clients to their nearest clinics if so requested.

Record-Keeping

BWHC's experience of providing quality care led it to reorganize and simplify its registration and record-keeping. Until 1986, filling out forms was complicated and time-consuming and yet did not allow management to track the pattern of demand adequately, service staff to monitor through time the pattern of different services provided to an individual client, or clients to readily understand their own records.

Not all problems have been resolved, but the effort to reform the flow of documentation has already paid off. Not only are the new systems easier for everyone to follow, but they also are beginning to allow the effects of quality care to be demonstrated. It is now possible to interpret, for example, the high rate of return visits as client satisfaction—happy with one service, clients return to request another. It is possible to show impact in terms of the nearly 90 percent of menstrual regulation clients who choose to use a contraceptive after the procedure. In the one district where the analysis so far has been made, 72 percent of post–menstrual regulation clients were still using a contraceptive one year later. The BWHC attributes the rejection of contraception by the minority as largely a result of the lack of a sufficient number of counsellors.

Financial Implications

The BWHC's financial record shows that a low-overhead, high-volume, multiservice approach is cost-effective. Cost analysis of clinic-based services for 1990–1991 gives a cost per service figure of about $0.65. Total expenditure on services was approximately $100,000. The cost per household visits under the community development program averaged about $0.22. Total expenditure on the community development program amounted to approximately $23,600.

Neither the individual clinics nor the BWHC are self-financing. It is unreasonable to expect that they could be in the prevailing conditions of poverty. Nonetheless, by 1990, two of the urban clinics met about a third of their costs through charging fees for service on a sliding scale. The level of fees has been set in light of the prevailing wage incomes. For example, the fee for a prenatal pathology test is one-tenth of the weekly income of an unskilled laborer. Although clients are encouraged to pay according to their income, not every client can, and it is an absolute rule that no client is refused service because she cannot pay. For the present, the payment of fees for service is beyond the reach of the BWHC's rural clients. Attempts were made in the early days to experiment with the collection of service fees in kind (for example, eggs) in the rural areas, but the experiment was quickly abandoned as unmanageable, unfair, and not cost-effective.

Nominal registration fees have been introduced at all clinics, partly because through discussion with clients, the BWHC learned that it strengthened clients' sense of self-worth. The clinic services are perceived as not just another charitable handout but something clients value and want to contribute toward.

Lessons for Bangladesh

Professional Impacts

The BWHC from the start has had the support of a group of concerned male and female medical practitioners working in government service and nongovernmental organizations. As the experience of the BWHC has grown, the medical practitioners have become powerful advocates of the BWHC's approach, both domestically and internationally. The BWHC's experience also has had an often profound influence on members of the international donor community. By demonstrating an alternative to contraceptive-led population control, the BWHC has enriched and enlarged the debate worldwide.

Impacts on Government Provision

The government has responded to the achievements of the BWHC by requesting the BWHC to provide clinical training in family planning services to family welfare vsitors enrolled in government training programs and in-service refresher training. This is a positive step, but more needs to be done if Bangladesh's needs are to be met. The BWHC can never be the whole solution, however many clinics it operates. The components of its approach that would most strengthen the government's program as it expands its services, are:

1. Provision of a mix of family planning and maternal and child health services at all levels of the health care system

2. Attention to the details of management and the logistics of service provision so that assumed access to facilities becomes effective access

3. Provision of choice among methods, accepting that contraceptive effectiveness is not the only criterion of concern to women

4. Greater accountability to women, for example, through local-level management boards

Women's Sexuality and Fertility in Nigeria

Many people see little of Africa beyond the images of war, pestilence, and famine, hear few of its voices beyond those raised in supplication or violence, know nothing of its past, and perhaps care nothing for its future. The images are not wrong: Africa is experiencing a prolonged period of multifaceted crisis and an almost unimaginable disruption of community and family life. The images, however, convey only part of the picture. There is enormous resilience in the African way of life and a gloriously creative indigenous competence. Both the problems and the opportunities loom large in Nigeria, one of the most anarchic states in West Africa and home to about a fifth of the continent's people.

Establishing the Parameters of Debate

Nigeria's population probably is growing at more than 3 percent a year. Although the middle classes are talking of limiting their family size, at least for the time being, under the impact of the difficult economic situation, there is little evidence that the low rates of contraceptive usage will change in the near future. There is also little evidence that low usage rates result primarily from shortfalls in the supply of contraceptives, although there is clearly an unmet demand from particular groups such as young unmarried women. Nor is there unambiguous evidence (as there is so clearly for South Asia, for example), that higher income, degree of urbanization, or female primary education individually lead to any marked decline in the desired or achieved family size. Further, the quality of the available statistical data is not reliable enough for confident analysis of large-scale relationships and trends. In brief, the determinants and parameters of fertility in Nigeria (and, indeed, in the rest of Africa) are not well established.

There are, of course, innumerable studies from the social sciences that illuminate the micro-determinants of fertility, but their interpretation remains a matter of controversy and doubt. At the same time, the relative neglect of the complementary domain of sexuality, and of how male and female sexuality is protected and directed within complex networks of lineage-based economic relationships, only adds to the lack of clarity. There is, moreover, extraordinary diversity among the multitudinous communities that make up the nation, giving rise to subtle but important nuances in gender relations and sexual bargaining.

Distinctive Social and Economic Patterns

Nonetheless, a few generalizations might be hazarded about the distinctive nature of land-based social and economic organization, the arena in which sexual relations and fertility decisions are played out. The link between socioeconomic relations, sexuality, and fertility is captured explicitly in the languages of Nigeria. For example, in Hausa, one of the terms for vagina is "the husband's farm." Cast in ideal terms, the fundamentals might be expressed as follows:

1. The basic unit of social reproduction in customary agrarian society was the hearth-hold, a mother and child unit of relative autonomy and separate identity, nested in a male-headed household and a wider set of lineage relationships. Many, and sometimes all, of the costs of bringing children to early adulthood were met through the mother's production of food for consumption or sale or by other activities such as trading. Land and other resources were allocated to each hearth-hold for that purpose. The hearth-hold might also contribute to the individual production activities of the husband and those of the household as a whole.

2. The name given to the hearth-hold, its space, property, and rights to resources were inherent in, rather than inherited from, its membership in a household and lineage. Membership was conferred by birth, in some cases by adoption, and by marriage. Customarily, dependents acquired through war, raiding, or trade also might be conferred subsidiary but not necessarily lifelong rights and obligations of membership. There was no existence, no identity outside membership in a lineage; conversely, everyone recognized as a member had inalienable rights to a livelihood and a place in society. In this sense, there was no such thing as an unwanted child.

3. Goods and services were produced and consumed in the first instance within households and lineages. Wealth was accumulated among (male) elders through judicious deployment of resources, the chief of which customarily was household labor for the management and cultivation of land and stock, for trading, and other activities. In the uncertain conditions of rain-fed farming and herding, which were the basis of economic life, additional labor meant additional wealth.

4. Access to and control over economic resources and benefits were vested in membership rights, not ownership rights. Land, the primary economic resource, was held under the stewardship of male elders for the lineage, its past, present, and future generations. The fullest rights were vested in those considered to have permanent membership. Thus, a woman might have full rights to land in her village of birth but only derived rights to land in her husband's village, which would cease at his death. The remarriage of a woman to her husband's brother is still a common practice, reinstating her membership in her late husband's lineage.

5. The responsibilities and obligations of men and women in a household with respect to income, expenditure, and tasks were based on clearly described individual roles and spheres of activity. Key economic decisions typically had to be negotiated on the basis of men's and women's separate enterprises within the household.

6. Women's social value was vested in their ability to reproduce labor. Womanhood was honored and defined in terms of a woman's ability to bear healthy children. A woman without a child was not considered fully adult and was seen to be of minimal economic and social value in terms of the wealth of the household or the continuation of the lineage. Women's reproductive and maternal health was carefully guarded and protected.

7. Rites of adulthood and fecundity were mandatory. They were what ratified and legitimized women's reproductive powers, specified the norms of acceptable sexual relationships, defined parenthood, and established the legitimacy of children within the lineage. Neither set of rites was tied necessarily to marriage or the stability of any particular sexual relationship.

These fundamentals continue to shape men's and women's decisions and aspirations in Nigeria today. Terrible damage has been done, however, to the coherence of customary life over the past several hundred years. The structures for organizing socioeconomic relations, entwined in a system of moral sanctions and rewards governing sexuality and fertility, have been deeply fractured as Africa has become increasingly incorporated in the world economy. The pace and scale of change is becoming faster and larger in scope. Nowhere else in the world is the rate of internal migration so high, the rate of urbanization so fast, or the rate of population growth so great.

Among the profoundest effects has been the loosening of the economic and social ties that bound men and women to each other within the household, the weakening of the supporting rites of adulthood and fecundity, and the displacement of the lineage as the source of authority and governance. What is left is often no more than an empty shell of rights and responsibilities that cannot be honored and of obligations separated from the means to enforce them. Nowhere is this more clearly seen than in the area of reproductive health and sexual relations between men and women. The population challenge cannot be addressed effectively without effort to evolve new ways of dealing with the resulting tensions in gender relations.

The Situation Today

Men in Nigeria typically demand and exercise the right to unrestricted sexual relations, no longer constrained by the controls of village life nor guided by the sanctions of household and lineage relations. Yet their concern to perpetuate the line of membership in their lineage remains strong, not the least because their own status within it in part still depends on their success in procreation.

At the same time, the economic ties that bind men and women together within the household have grown weak. Men's ability to allocate resources in land for the upkeep of women and children is disappearing, as urbanization, wage employment, and the commercialization of agriculture absorb the traditional rural economy. The low and insecure wages of men generate too meager a surplus to substitute for land. In brief, although economic circumstances have changed, men continue to bear few of the costs of children, while women retain the customary obligation of supporting the hearth-hold with fewer, or less certain access to, resources for so doing. Nonetheless, childbearing continues to be the main way in which girls and women can establish a claim to economic resources, social respect, and security in old age. Fecundity rather than marriage provides the means to survival, womanhood, adulthood, and the hope of a stable household. One of the greatest fears women thus have is fear of infertility. In the eyes of many Nigerian women, the West's concern for issues of fertility are an inappropriate emphasis.

Infertility rates in Nigeria in fact are high and probably rising. Infertility is the most common reason women request consultation at Nigeria's teaching hospitals, between one-half and three-quarters of all requests. In the majority of cases, the problem turns out to be blocked fallopian tubes as a result of infection.[2]

Infertility is so much to be feared that, as one woman in Lagos put it, "Women will not just do nothing . . . if the modern public sector fails them, they will find the money to pay a private practitioner, or just go and buy drugs over the counter, or go to a traditional healer."[3]

Some infertile women turn to prostitution in a desperate attempt to conceive. A study in Calabar found that more than 5 percent of prostitutes had become commercial sex workers in the hope of becoming pregnant by increasing the number of their partners.[4]

It is in this context that women themselves come to see their reproductive health concerns in terms of the probable main causes of infertility: unsafe abortion, unsafe delivery and postpartum practice, sexually transmitted diseases, and early adolescent sexuality and pregnancy. Such practices as circumcision and vaginal insertions to increase or dry up vaginal fluids in order to promote sexual satisfaction are also areas of concern. Fundamentally, these problems are seen as arising out of the complex socioeconomic circumstances that condition relationships with men and, therefore, are not solvable in terms of health or contraceptive interventions alone.

Nigeria's Population Policy

In 1988 Nigeria enacted its first population policy. It had two primary aims: the promotion of health and welfare, especially through the prevention of premature death and illness among high-risk mothers and children; and the provision of voluntary fertility regulation methods. The specific objectives of the latter were to ensure the availability of family planning services to all couples and individuals seeking such services, at affordable prices, on a voluntary basis. The definition of services explicitly included services to sterile and subfertile couples as well as "individuals who want to have children to achieve self-fulfillment." The main methods chosen for promotion were condoms, oral contraceptives, and IUDs.

Women enthusiastically welcomed the government's commitment to expanding access to family planning and better maternal and primary health care. Maternal mortality rates are extremely high, more than twice those of India and Bangladesh. However, they objected strongly to a number of features incorporated in the policy: women were targeted as the main clients of family planning services; the legal age of marriage was raised to 18 years; and maternity benefits were spaced at 2-year intervals. These policies were accompanied by the recommendation that pregnancy be planned to occur between the ages of 18 and 35 years; and that the number of children be limited to four for each woman.

Women found these provisions unacceptable on a number of counts. Many prefer to marry young and get child-bearing over early, and within a short space of time, so that they can concentrate on trading or other economic activities. The four-child norm tied to women leaves men free to have as many children as they want with as many women as they choose or can afford. This, combined with the identification of women as the main target for contraceptive acceptance, absolves men of all responsibility for population outcomes while putting all the burden on women. The impression that this was the intention of the policy was reinforced by wording that stressed that the "patriarchal family system in the countryside shall be recognized for stability in the home." As one woman Commissioner of Health put it, "Men should also take the responsibility but they don't listen and roam free."[5]

Women increasingly feel the force of the dilemma. On the one hand, many fear that modern contraception may impair their fertility permanently (as indeed IUDs might in the presence of an untreated infection). On the other hand, women are beginning to realize that reproductive tract infections also seriously compromise their fertility, and they want the means to protect their health themselves. Unfortunately, the only technologies that are effective in containing the spread of infection (condoms and, to a lesser extent, viricides) are also contraceptives and, moreover, ones that many women feel they cannot insist that their partners use. Further, male sexuality is expressed in part as a right to more than one partner, whereas female sexuality is expressed in part as the obligation to be available.

The fast-growing spread of HIV and AIDS intensifies the dilemma. The former First Lady, Maryam Babangida, summarized neatly the complex web of socioeconomic and sexual relationships that promote its spread, as follows:

> The virus has also cast a shadow over childbearing. . . . Infected women face a series of difficult choices whether to become pregnant, continue pregnancy or have an abortion. But we know that women are culturally expected to fulfil their reproductive obligations of pro-creation. In many African cultures a childless wife is scorned and repudiated. This may be a license and excuse for men and women to keep changing husbands/wives hoping for a child. This practice may unwittingly expose involved partners to greater risks of getting AIDS and other sexually transmitted diseases.[6]

The Society for Women and AIDS in Africa-Nigeria

The Society for Women and AIDS in Africa-Nigeria (SWAA-N) is the Nigerian chapter of the pan-African Society for Women and AIDS in Africa (SWAA), which was founded in 1988 by a group of concerned African women. The initiative has to be seen as truly radical, for matters such as sexuality, the behavioral causes of infertility, and the emotional intimacies of gender relations are not normally a matter for public discussion in African culture or even for private reflection between men and women or parents and children.

SWAA-N was established in November 1989 with a predominantly female membership drawn from professional women's associations, market women's associations, the government's Better Life for Rural Women program, religious groups, Women in Nigeria (a feminist research group), and the National Council of Women's Societies. Although its focus is on women, it recognizes the importance of finding solutions jointly with men.

Its aims are to increase AIDS awareness and action among women in Nigeria, to determine how HIV infection and AIDS affect the lives of women and children and their communities, to explore approaches to control that are responsive to the dilemmas women are experiencing, and to stimulate collaboration among government and nongovernmental programs.

One of its first activities was to organize the second pan-African SWAA meeting, held in Lagos in May 1990. As SWAA-N's organizational, planning, and financial management skills have grown, its activities have expanded. They now include:

□ An HIV/AIDS Drop-In Information Center in Lagos. The center is located in a central low-income area beneath a busy overpass. It is open from 10 a.m. to 7 p.m., seven days a week. From 4 to 7 p.m. on Monday through Saturday, SWAA-N members take turns providing additional information and counseling. Most of its clients so far have been young men and women and older single women with children.

☐ Branch activities in 12 states have stimulated collaboration with government and other nongovernmental initiatives in a variety of ways, including television panel discussions and radio commentaries in order to provide AIDS education, especially for poorly educated women.

☐ Media workshops enlist journalists' assistance in promoting AIDs awareness and promoting condom use. Other public education and advocacy, invoking poster campaigns and street theater, are also undertaken, such as correcting popular misconceptions concerning HIV and the spread of AIDS.

☐ A quarterly SWAA-N newsletter is edited and disseminated.

☐ In six states (as of 1992) there is training support on counseling, program planning, fundraising, and management.

Perhaps the most innovative step of SWAA-N has been to initiate discussions with women sex workers in the states of Cross-River, Borno, and Lagos, where there is frequent cross-border migration to and from countries that have higher recorded rates of HIV infection than Nigeria. Leaders among the workers are trained to provide safe sex education and counseling among their peers.

The project builds on earlier work by Eka Williams (1991 President of the Regional Coordinating Committee of SWAA and 1992 International President of SWAA), among sex workers in Calabar, a fishing port in the southeast corner of Nigeria. SWAA-N is finding that prostitution is an elastic term covering at least four categories of activity: hotel-based prostitution in which a landlord rents out rooms, thus nominally dissociating him- or herself from the sex workers, but serves beer and food to clients; a house run by a manager who collects the clients' money, accommodating both steady patrons who support a particular girl and more casual clients; girls who take a regular client who pays for their rent and living expenses; and casual pick-ups in discos, modern hotels, and bars, with clients paying for service at a place of their choosing. In addition to the full-timers, many single mothers, poorly paid working women, and young women students engage in occasional casual sex work when other sources of support run out.

As already noted, quite a number of sex workers in all categories have entered the trade, hoping to become pregnant and thus restore or begin married life. The commercial relationship shades into the much more widespread practice of sexual bargaining, whereby boyfriends are expected to give presents to their girlfriends, and husbands to wives, in return for having their meals cooked, laundry washed, and children cared for, as traditional roles and divisions of activity take on new meaning and definition. Unlike in other parts of the world, it is thus difficult to draw hard and fast distinctions between women in general and those at high risk.

Action Health Incorporated

Action Health Incorporated (AHI) addresses a somewhat different aspect of the problem, that of adolescent sexuality and fertility. A lively and widespread awareness is emerging among a growing number of medical practitioners, women's health advocates, and other opinion leaders that the customs of the past that served to integrate youngsters into adult society are now problematic. One study among secondary school students between 14 and 19 years old found that more than two-thirds of the boys and nearly half the girls admitted to being sexually experienced. The overwhelming majority used no contraceptives to protect against infection or pregnancy.

There is an increasing incidence of pregnancy among school-age girls and more than half are expelled, never to return to school. Estimates based on small local studies suggest that two of every five secondary school girls will have had at least one pregnancy by the time they leave school. There is a corresponding increase in the proportion of young girls among emergency admissions to hospital and clinic services after an induced abortion. Public health agencies and schools customarily have emphasized abstinence, however, and have been reluctant to undertake sex education programs for youngsters and parents for fear of being accused of encouraging promiscuity, behavior that has no sanction either in past or present society.

On the one hand, as a director of a private women's health clinic in Lagos noted, it is difficult to blame girls when they get into trouble, because "Being a woman in Nigeria means sexuality. Girls are trained to believe, the more sexual, the more woman. They are trained from childhood that womanhood means pleasing men, attracting men."[7] On the other hand, as a deputy hospital matron in Zaria insists: "In this modern age, we have to give daughters a way to go forward, daughters should have the chance to be protected."[8]

Origins of Action Health Incorporated

AHI was established in 1989 by Nike O. Esiet, a journalist. Its fifteen core members and five trustees include doctors, social scientists, family planning providers, and media/communication professionals. They began by providing, on a volunteer basis, in-school and public health education in poor urban neighborhoods on drug abuse, family planning, circumcision, and related matters. Initially they experienced considerable difficulty in dealing with social pressures not to recognize adolescent sexuality at all as a public issue. As their experience grew, their focus on adolescent sexuality and fertility sharpened and deepened.

Community-Based Activities

An ongoing project in Somolu Local Government Area of Lagos State aims to develop effective community-based interventions that address the problem of adolescent pregnancy among secondary school students. The schools were targeted for two reasons. First, secondary schools are the most effective forum for reaching relatively large numbers of the coming generation and their parents. Second, helping girls to continue their education in itself carries important private and public benefits. As the project got going, Esiet resigned from her job as a full-time journalist in order to devote herself to supporting the growing enthusiasm of the AHI volunteers and collaborators working on the project.

It started with a series of three seminars, for teachers, parents, and students, to discuss "family life planning," a convenient term under which to discuss sexuality, reproductive anatomy, abortion, contraceptives, infection, AIDs, and related matters. The aims were to generate support for adolescent fertility education, develop understanding within AHI about the specific problems and views of the three groups, and establish the basis for further collaborative work within the community.

The parents developed the concept of parent counsellors, that is, volunteers recruited from Parent Teacher Associations. The students suggested male and female peer educators and Health and Life Planning Clubs. Both suggestions were taken up. The AHI began working with the student volunteers to develop their knowledge and skills for counseling their fellow-students. The aim is to enable students to make fully informed decisions for themselves and to provide information on services should they decide they need them. Parent counsellors and peer educators have been trained by AHI so far in all thirty-three secondary schools in Somolu Local Government Area, and AHI is providing continuing support to the establishment and initiatives of the clubs.

Although all this might seem basic and ordinary, it is important to understand that AHI is operating in an environment that can provide them with virtually no information on how to achieve what they are trying to do. Few others have tried in Nigeria so far to recreate individual, family, and community norms to guide behavior adapted to the conditions of modern life or to recreate mechanisms for enforcing voluntary compliance.

AHI's approach has to be seemingly conservative, because explicit discussion of the problems of reproductive behavior and health do not normally arise between parents and their children or between boys and girls, or even between clients and health service providers. The very idea that teenagers should be allowed to make decisions for themselves goes against the grain of tradition, although clearly there is recognition that teenagers are no longer doing what their elders would want them to do (and perhaps their elders are no longer sure what the best advice is anymore).

As the project developed, AHI set up a community-based Youth Center. In addition to general entertainment and sports activities, the center provides education, information, and individual counseling on sexuality, body awareness, pregnancy prevention, sexually transmitted diseases and AIDS prevention, and the pelvic examination four days a week during after-school hours. It explores the mix of reproductive health care services, including contraceptive services appropriate for teenagers and how to deliver them. Basic clinic services are provided at the center by a qualified doctor once a week during after-school hours. Clinic services include primary and reproductive health care, pregnancy testing, basic sexually transmitted disease diagnosis, contraceptive counseling and supply, and routine risk assessment for pregnancy and sexually transmitted diseases. The center also organizes referrals for more complicated cases, including AIDS testing and cervical cytology. AHI tracks the use of all services closely in order to develop a guideline checklist of teen-friendly care.

It also has begun to develop a program of communication by using video technology (which is relatively cheap and widely available in Nigeria). The peer educators are establishing a Teen Video Team to make short videos of teenagers' views and experiences and of the work of the peer educators. The aim is to show the videos in other schools and at the "hot spots" where youngsters gather for relaxation.

Conclusions

If population policies were to take as their inspiration the real dilemmas of managing sexuality and fertility in a rapidly changing world, both the policy goals and the kinds of services that would flow from them would look considerably different from the crisis-driven advocacy promulgated today.

The cases presented here have been inspired by women's creative reconceptualization of the nature of the population problem and the kinds of services that make the difference. They show that poverty, of clients or nations, is no necessary barrier to providing a quality of care that, by addressing the range of women's reproductive health concerns, secures responsible management of fertility. They contribute evidence that such approaches can reconcile individual and societal goals.

They show that the search for new ways to help individuals manage their sexuality safely, beyond technology and beyond the presumption of stable family life, is a necessary and effective component of that effort, perhaps especially where the rate of social and economic change is greatest and profoundest in its effects. They provide the grounds for arguing that respect for and indeed enhancement of girls' and women's rights to make their own voluntary, informed choices are a surer foundation for the achievement of population stabilization than are authoritarian and coercive approaches.

They emphasize that solutions begin with the creative energy and vision of individuals, those who are face to face in their own lives with aspects of the larger problem. The cases presented here are just a few among many thousands of examples of pioneering, locally adapted efforts by women activists. As with the education examples, their power comes from rejection of mass replication of standardized approaches and the adoption of an evolutionary approach based on the unique human capacity for applying knowledge, experience, and information to circumstance. There may be no other way to bring about purposive transformation of the state of the world and its future development.

Women, Agriculture, and Natural Resources

10

Green and Just

The extent of women's involvement in managing agricultural and natural resources is considerable. The provision of appropriate production and marketing services, training and advice, such inputs as improved seeds, and more secure access to land and water would increase production, relieve stress on marginal lands, and strengthen household nutrition and incomes.

A woman-centered agenda, however, goes beyond these material benefits. Where women are involved in setting the agricultural agenda and in planning the management of natural resources, the values and priorities are different. Three principles in particular lie at the heart of women-centered perspectives: preservation of the regenerative capacity of seeds and natural systems, the sustainability of farming communities, and concern for future generations.

The development of a more sustainable agriculture and management of natural resources is not only or even primarily a technical matter. Farming systems that are productive, competitive, and yet less demanding of chemical inputs and more sparing of waste and pollution require greater management attention than chemical-based industrial farming. For example, farmers must spend more time observing and measuring nutrient flows through the soil and waterways and the natural cycles of pest and disease. They must create and maintain habitats in their fields and in the landscape in order to encourage pest predators and manage the flow of winds and water. The timing of interventions and treatments becomes more critical and typically may require management interventions beyond the farm boundary.

Effective management, in turn, relies on active examination of experience and knowledge and a strong flow of new information and action among farmers who depend together on a water catchment, forest, or ecology, that is, on the processes of social networking and communication. Thus, there can be no sustainable farming without sustainable rural communities that can care for the land and bear the higher management costs of responsible land care.

There can be no sustainable communities, however, where the goods and services generated by women are treated as cost-free, where the value of women's contribution is appropriated by men and the state, or where women's agricultural labor is assumed to be infinitely capable of making up the deficiencies of the market sector. As women environmental activists in Australia ask: What future do we want—just green or green and just?

Women and Land

Women in the developing world do not, generally speaking, "own" farmland in the sense of having legal entitlement to a plot registered in their own name, with full rights of disposal and management. Women's rights to land tend to be derived rights, contingent on marriage, descent, or membership in a larger family group, and women are frequently impaired by customary and legal limitations on their status as adult persons.

Women's rights of use over land are extremely various, complex, and subtle. In Imo State, Nigeria, for example, the right to harvest wild oil palm passes from men to women during the field crop planting months in recognition of women's roles in feeding the household. It is the season of scarcity, when household food stocks are low, but the family and any hired labor must eat enough to carry out their agricultural work.

For a number of reasons, women typically cultivate and exploit a much larger range of different microsites than do men. Further, the range of women's tasks means that they move around quite specific areas in the landscape, and it is simply more convenient if they can accomplish one (agricultural) task while in pursuit of another (such as fetching water). In addition, their need both to earn income and help produce food, fodder, fuel, and fiber means that only rarely can they invest their labor in producing large quantities of only one thing. To produce smaller quantities of a larger range, they need to exploit the different qualities of different sites.

The range may include, in addition to regular fields, such sites as roadsides (where particular grasses are gathered to feed to small stock such as goats), grain fields (where plants are weeded out and used as vegetables or as feed for the stock), the edge of fields (where semiwild leaf vegetables are sown and tended as vegetable supplements), forests for harvesting caterpillars and fruit and medicinal trees, and a homestead garden (which might itself encompass three or more different sites such as an old ant hill, a damper patch where waste well water runs, and the side of the house where vining plants grow). A woman may grow a second crop on the same land as her husband: one piece of land, registered in a man's name, with two separate crops, such as beans between coffee trees, and two managers.

Women's rights of use are becoming subsumed in male rights of legal ownership, as land registration proceeds in developing countries. Women's production sites are marginalized as commercial production and the corporate ownership of land increase. Women's rights of use are becoming less secure, more hidden, and pushed increasingly to the less fertile margins. Without legal title that can be offered as collateral, women face what can be insuperable barriers to raising credit. Where formal marketing organizations register only landowners as recognized growers, as in much of Africa, the income from market sales passes to husbands, even for crops that have been solely under women's management.

The Labor Contribution

Detailed analyses of the information available from agricultural censuses and local surveys suggest women's involvement in agricultural activities is greater than more aggregated data suggest.[1] A recent review of Indian data, for example, concluded on the basis of the hours men and women spend in farming activities that "most farmers in India are women."[2] Further, in many developing countries, women's agricultural labor input is increasing, as more and more men leave farming, temporarily or permanently, in search of wage work, and as children enter school. In Kenya and Tanzania, for example, as in many other African farming systems, children's labor customarily accounts for about a third of the total labor input to farming.

Women's labor contribution does not necessarily diminish as agriculture modernizes. Where family farms remain the basis of production, as in the Netherlands, the type of unpaid labor that women do on the farm may change, with bookkeeping, for example, taking over from milking, but the labor remains essential to the farm's commercial viability. In other cases, as in southern Florida, the squeeze on farm prices drives men into off-farm employment, and women take on the running of the family farm.

Almost without exception, agricultural development plans treat women's labor as infinitely available at no cost. Further, the resources allocated to domestic work, child care, and self-provisioning, especially women's labor, are assumed to be an infinitely flexible and transferable resource that can be switched without cost to the demands of new crops or farming practices. Only a single farm decision maker has been recognized, the male head, with the presumed power to make investment calculations of returns-to-resources on behalf of the whole farm family. Logically, from this perspective, advisory services and farm inputs and credit have been made available almost exclusively to the male head of household. Such models and plans simply do not reflect the reality.

Income and Expenditure

A varying but significant proportion of income accruing to men is lost to the household, being spent on private leisure and other individual pursuits.

Virtually all income in women's hands, however, is devoted to household and family expenditures, reflecting the socially ascribed roles of women in meeting daily welfare needs. Increasing the income of rural women thus may be one of the surest ways of increasing basic family welfare in the countryside. Efforts to increase women's income without relieving their workload, however, typically lead to two undesirable consequences. Women stretch their already overlong work days—up to 16 hours or more are not uncommon—and family welfare, such as child care or nutrition, is compromised by the hours women spend in income-earning work.

Women's spending has a significant impact on regional income multiplication that may exceed men's. One study reported by the Bureau for Research and Development of the U.S. Agency for International Development (USAID) showed that though men in one region of Kenya generally had higher incomes than women, women had a higher propensity to spend their earnings locally. Other studies by the International Food Policy Research Institute similarly suggest the importance of increasing returns to women's crop incomes in order to increase regional income multiplication effects.

Yet agricultural receipts for produce sold to the formal market typically are paid to men, on the grounds that they are the household heads and, even where there is no legal title, the presumed owners of land. Unfortunately, it cannot be assumed that the income received by men then trickles across to women within the household.

Implicitly, the concentration of income in male hands assumes that men "own" women's labor within the household, as well as the land and the capital accruing from such labor. Yet the assumption does scant justice to the nuances of economic relationships and control over resources that exist between men and women within households. In some parts of Nigeria and the Cameroon, for example, a husband must pay his wife if she works in his fields. Analysis shows that, in such cases, it is the intrahousehold rate of compensation rather than market opportunity costs that determines how women allocate their labor. When deprived of a just return for their labor, women have neither the incentive nor the means to increase their labor productivity and efficiency. Conversely, predictions of agricultural growth based on an increased flow of credit or the provision of price incentives can never be achieved if the investments and benefits do not in fact also reach the women who do the work.

Women and Agricultural Services

Only a small proportion of state expenditures on agricultural research, advisory and training services, and subsidies and price supports ever benefits women. In part this reflects naive assumptions that only men really farm or a reluctance to disturb the harmony of the household. Often, even with good intentions, it reflects a lack of effort to adjust the way that services are provided. If training, for example, is provided only through residential courses that entail sustained periods away from home, or that provide no child-care facilities or no separate washrooms for men and women, women may be unlikely to attend.

It might be that planners simply have not caught up with changing realities. A recent survey in Nyeri District of Kenya, for example, found that in 70 percent of the households interviewed, the husband was absent and the wife cultivated the entire holding. In the other 30 percent of the households, the wife cultivated her own plots within the holding. Decisions about crops and input use were, in the majority of cases, made by the women, with only credit decisions being made by the husband or by both spouses jointly. Yet male farmers were more than four times as likely to receive a visit from an agricultural adviser than female farmers.[3]

Agricultural bureaucracies have proved to be excessively rigid in responding to the diversity of production roles that men and women perform. There are important consequences. The efficiency of male labor has increased, and the returns to increased production have been captured largely by men. Productivity gaps have been created or widened between men and women. Where the division of labor and responsibility between men and women is also inflexible, such changes have tended to increase the labor of women disproportionately compared with men's labor. For example, a man might receive oxen for plowing, which enable him to open up a larger acreage or to carry out row planting, while his wife is expected to continue to weed using only a hoe.

Two contrasting cases illustrate this point. In Botswana, analysis of 1984 production data shows that while women contributed almost 70 percent of the value of arable production, they received the benefit of less than 15 percent of government expenditures made to that subsector.[4] With high male outmigration and an increasing proportion of children in school, more and more work on the farm and in the home falls on women's shoulders. Yet women receive little support from government agricultural advisory services and only uncertain financial help from their husbands' own typically low and insecure wages.

One response has been for women in Botswana to develop close intergenerational ties among their own female relatives. Often living apart, they diversify and spread economic and social risk and reward among themselves. Urban informal sector income can be called upon if a crop fails, or a sorghum surplus may be shifted to an urban relative for beer-brewing to generate higher cash returns, or a child in need of care might be moved to live with a rural grandmother. Although these are important coping mechanisms, they do not allow much room for the development of social and economic capacity to invest in sustainable and productive farming.

Zimbabwe provides a contrasting case. Women farmers dominate the small farm food sector. Their access to advice, training, credit, fertilizer, and other inputs was increased significantly through targeted programming and the removal of barriers to women's access. Further, the Agricultural Finance Corporation discontinued the practice of requiring husbands to sign women's credit papers, in recognition of the fact that many women were the farm managers while their husbands lived in town. Similarly, the marketing organizations allow women to register as members in their own names, which ensures that crop payments reach those who actually invest their time, labor, and skills in food production. The response has been tremendous: maize output from the small farm sector rose from 6 percent of the national total in 1982 to more than 50 percent by the end of the decade.

Women-Centered Principles

Women farmers and developmental advisers have derived from their experience of agricultural development three principles that challenge the narrowly technical and economic terms in which agricultural futures are debated. One has to do with the regenerative capacity of life itself. The outstanding exponent of this point of view is Vandana Shiva, a physicist and Director of the Foundation for Science, Technology, and Natural Resource Policy in Dehradun, India. The second principle has to do with the sense that there can be no agricultural sustainability unless social and economic relations sustain the community life on which farming as a human activity depends. The third principle is that the rural environment should nurture the future of the children and grandchildren and remain a safe place for the generations to come.

The Feminine Principle

Vandana Shiva makes an elegant and compelling defense of the regenerative capacity of life, which she terms "the feminine principle."[5] She links women's age-old roles in growing food, storing grain, and selecting seed with their roles in human reproduction, that is, the conservation and reproduction of genetic potential through the generations as creative and evolutionary processes of self-renewal.

She makes a further link. The "green revolution" approach to producing agricultural surplus is based largely on the breeding of new hybrid varieties of a small range of relatively uniform crop types and the reduction of variation in growing conditions through the application of chemical fertilizers, chemical pest and disease controls, mechanization, and irrigation. The sterile hybrid seeds, which cannot reproduce themselves, and industrialized agriculture, which is endlessly repetitive and uniform, supplying processing factories and mass markets intolerant of diversity, are far removed from the power of self-renewal.

Traditional varieties of crops, rich in genetic diversity, have been displaced over broad areas by green revolution approaches to agricultural development. Since the 1940s, for example, 95 percent of Greece's traditional varieties of wheat are no longer grown, and the introduction of Texas hybrids has displaced practically all the sorghum varieties formerly grown in South Africa. Agricultural researchers have transformed seeds and genetic potential into sources of profit and commercial control.

A bias against local crops and varieties is inherent in the green revolution approach. Labeled inferior, marginal locally evolved varieties, or weeds, many local crops are grown by women to meet household needs and preferences and local market demand. This bias has undermined the knowledge and labor, particularly, of rural women and devalued their contribution to the nutrition and survival of their families. In northern India, for example, the green leaf potherbs allowed to grow alongside the wheat have been labeled weeds, to be eliminated with herbicides. Some cassava varieties developed by the international research center in Ibadan, Nigeria, produce large tubers too heavy to be easily peeled for domestic processing and too tall for easy harvest of the leaves traditionally used as a seasonal vegetable. Thousands of such examples of the displacement and marginalization of the crops and varieties preferred by women have been documented for every part of the world, including north America and Europe.

Large-scale commercial production of uniform varieties of a small range of crops has not freed farmers from biological constraints, however. Instead, it has led to new ecological vulnerability. The susceptibility of a parent line to a particular fungus infection caused an average 15 percent reduction in maize yields in the United States in the 1970s, causing losses running into millions of dollars. In India, soil and water systems have been destabilized, micronutrient deficiencies in the soil have increased, and previously unharmful insect pests and diseases in rice and wheat have become out of control in an increasing number of areas.

Agricultural researchers tend to read such phenomena as evidence of the inherent dynamism of agricultural systems, requiring a continuing process of adjustment and innovation. Vandana Shiva reads them as evidence of deepening trends toward uniformity, vulnerability, and food insecurity. In the view of many others like her around the world, the recovery of the feminine principle in agriculture is the only way forward.

In Shiva's view, surrogate motherhood, the therapeutic use of gene transplants, and the patent protection of genetically engineered material are linked, as bioengineering and the new technologies for the management of human reproduction become capable of transforming the process of evolution. Natural evolutionary processes have not given rise to just societies or equitable relationships among nations or between men and women. In light of the history of abuse to which new reproductive technology may give rise in conditions of gender inequality and poverty (as in Bangladesh between 1980 and 1985 or in India under Mrs. Gandhi), there are grounds to fear the consequences of a further extension of humankind's control of evolutionary processes. It is these fears that drove a number of women at the United Nations Conference on the Environment and Development held in Rio de Janeiro in 1992 to oppose modern contraceptive technology, genetic engineering, and an intensification of green revolution approaches to feeding the world.

More fundamentally, Shiva argues that the commercialization of the inner spaces of life does not merely transform evolutionary process, it negates it. In her view, the principle of self-renewal is the only true and sustainable creativity, the source of diversity and of the power to continue to create. At the World Women's Congress for a Healthy Planet, held in Miami before the Rio Conference, she received a standing ovation for her call to "reclaim women's capacity to act through regeneration."

No Sustainable Agriculture without Sustainable Communities

In all the diverse world's cultures, women are praised—or cursed—for the time they invest in cultivating and maintaining social networks and in exchanging social intelligence. Talking serves to bind individuals and family units into the larger groupings necessary for the agricultural and natural resource management tasks that extend beyond the single farm enterprise. A water catchment, for example, cannot be managed without intense social networking among the communities and land users who live within it or without processes that create through communication agreement about the ecological unit to be managed and the values and goals the catchment should serve.

Research from the anthropological, biological, business management, and communication sciences suggests that there is a constant limit to the number among whom person-to-person relationships can be maintained in this way, ranging between 100 and 230 individuals. Agricultural societies typically are based on natural groupings within this range. Indeed, the organization and management of farming as a human activity is intimately and necessarily woven into the organization and management of coherent sets of social relationships.[6]

Beyond the critical size threshold, the relationships become more formal and hierarchical and the resolution of conflict more problematic; below the threshold, the pool of social intelligence is not sufficient to maintain complex social life or to manage complex farm operations or resource management tasks. In other words, the maintenance of social relationships within a farming community and across a landscape is essential for the performance of the activities that secure biological and human reproduction.

Researchers in the Department of Biological Anthropology at University College, London, maintain that there are important gender dimensions to this social role. Men and women take on different social talking roles.[7] Whereas men in the majority of societies hold key leadership positions and invest time in maintaining formal organizational relationships, it is women who quietly hold personal relationships in society together.

Rural women in environmental movements around the world typically, to a much higher degree than men, express an acute anxiety over the quality and sustainability of community life, as economic and environmental crises disrupt the social relationships that hold communities together.

The Australian Land Care movement demonstrates this. Australians have cleared more than 70 percent of their rain forests, 50 percent of their other forests, and 35 percent of their woodlands and eliminated 27 species of animals and birds and 100 plants, all in the past 200 years. Over wide areas, rising water tables and salinity, wind erosion, and loss of soil quality undermine the future of agriculture. Partly as a result of environmental problems, the average farm is estimated to have had a net loss of $30,000 in 1991–1992. More than a third of country towns are in decline, and the rates of suicide and divorce in the rural population are increasing.

Australian women are energizing, inspiring, and leading environmental activism in an effort to keep their communities together, their men on the farm, and their farm land in good condition. Women form the majority of the members of the more than 1400 local Land Care groups in farming areas and are spearheading a range of other voluntary activities in rural communities. In 1990, in Queensland, a state known for its conservative social outlook, half of the 84 Land Care groups had a woman executive.

In a 1992 survey of 2400 Australian women, the National Women's Consultative Council found that more than 95 percent of respondents believed that women had special attributes and capacities to contribute to environmental management. For example, their extensive social networks formed through community involvement and family life resulted in better networking among information sources, resource persons, and the community. Another quality specially valued by Land Care groups is the emphasis that women bring to the groups on mutuality, co-operation, and affiliation.[8]

Living the Present So That Future Generations Might Live

In the course of a series of nationwide hearings organized by the National Women's Consultative Council throughout Australia in 1991, some 40 women, rural and urban, old and young, met together in Albany in Western Australia. Some were angry, some anxious, many were tearful. What they brought to the meeting was a common understanding that women have a special responsibility to safeguard the environment for their children and grandchildren, as an extension of the safe environment of the home. They went on to develop an analysis that linked environmental processes to women's roles in the household and the family and to the transmission of cultural and social intelligence between generations.

Cultural and genetic continuity are both information-intensive processes. Women possess knowledge and information that is unique to their own experience and that cannot be substituted by the information and knowledge unique to the male domain. Women are largely responsible for transmitting to young children both this unique body of understanding and broader social intelligence about how the world works.

The women of Albany left the meeting strengthened in the realization that they had a contribution to make to the common concern that decisions taken today must give the children of tomorrow a chance to live. They did not know the proverb sung by the farm women of Nyeri in Kenya, but they surely would have appreciated it:

> Treat the earth well. It was not given to us by our parents: it was loaned to us by our children.

Application of the Principles

These principles argue for a bias away from a solely expert-based determination of environmental futures toward a broad-based process of recursive learning in which the experience, values, concepts, and interpretations of ordinary citizens enter into the debate about whether present decisions compromise the future. Women-centered perspectives raise fundamental questions about knowledge as power. The criteria for what constitutes knowledge, what is to be excluded and included as valid knowledge, and who is designated to know involve acts of power.

When the principles are applied to the challenges of agricultural development and natural resource management, they lead toward two complementary strategies that enable rural women to participate in the determination of agricultural and environmental futures and the involvement of women in the development of agricultural technologies.

Enabling Women's Participation

Women in agriculture seek the power to act, that is, the power to make decisions in ways that enhance the capacities of families and communities to meet everyone's needs fairly and sustainably. Two principal conditions are attached: (a) women must control the way they engage in agricultural production and the benefits that flow from it and (b) they must be able to participate in the social construction of definitions of what constitutes good farming practice and of the means and ends of production.

Responsive and Accountable Services Necessary

The will must be created among agricultural bureaucracies and service agencies to respond to women's needs for specific skills and resources and to be accountable to women for the delivery of those services. This is a conceptually simple but sometimes practically complex matter. The specific ways in which men and women engage in farming are embedded in the gender roles and relations of particular cultures and classes. Thus, the development of services and access to resources for women is typically not a matter of simply expanding the quantum of existing services and resources available or of creating special assistance for women only. Indeed, it might not involve any increase in personnel or investments at all. It does involve, however, adjustment in the ways in which existing services and resources are provided and in the type of resources or services offered.

The Case of the Dairy Development Movement

The case of dairy development in southern India illustrates both these lessons. In 1970, the National Dairy Development Board initiated Operation Flood. An efficient system for the daily collection and subsequent local processing and marketing of milk and milk products was instituted, on the basis of village-level dairy co-operatives. Training was provided to co-op members, as well as advice on dairy hygiene, the feeding and basic health care of milk cows, milk-fat content testing, and artificial insemination services. Although it was known that women contribute the most labor and care to household cows and buffalo and that, for many women living alone, a cow or buffalo was their sole means of support, only men were registered as co-op members. As members, it was men who received the dairy payments, training, and advice.

Bringing Women In

Pilot projects in Andhra Pradesh, Tamil Nadu, and Gujarat subsequently showed how practical adjustments could be made to ensure that women's roles in dairying were supported by training and credit and advisory services and their labor remunerated. All-women co-operatives have been found to be especially effective in bringing women into the mainstream of dairy development, but they are not a sufficient mechanism.[9] Additional efforts include establishing revolving loan funds so that landless women can purchase green fodder, arranging bank guarantee funds so that poor women with no collateral can buy cross-bred cows or buffalo on credit, ensuring that insurance policies are written in women's names when they take out a loan, and helping women develop functional literacy and numeric skills so that they can keep their own dairy accounts.

Today, illiterate village women carry out artificial insemination with confidence and have set up networks of village-based para-vets to administer basic health care to milk cows and buffalos. A number of states employ female extension advisers and veterinarians to back up the male-dominated services of the government and the dairy development boards. Older women who have a longer experience of participation have assumed leadership roles in the still-expanding dairy co-operative movement, while young women from the universities are taking professional roles in dairy training, processing, and marketing.

Impacting the System

Difficulties continue, and many problems remain. Both village men and officials of the dairy development boards, however, now acknowledge that women's participation is making the entire system more efficient and effective. Women are ferocious in checking corruption or cheating by cooperative officers and complaining if there is a missed collection or if a training session is not well prepared. Because of women's concern for family welfare and nutrition, the milk income and milk products go straight back to the family. Further, as the returns to women's labor in dairying improve, women are better able to make effective use of their time and energy across the range of their tasks.

The effects are synergistic. Women co-op members have access to more dung for making fuel cakes for burning and so need to cut less wood for fuel. They have access to dung for applying to home gardens and so can better care for the soil while improving family nutrition. Now that they have another income source, they can take part of their casual labor wages in the form of straw lying waste on the landlords' fields; mixed with urea and water and digested under cover for a month, it is fed to the cows to improve the milk yield.

None of this has happened by itself. It has required sustained advocacy on the part of articulate, educated women at the state and national levels. It has required determined struggle by women activists and voluntary workers against vested interests at the village level. It has required that unemployed women laborers who have never before been far from their village take a bus to town to convince a bank manager that they will "cherish the milk cow like a child" if he will only release credit against the group's saving record.

The energy and spirit to achieve so much clearly exist among women, but to gather the courage and confidence to take the first steps, women in the dairy movement, as in the Mahila Samakhya program, have needed to develop a critical consciousness, a positive self-image, and a collective competence and capacity to act. That is, women's empowerment has been in part a process of self-empowerment.

Women often speak of their personal experience of empowerment in terms of spirituality. Peggy Antrobus, a leading feminist and activist from the Caribbean, has called women's sense of spiritual power the "very personal, very private, very intimate" ground upon which women stand.[10] Men, too, may recognize and honor the latent spiritual power of women. Senior male professionals in the Indian Council of Agricultural Research opened a review of research studies on women in agriculture with an acknowledgment to Laxmi, Durga, and Saraswati, the three great Indian goddesses of prosperity, power, and wisdom.[11]

Involving Women in Technology Development

The sectoral, fragmented, and reductionist approach of agricultural technology development breaks the ecological flows of energy and resources that women's work and knowledge transform into agricultural goods and services for the household and the larger economy. Women daily experience the irreducible complexities that make farming systems whole systems. As a field-worker of the Zimbabwean Women's Bureau puts it, men find it "easier to work without thinking backwards" to all the other chores that have to be done before a woman farmer goes to her fields and without thinking forward to all the chores that await her when the day's farm work is done.[12]

The involvement of women in technology development has to begin from different premises, on the basis of an understanding of the distinctive ways in which women use and develop agricultural technology. If scientists and field-workers talk only or mainly with male farmers, women's distinctive knowledge of plant characteristics, production sites, processing qualities, and so on will never enter the technology development processes of modern agriculture. Conversely, incorporation of women's knowledge increases the relevance and effectiveness of scientists' work.[13]

Distinctive Knowledge

Although men and women in farm households share many skills, tasks, and objectives, women as well as men have distinctive agricultural knowledge and priorities with regard to plant material and other agricultural technologies. For example, men tend to emphasize maximization of present outputs when looking for good seed, whereas women are often more interested in economizing of inputs, particularly their own labor and purchased inputs. As Musonda Kalaka, a woman farmer in Zambia explains it:

> Women are more responsible because it is they who face most problems in the family . . . . Women have always taken care of the family. They have to find food and relish, or clothes for the children. That's why women know how to economize. Men only think about today, but women have to think about tomorrow and the next season as well.[14]

Trade-Offs

Women also tend to emphasize the plant characteristics that satisfy a range of food and nonfood uses, rather than a single criterion such as grain yield. A woman in Andhra Pradesh may favor a particular variety of long-stalked pigeon pea, even though the yield of grain is not as high as other varieties, because the green pods can be eaten fresh at the time of year when she is often too busy to cook, the leaves can be harvested as a vegetable, the dried grains when pounded make a good additive as a weaning food, and the dried stalks give a smoky fire appropriate for cooking certain special dishes, even though the smoke hurts her eyes. Her choice of variety undoubtedly involves making trade-offs and accepting compromises. What is not so widely recognized is that improved varieties also involve trade-offs, but it is scientists who make the judgment about what is needed.

Diversity and Multiple Use of Resources

Because no one variety of crop can meet all needs or does well in all production conditions in small-holder agriculture, women typically also favor growing a diversity of crops and varieties, even after a family's main fields have been turned over to the production of a single crop sown to one uniform variety. When deciding what characteristics and varieties to preserve and what new combinations to search for and try out, women quite consciously weigh numerous complementary, interactive advantages. The resultant portfolio is predicated on a quite different decision-making process than that of the industrial farmer or agricultural research scientist, who is looking for the ideal genetic material for a limited range of purposes.

Women are similarly concerned about making multiple use of other resources, such as water supplies. Yet these too are often developed with only a single purpose in mind. For example, few irrigation schemes pay any attention to women's need for water for small stock and poultry kept near the house (though cattle watering points may be provided in rangelands); few consider seriously the human health problems that arise if women draw water for drinking from canals contaminated with agricultural chemicals; and few provide places for the washing of clothes.

Post-Harvest Considerations

Women also tend to be much more concerned than men with the post-harvest characteristics of agricultural products, specifically their storage, processing, and cooking qualities. Some potato varieties are good for frying, others for mashing, some for roasting, others for parboiling. Some cassava varieties have tubers that can be processed into the whiter flour that, compared with more grayish flours, may fetch a premium price on the local market, while others are better for brewing into beer. Some dried beans swell to a large size when soaked and thus are good pot-fillers; others keep a long time without becoming rock hard and needing a lot of fuel to cook; some are more digestible than others and thus more suitable as weaning food. Some rice varieties are excellent for puffing into snack foods; other more glutinous types are better for making into rice balls.

Conservation of Habitats

Not only are women thus intimately concerned with the preservation of plant diversity, they are often acutely aware that diversity depends on the preservation of particular habitats, even if they do not always fully perceive the underlying relationships. I well remember visiting in 1980 a village in the Central Province of Zambia, where women earned extra income by selling mangoes along the roadside. They were arguing with some men who proposed cutting a grove of mango trees in order to put up a co-operative store. The women had no particular interest in the store, as only their husbands were allowed to register as members, but they did feel concerned that by cutting the trees, the bats circling around the village would lose their favorite roosting place. The women felt strongly that the prosperity of the village was tied up with the presence of the bats and that their mangoes would do well only as long as the bats remained. Indeed, mango trees are fertilized by bats, which the women did not know, yet their observation of the relationship between the trees and the bats enabled them intuitively to understand their interdependence.

Women's Labor and Energy: The Breaking Point

Women's labor, time, and skill are the point at which the environment, the production of agricultural surplus, and the vitality of rural communities meet together in daily life. The legacy of past neglect of women's roles in farming, however, is the increasing number of cases where the pressure on women's labor time is becoming insupportable. The effects ripple out through the worsening health and welfare of children and families into community life and ultimately threaten societal survival. Reversals in the degradation of natural resources, and further increases in small-holder farm production, cannot come about unless and until the pressures on women are relieved.

At an All-India meeting of State Secretaries of Rural Development, the point was put strongly and succinctly thus:

> [T]he stark reality of poor rural women's life is overburden of labor for family maintenance. Unless this overburden is relieved considerably, the creation of additional earning opportunities will either remain unutilized or will be met at the cost of their health or other responsibilities. Relieving women of the burden should be considered a non-variable part of the support services such as child care, supply of water, fuel, fodder, etc.[15]

Structural Adjustment

Unfortunately, macroeconomic policies designed to stimulate growth and structural change in economic relations have pushed the costs of adjustment onto women as providers of last resort. In environmental terms, the mismatch between the way land, labor, and capital are managed within the household and the way the returns are delivered to the household assumes a new significance. As public sector goods and services are cut back or priced beyond women's reach, it becomes increasingly difficult for women to accumulate a surplus with which to upgrade their own productivity and safeguard the welfare of their families. They often then have no option but to mine the productivity of natural resources in order to fulfill their roles and sustain their families. In the end, neither the biophysical environment, nor the market economy, nor family and community life can be sustained along this pathway.

This is as true in the rural areas of industrial economies as it is in still largely agrarian economies. In the Netherlands, for example, which over the past several decades has been the second or third largest exporter of agricultural produce in terms of value, farming remains a family business. Women are recognized as co-workers on about half of all farms and contribute on average 22.3 hours per week to farm activities. At the same time, as in all European countries, more women are having to seek off-farm jobs. Yet the environmental costs of intensive farming demand that there is rapid and radical change in farming systems and practices, changes that necessarily require greater, not less, leadership, attention, energy, and time from farm families. Meanwhile, rural areas are losing the commercial and social services essential to maintaining family and community life.

Three Scenarios

Analysts of the relationship between population pressure and agricultural transformation have treated the farm household as a homogenous enterprise, the resources of which are available to the male head. Three of the most influential scenarios of agricultural development pathways under conditions of population growth are based on this premise. They are depicted in the accompanying figure, which appears on the next page.

Part 1 of the figure shows the process of agricultural intensification analyzed by Boserup.[16] Increasing population leads to spontaneous innovation in technology and the organization of production so that output increases above that needed for subsistence. Commonly, such a process occurs in areas of high inherent agricultural potential and environmental resilience, close to nonfarm markets and close to services and the sources of chemical and other inputs.

Part 2 of the figure illustrates the process termed by Geertz agricultural involution, based on empirical and historical studies in south-east Asia.[17] A rising population is absorbed by the production of as much additional output as needed to support the added labor input. Part 3 of the figure illustrates a process documented by the World Bank[18] in much of sub-Saharan Africa, of agricultural stagnation. Tenurial arrangements, lack of services and inputs, trade and price disincentives, and unfavorable soil or climatic factors, singly or in combination, lead to a situation in which although output is rising it is insufficient to meet the needs of the nonfarm market. Commercial imports make up the deficit. The area develops a decreasing capacity to absorb its own labor; some members of the increasing population migrate to lands marginal for cultivation, others to urban areas.

Implications for the Natural Environment

Each of these three scenarios has its own implications for the natural environment. Intensification typically is associated initially with increasingly careful management of soil, water, and biological resources in ways that enhance the productivity and diversity of the landscape but only up to a point. Agricultural intensification, as in the Netherlands, in the end leads to increasing simplification, uniformity, and unsustainable environmental costs, which spread far beyond agriculture itself.

Agricultural involution similarly tends to have an initially positive, or at least neutral, environmental impact, but it eventually runs into natural resource limits. If no nonfarm source of income and livelihood becomes available, the situation slides toward the scenario shown in the figure's third part. Lele and Stone suggest from their studies of small-holder development in Nigeria, Kenya, Malawi, Senegal, Tanzania, and the Cameroon

① Autonomous Intensification (Boserup)

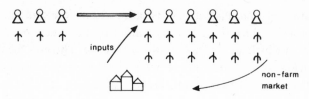

② Agricultural Involution (Geertz)

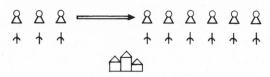

③ Agricultural Stagnation (Lele & Stone)

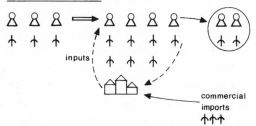

④ Gender-Sensitive Analysis

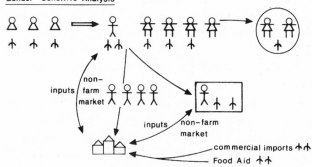

Key to Symbols

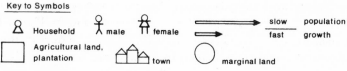

Janice Jiggins.1992

Population Pressure and Agricultural Intensification.

that the rate at which agricultural populations grow might be important in triggering stagnation rather than intensification or involution. The faster the rate of growth, the less likely more virtuous processes will occur, and the more important it is to select appropriate policies to relieve the pressure on agriculture.

In trying to sort out the various dimensions of the relationships, Lele and Stone suggest further that population density, expressed as total population in relation to total land area, is not as meaningful an index of pressure as population in relation to available agricultural land. Nigeria, for example, is estimated to have an overall population density of 1241 per 1000 hectares (1990 figures), compared with Kenya's 441, but just under 60 percent of Nigeria's land is classified by the FAO as arable, compared with Kenya's meager 11 percent.

One of the other correlates identified by Lele and Stone is the resource degradation that occurs as marginalized households seek a livelihood in fragile and vulnerable environments. Another is the increased pressure on natural forests since, in Africa at least, rural stagnation tends to occur where urban populations remain dependent for their energy (because of both physical supply and price) on wood fuel and charcoal for their energy. Cutting wood to supply urban demand becomes an important income source as agricultural livelihoods fail.

A Woman-Centered Perspective

The fundamental limitation of all three scenarios is the neglect of the simple but absolutely key fact that farm households are not undifferentiated wholes. Women are not wholly passive resources to be allocated at the will of planners or household heads to new tasks. They make their own calculations of the trade-offs and returns to the resources available to them, in light of their own agricultural and family obligations, duties, and rights. That is, they manage and control resources on their own account and bear the costs and enjoy the benefits that flow from them, as well as participate in and contribute to the resource flows managed and controlled by men.

Resource allocation in the self-provisioning sector thus necessarily affects resource allocation in the market sector. If agricultural services and inputs are not made available to women, already burdened with domestic work and mothering, so that they can increase their own labor productivity, time use, and income returns, the productivity of the market economy drags. Optimal efficiency gains can be achieved in the market economy if, and only if, the efficiency of women's labor and resource use increases. Neglect of this relationship has lead to women being forced to absorb more and more of the costs of system transformation. One way they seek to ease the costs is, of course, to augment the labor supply available to them by bearing more children.

The scenario shown in the fourth part of the figure is a gender-sensitive illustration of the relationship between population and agriculture. Male productivity increases as advisory services and farm inputs are made available to them but not sufficiently to hold all male labor on the farm. Some men migrate to town; a few enter the commercial large farm sector as wage workers. Women receive no technical assistance. At the same time, an increasing portion of the farm tasks fall on them, as male members of the household leave in search of work. Support from social networks and the community decreases, and women receive less help with their own tasks within the farm. As the commercial sector appropriates more land and men take over women's fields to grow (nonedible) cash crops, women are forced to cultivate more marginal lands. Women absorb the costs in terms of their own health, nutrition, and energy to the point at which they can no longer produce sufficiently to ensure their own reproduction, maintain community relations, or care for the environment.[19]

In an increasing number of areas, the breaking point has been reached. When the gender-based inequities in the economic returns of labor and skill reach a certain threshold, people's relations with their biophysical and socioeconomic environment become unsustainable. These pressures must be relieved if there is to be any progress toward sustainable agricultural development. It is not merely a technical matter of raising the economic efficiency of female labor or a question of a more balanced approach to the provision of agricultural services and inputs. Policies must reflect the simple truth that men and women will survive together or not at all, a not so simple matter of adjusting the power relations between men and women within society and the household.

11

Five Cases

I Also Want to Be Heard

"I'm flattered at being consulted but I also want to be heard." This demand was made by a woman farmer to the National Women's Consultative Council in Australia during 1991–1992. During the course of nationwide consultations to solicit women's views on environmental issues, women in Australia repeatedly stressed that merely consulting them was not enough. Men and women, governments and local communities, must learn how to work together, build institutions and decision-making machineries together, if environmental problems are to be solved. It is a demand that can be heard the world over. Women become exasperated at being treated as a resource to be tapped to achieve the agendas of others. Where men really are prepared to listen to women's voices, they discover values, knowledge, and skills that enrich and strengthen the decision-making process and actions based on those decisions. Women make a difference both to the process and the outcome. Further, if the wider-scale changes required are to be achieved on the basis of voluntary choices, the decision-making process must include women.

Five cases are presented here, from Kenya, Bangladesh, Botswana, Burkina Faso, and Zambia, of women and men working together to sustain or enhance the productivity of the biological, physical, and socioeconomic resources of their communities. The cases illustrate the institutional and practical steps that are both achievable at the micro level and necessary to bring about system-wide change. They also exemplify the common environmental concerns that were explored in Chapter 10:

☐ To manage the flows among and between resource systems in ways that protect regenerative capacity

☐ To manage biological, physical, and social relationships as interdependent aspects of sustainability

☐ To enhance the processes of social learning and create the power for people to act collaboratively, on scales significant for common survival

☐ To ensure that proposed solutions to environmental problems will not be at the expense of women's uncounted labor and energy

Water Supply Development, Nyankine Village, Kenya

High in the hills of the Nyambene range in Meru District of Kenya lies the village of Nyankine.[1] During the rainy season the area is virtually cut off as the roads become muddy and impassable. At the best of times, public transport is erratic. Social services and schools are few, but the Kamujine Farmers Center, some 3 kilometers from the village, provides a limited number of field services and training courses for farmers. Men and women grow coffee and food crops on small family holdings carved out of the steep slopes and keep a few stall-fed milk cows to supply the burgeoning dairy industry.

Although two permanent rivers cut across the district, water supply has always been a problem. Women, in particular, were affected, as it was mainly their responsibility to fetch and carry the water from the nearest river lower down the slope, a task that was both time-consuming and burdensome, or they had to buy whatever water they could afford from itinerant sellers. The expansion of dairying also meant they needed additional supplies to water the cows and wash the cows' udders and the milk churns.

Project-Based Initiatives

Personnel connected with a drinking water supply project, who had experience in water tank construction, discussed the problem with members of the farmers' groups, organized by the Department of Agriculture, and the women's groups, organized by the Ministry of Social Services. Although some women were members of the farmers' groups, because these groups were organized primarily around coffee growing and marketing, most coffee holdings were registered in the men's names, and the women were more interested in the women's group meetings.

From the men's point of view, the easiest solution was for the project to build water storage tanks to collect runoff from the tin roofs during the rainy season, on an individual household basis, financed by loans from a revolving fund administered by the Kamujine Farmers Center. The men were used to dealing with the Center and could rely on their coffee incomes to cover the loan repayments. This was the solution the project decided to follow, and work began on tank construction.

The women, however, had pointed out that comparatively few houses as yet had tin roofs. The project would benefit only a few, and the water problem for most women would not be solved. They convened a meeting of all three women's groups active in and around the village to discuss the problem further. There they identified the following additional issues:

□ The coffee factory higher up the hill drained its waste water into the river; when it was operating, the water fetched from the river was smelly and tasted bad.

□ The river water became dirty and caused stomachaches and diarrhea during the rainy season.

□ The steep slopes meant that fetching the water could be dangerous, especially during the rains when the hillsides became slippery.

The women sought solutions that would benefit the largest number of households and provide a clean, safe supply of water year-round. They considered three options. One was for the women to join the water tanks program operated by the Farmers Center. This option, however, would involve either redoubling their own group revolving loan efforts to help everyone get a tin roof or taking additional loans from the tanks program to finance the roofs as well as the tanks. The second option was to ask the coffee factory to reduce or eliminate its discharge into the river. The third option was to tap the springs rising above the village and bring the water down by pipeline. Only the third option seemed to address all aspects of the problem.

Changing the Agenda

The next step was for the women to present their arguments and preferred solution at a village meeting. The men listened and realized they had jumped too hastily to a conclusion. They backed the women's ambitious plan, and a self-help group, the Nyankine Water Project group, was formed. A 17-member committee of men and women was elected to start collecting money. Then they contacted a water engineer who donated his services to draw up a preliminary design. At this point, the members of the committee realized they had neither the expertise nor the finances to complete the scheme on their own. So they asked the coordinator of the water tanks program to help raise additional funding.

Community-Based Action

Within three months the coordinator had raised the money. The coordinator and the committee attended another village meeting to discuss how to proceed and to divide responsibilities. The village agreed to provide the labor and collect all the sand, stones, and timber required for construction. The coordinator agreed that the tanks program would make available a mason and water engineer. She also suggested that the committee organize a village workshop to decide how to organize and manage the construction work and the subsequent maintenance of the project.

During the workshop the committee realized that continuing financial contributions from the community would be essential to cover the costs of maintenance of the main pipe and the taps. It was agreed that each family would pay a yearly user fee, either in cash or in coffee. A neighborhood committee would become responsible for each tap and the collection of fees.

The villagers organized themselves into teams to collect the materials, make the bricks, and work with the mason and engineer, from whom they also learned how to maintain the project. Five months later it was fully operational.

Implications of Women's Involvement

The preceeding case illustrates how women brought another point of view and a different set of values to a resource problem that ultimately affected everyone in the village. Even though the women themselves were the most directly affected, the initial consultation process had not encouraged the women's views to influence the technical decisions made. The existing male-dominated institutions and decision-making processes prevailed. When women seized the initiative, the project and the process took a different path, leading to a result that more nearly satisfied the needs of everyone and spread the costs and benefits more equitably. The village committee of men and women went on to develop new village-based institutions responsible for ensuring that the project would be financially sustainable.

Integration of Fish Ponds and Homestead Gardens, Bangladesh

About 10 percent of the 13 or so million rural households in Bangladesh have an average of 810 square meters of land available for gardening, and a further 56 percent have an average of 400 square meters.[2] Although by no means all households have garden land, altogether, homestead gardens account for about 5 percent of all cultivated land. On a day-to-day basis, homestead gardens fall largely under women's care.

In a country as crowded as Bangladesh, garden land could not be said to be lying idle. Some 70 percent of timber and building materials and 90 percent of the fuel wood and bamboo come from homestead garden land, for example. The gardens also yield fruit, herbs, seasonings, and medicines, provide shelter for tethered cows and goats and for poultry and ducks, and provide space for seedling nurseries. However, homestead-based production of vegetables, the main source in Bangladesh of dietary vitamins and minerals, is low. Among the reasons why this is so are the lack of good seed, shading of the garden area by trees, and damage to the garden area by poultry or livestock. In Bangladesh, more than 30,000 children a year fall victim to blindness as a result of vitamin A deficiency. Many more thousands of women have moderate to severe iron deficiencies leading to anemia, which gives rise to complications of pregnancy and childbirth. The severity and scale of these afflictions could be reduced if more vegetables could be grown in homestead gardens.

Women Urge New Initiatives

Until recently, homestead gardens received virtually no attention from the agricultural research community. Women researchers and advocates repeatedly drew attention to the garden's role at the center of household production and family welfare and as the only land asset to which otherwise landless families had access. Not altogether unreasonably, the government and scientists focused on increasing the yield of the main food staples.

As success in raising the main crop yields above the rate of population growth began to relieve the pressure, agricultural scientists attached to the Bangladesh Agricultural Research Council (BARC) started to explore the potential for intensifying garden production. In 1985 they adopted the guideline that any innovation should optimize the input of women's labor and raise the returns to nutrition as well as to land.

Breaking New Ground

The scientists began with a period of field investigation. This was in itself a breakthrough in terms of scientific and cultural traditions. They realized they simply did not know enough about how homestead garden production fit into farm enterprises as a whole. Further, the scientists realized that women investigators would have better access to, and obtain better quality information from, women in the homestead, but there were at the time no female agricultural scientists with experience in field studies. So they persuaded a number of female scientists working in agricultural research laboratories to join the field study program.

Together, the male and female scientists prepared new study methods for plotting the diversity of production sites, practices, and crops typically found in homestead gardens, as a complement to more formal questionnaires. As the women scientists developed confidence and experience, they quickly showed their competence in working in the field. Moreover, they developed creative and innovative methodologies for mapping the flow of resources within the homestead, between the homestead and the larger farm enterprise, and with the formal and informal market systems.

The New Technology

After analyzing the field data, the scientists developed a system of raised bed vegetable cultivation based on 6 x 6 meter plots. Using a mix of 14 different vegetables grown in any of five different combinations and sequences, they showed how the system could provide a flow of vegetables virtually throughout the year. This system is capable of producing a total of 200 kg a year, sufficient to meet the vitamin A, vitamin C, and iron needs of a family of nine, as well as producing a small cash income to refinance the purchase of seeds. Its fertility is maintained through the careful incorporation of household waste and vegetative matter from other plants and trees in the garden and manure where available. Because the total plot size is small, it can be protected from poultry and animals by simple fencing using material from the homestead.

BARC has shared its findings with nongovernmental organizations and the Department of Agricultural Extension in order to reach as many of the poor women and men with garden land available as possible. More than 10,000 demonstrations had been carried out in homestead gardens by mid-1991. The network of seedling rearers (mainly women) and seed growers (mainly men) is rapidly expanding, providing additional cash incomes to the poor.

Involving Family Planning Volunteers

After some years, women extension agents working in the Department of Agricultural Extension suggested that, in view of women's roles in food management and the daily care of the garden, special effort had to be made to encourage the participation of village women in the department's communication and training efforts. The few hundred women extension staff employed by the department would never be sufficient to reach all the women who potentially might benefit.

They suggested that, as an experiment, the 327 village-based Family Planning Volunteers in three subdistricts be given training in intensive vegetable production. The volunteers were then asked to start their own plots as a demonstration and to train four other Family Planning Volunteers in their village, who in turn would be asked to set up their own plots and train four others.

This strategy has proved so successful that the involvement of the Family Planning Volunteers has been extended to thirty other subdistricts, and the movement is still growing. The integration with the family planning effort in turn is making a positive contribution to men's and women's use of contraceptives. The men enjoy the better diet and appreciate that their wives and daughters are making a contribution to the well-being of the family—not simply consuming the men's wages. Women's confidence and self-image is strengthened by acquiring new skills and managing scarce resources to yield such a handsome return. They acquire a greater say in decisions about family size and the use of contraceptives. As their health and that of their children improves, there is a lessening of the pressure to bear more children to ensure that some survive.

The Link to Fish Farming

The program has had other spin-offs. The intensive vegetable gardens produce more total vegetative matter. The parts that are not used for food or replenishing the fertility of the plot can be fed to chickens or composted. The compost or chicken manure can be used as an input to homestead fish farming. The bones and residues from fish farming in turn are fed back into the intensive vegetable plots.

Fish is the most important source of protein for poor people in Bangladesh. Intensive fish farming in larger ponds and natural depressions, usually under the control of the better-off households in the village, is a long-standing tradition, and considerable effort has been made in recent years to improve the productivity of such water resources. Small homestead ditches and ponds (used for draining waste water and for bathing or washing clothes), roadside ditches, and borrow pits are mostly lying unused, stagnant and covered with weeds, and can pose serious health problems. They are mostly seasonal, retaining water for 4 to 6 months of the year, and until recently were considered unusable for fish farming.

Fish Farming as a Garden Activity

The fish varieties cultivated in the traditional ponds are unsuitable for the shallow, seasonal waters and require high inputs of fertilizers and supplementary feedstuffs beyond the reach of most poor families. But short-cycle species such as tilapia and silver barb require much less attention. The aquaculture program of the International Center for Living Aquatic Resources Management (ICLARM), based in the Philippines, has been assisting governmental and nongovernmental agencies in Bangladesh to integrate fish farming into homestead gardens.

For Safira Khaton, who with her husband and seven children live on a plot whose total size is just 360 square meters, fish farming has been a real blessing.[3] She cleared the weeds from the shallow ditch of some 120 square meters, which holds water for 4 to 5 months and was formerly a prime breeding ground for mosquitoes and flies. Under the guidance of a nongovernmental organization's fieldworker, she limed the water and released 240 tilapia fingerlings. As they grew, she fed the fish daily with rice bran, a byproduct of her home-based contract rice pounding operations. She started catching the fish from the 3rd month until the ditch dried up at the end of the 4th month, harvesting more than 17 kg in total, the equivalent of more than $15 in net revenue.

The Benefits of Intensification

The intensification of homestead production in Bangladesh illustrates how the productivity and sustainability of biological and human systems can be increased once women's role, mediating the flow of energy and resources between key system components, is properly valued. The downward spiral of ill-health, poor nutrition, poor resource use, and repeated childbearing can be checked.

Scientists Collaborate with Women Farmers, Botswana

In distinct contrast to Bangladesh, Botswana is a large country with a relatively small population.[4] Women are relatively well educated, in some respects more so than men. Increasing numbers of women find urban employment in education, social services, and government. A prosperous mining sector provides skilled occupations for many men.

Whereas Bangladesh has consistently raised the yields of its main crops, agriculture in Botswana remains largely a low yield and risky occupation. Its strong patterns are an extensive cattle herding sector, operated largely by men and boys, and a rain-fed crop sector.

The Agricultural Setting

Both men and women farm and have rights to cropland, but they cultivate under somewhat differing conditions. Women's labor must be spread among the fields designated for meeting household needs, their husbands' fields, and their own smaller plots. They might also keep a few sheep or goats. Men tend to have better access than women to oxen for timely plowing, and although they may help plow their wives' fields, they are often absent, looking after cattle or small stock or seeking urban or mining employment. Many women have no access to oxen or donkeys for plowing or have access only through relatives. Those who can get access to a plowing team may lack the labor, cash, or expertise to complete their own plowing adequately and in time.

Rainfall is low and erratic, with unpredictable fluctuations within any one season and between years, interspersed by periodic droughts. Considerable spatial variation exists in the distribution of rainfall. Yields of all crops, including the main staple, sorghum, are low, limited by rainfall and the typically moderate to low fertility of the soils. Both men and women try to develop nonfarm sources of income in order to spread the risk of crop failure, but opportunities for rural women are more restricted than those for men.

Difficulties of Technology Development

The development of improved technologies in such conditions is difficult. In the past, agricultural researchers in Botswana have concentrated on the levers of rapid and large-scale improvement, which raised yields in rice and wheat in Asia, particularly wherever irrigation created relatively stable and homogenous environments for plant growth. That is, they have focused on breeding seeds for uniform, monocrop cultivation, developing a package of related chemical inputs and fertilizers and tillage and planting practices by using ox-drawn equipment or tractors for row cultivation. It is becoming increasingly clear, however, that appropriate strategies in areas of poor soil quality and erratic rainfall are more likely to be based on incremental change in complex systems, which necessarily mix a far wider range of crops and varieties.

The aim is to increase the flexibility of crop management in response to the uncertainty and variability inherent in the environment. The approach implies that the researcher's job is to increase the diversity of options farmers have in their management portfolio. What constitutes improvement in one place for some farmers, however, may offer little benefit to others in another place.

It follows that it is not only desirable but essential to include farmers in the research process. When farmers are allowed to make their own assessments of what constitutes an improvement and are assisted to carry out their own experiments and to share their views of research priorities with scientists, much wasteful effort is avoided and technologies that show real benefits in farmers' fields are used to a greater extent.

Difficulties of Collaboration

The business of scientists working together with farmers is not straightforward, especially where most farmers are women and most scientists are men. Even where women are quite visible as farmers, a number of factors may prevent women from being included in the research process. Male scientists and fieldworkers may have attitudinal and cultural barriers to working directly with women. Women for their part may feel shy about speaking openly to male authority figures or checked by custom from speaking out in general discussions or in formal meetings.

Professional training may compound the bias. Agricultural economists, for example, tend to work with models of agricultural activity that reinforce a perception of farming as a male-controlled enterprise. Farms tend to be viewed in economic models as undifferentiated units under the direction of a single decision maker, as might be an industrial enterprise. The resources of the family often are assumed to constitute a pliant labor force and source of capital under the control of the male farm manager. Women's labor input typically is valued as a fraction of the adult male standard, assuming gender-based differentials in skill and productivity.

More practical issues might also contribute to the exclusion of women. Scientists and field staff working to civil service schedules might simply never be on the farm at the times when women are free to talk with them. Farm women commonly will leave a lengthy interview session in order to attend to another chore.

The Agricultural Technology Improvement Project Initiative

The Agricultural Technology Improvement Project (ATIP) was established in the early 1980s to support a research team of local and foreign scientists to work on the improvement of crop-based farming systems. The team has pioneered ways to bring farm women into the technology development process.

Experimenting with Groups. The researchers initially were driven by their own appreciation of the benefits that working more closely with farmers would bring to their own work. By capturing more of farmers' knowledge of production conditions and crop performance, the research team expected they would be able to increase the efficiency and relevance of their own work.

With little previous experience to guide them, the researchers decided to experiment with different forms of farmer involvement. In one village where they had laid out trials the preceding season, ATIP researchers formed two groups, one of women from poorer households and one of women from households that had participated in the previous season's experiments. Later the two groups were combined to form a rather large and heterogeneous group. In another village, ATIP encouraged husbands and wives to attend as couples. In a third village, a women-only group was formed, composed largely of women heading their own households. Nearly half the members of this group were also members of the Village Development Committee.

Each farmer member undertook to carry out at least one of the trials proposed for farmer participation and evaluation. The researchers met with the groups at a monthly meeting to listen to the progress of each member in turn. They facilitated discussion between the group and the researchers on the principles underlying their different assessments and choices. Problems with managing the trials were aired and solutions proposed and assessed. ATIP responded by providing additional material and technical assistance where this was clearly warranted. ATIP also provided information on topics raised by the group at previous meetings. From time to time ATIP arranged visits from outside speakers who could contribute specialized information.

Learning from Experience. As time went on, the researchers incorporated more and more of the farmers' own suggestions into the design and content of the trials. For example, the women heading their own households were especially interested in experimenting with different ways of sowing by hand, reflecting their limited access to teams of oxen. Further, it became clear that men and women tended to value different bundles of characteristics in the sorghum variety trials, reflecting the different end-uses and post-harvest responsibilities each had. Women, for example, had clear views about desirable processing, cooking, and beer-brewing qualities. They also introduced evaluation criteria that the researchers had either not thought about or considered of minor importance. For example, women—who are primarily responsible for weeding—were keen to see quick leaf growth so that the plant canopy would shade out weeds.

In the course of learning how to work with women farmers, the scientists became increasingly confident that women know much that is important about agricultural and natural resource systems. Women's knowledge, based on sharp and frequent observation, proved reliable. Moreover, because such knowledge is intimately linked to women's specific tasks and responsibilities, it is knowledge that male farmers in the main do not share. Whereas there might be considerable areas of overlap with the domains of male knowledge, the scientists came to appreciate better the necessity of encouraging women to speak for themselves about their own experience and priorities.

During the course of the group discussions, the farmers and the research teams also came to understand better the trade-offs each made when deciding which characteristics and qualities to aim for in plant breeding and agronomic practices. Insofar as there had ever been a belief in finding a single miraculous technological breakthrough, it gave way to a richer understanding of the potential for continual incremental gains through simultaneous, multiple innovation in the management of the farm system.

Although the onset of drought weakened the ability of some members to attend group meetings regularly and maintain their trials, the farmers remained enthusiastic. The three groups turned out to operate somewhat differently, reflecting their different composition. The first had the most problems, being larger and more mixed in membership. The members of the women-only group showed a consistent interest in how to share the results of the trials more widely and to extend participation to other groups, reflecting their responsibilities as members of the Village Development Committee.

Overall, women formed nearly 90 percent of the membership. They attended the monthly meetings more regularly than the men and were more assiduous in tending the trials. When a topic arose about which the men felt they had relatively more expertise, they tended to dominate the discussion, but they were less forthcoming than the women in bringing forward their problems. The women were eager for information and wanted to make the most of what for many was their first contact with the agricultural services. Over time, the women-only group went furthest in reducing its dependence on the research staff's initiative. The members continued their meetings through the nongrowing season and began working out their own plans for sharing what they were learning.

An Expanding Agenda

Government scientists and fieldworkers continue to be enthusiastic supporters of the participatory group process. They are expanding the participation of farmers in analysis and development of farming systems and natural resource systems. The aim is to help farmers move from the question "How do I improve the productivity of my farm?" to "How do I maintain or improve the productivity of the natural resources on which my farming is based?"

Local Natural Resource Appraisals

In one case, researchers conducted a participatory appraisal of the local natural resource systems, together with three women farmers from the village of Soshong. As they walked through the landscape, the women identified, characterized, and described nine natural resource systems in terms of their uses and products, from the open grazing land on the hills through croplands, to ponds and rivers and seasonal grazing lands. The women also described the soil types, microenvironments, and economic enterprises associated with each of the nine systems.

Although the drought was well established and farming seemed to have come to a halt at the time of the appraisal, the women traced a continuing and complex flow of resources among the diverse resource systems. Although no crops could be grown and rain-fed water sources had dried, income and produce were still coming from cattle foraging on the hillsides and crop headlands. Fuel wood and thatching grass were collected, water was transported from the river for home use, and manure was collected in the cattle yards.

Together, the women and the researchers identified several researchable options for improving the natural resource base and, thus, agricultural opportunity. These options were holding water in the seasonal river to provide water for small stock, vegetable production, and fish culture; seeding forage legumes into the natural grazing on the hillsides and crop headlands; and planting multipurpose trees around the yard and in the landscape.

In sum, what started as a mechanism for improving the quality and efficacy of scientists' efforts evolved into an ongoing process of dialogue and interactive technology development. The interactive process for the first time gives women farmers a real opportunity to work as valued partners, not in a special and isolated way, but together with their men and the male-dominated scientific and field services.

Stone Lines, Planting Pits, and the Naam Movement in Burkina Faso

Burkina Faso is one of the poorest countries in West Africa, lying across the southern margins of the great Sahelian desert.[5] Popular accounts of the destructive effects of population pressure on the land often are illustrated by bleak photos from Burkina. Men and women bend over in the swirling dust, hoeing around the shrivelled stalks of sorghum or millet, in a landscape without trees. These images are not false, but they capture only part of what is happening. Villagers have begun to take the future into their own hands. The inspiration of the Naam movement is central to their effort.

The Naam Movement

The Naam movement in Burkina Faso is rooted in the indigenous youth groups of the Mossi. The groups' main activity during the rains was to provide labor for the villages and in the dry season to sponsor dances and festivals. In the organization of these activities, a high value was placed on equality between the sexes, cooperation, and egalitarianism. The groups' vitality and strength ebbed away, however, during the colonial period.

Bernard Ouedraogo, who was a government official in the Office of Rural Development in the late 1960s, believed that the Naam groups could be revived for nontraditional roles in village-level economic planning and community participation. Today, there are more than four thousand Naam associations. About half of the total membership of nearly a quarter of a million is made up of girls and women.

Since 1979, the associations, each with a minimum of fifty members, have been organized into unions and federations, up to the national level. The movement is supported by government fieldworkers, who help the groups find financial support or technical know-how, as well as helping them improve their organizational capacities. Men's and women's groups are formed separately but often hold their meetings together.

Men's and women's groups differ in certain respects. For instance, whereas men's groups tend to give more weight in choosing their officers to such formal attributes as educational status and seniority, the women tend to choose their group leaders on the basis of personal characteristics and qualities:

> We know each other's reputations very well. We leave our villages after we marry but in our new homes we find new friends who are like sisters. We will say, that woman is honest, we can trust her with our money. We see that she wants to help everyone and get along with everyone. She dances and speaks well. Even if she cannot read, we want her to lead us. She can rely on her good memory. When we see all of these things, we ask her to be president.[6]

Group Activities

Group activities include economic, educational, social, and cultural events. A group may start modestly, with a small gardening activity or fruit orchard, and gradually move on to more ambitious projects such as setting up a grinding mill. An important guiding principle for economic activities is that of "father-daughter-son." The initial enterprise has to set aside funds from its profits to help a "daughter" enterprise get going in a neighboring village, just as a father helps a daughter when she gets married and goes to live in her husband's village. At the same time, it is recognized that fathers grow old and die and so must leave a "son" behind in the village to maintain and expand the chain of profit. Each investment thus should aim to create at least two "children."

Educational activities include study tours to other groups, functional literacy classes, and the establishment of village libraries. Social activities center around primary health, maternal and child health, family planning, nutrition, and mutual aid. Recreational activities are recognized as important for binding the members together. Group cohesion is also fostered by the "chief of discipline," a member designated by the group to ridicule lazy or nonattending members and, in extreme cases, to collect fines from defaulters.

Soil and Water Conservation

Often the first activity the groups undertake in the extremely dry conditions of Burkina Faso has to do with water. Water is an essential resource for almost every other activity. Good soil and water conservation practices are particularly essential for farming. Women play a decisive agricultural role. In most parts of the country they are responsible for securing the cereals and the ingredients for the sauces served with the staple foods, through growing crops, keeping poultry, sheep, or goats, and trading. They are concerned that effective conservation practices should be maintained, but as more and more men have left to seek a nonfarm income in the towns or to try their chances in the gold fields, traditional soil and water conservation has given way to less labor-demanding practices.

Over many thousands of hectares, soils have begun to suffer from erosion, loss of fertility, and physical deterioration. The vegetative cover has become impoverished, less diverse, less palatable to stock, and less dense. These effects became especially noticeable in the bush fields farthest from the villages. In some areas the deterioration is extensive enough to affect hydrological flows, increasing the scarcity of water and thus imposing ever greater burdens on the women who are responsible for hauling it from the drying wells and river beds.

A development agency in the 1970s attempted to prevent further degradation by checking and holding the flow of rainwater behind earth bunds. With the aid of tractors and other machinery, bunds were raised on 120,000 hectares. Although in theory the bunds brought considerable technical and economic benefits, the villagers were not much involved in the design or planning or siting of the bunds and so felt no responsibility for them and thought someone else should maintain them. Moreover, maintenance was labor-demanding, and the solid earth construction prevented water percolation, so the downstream side remained dry and useless for cultivation. Few of the bunds remain intact today.

Learning from the Naam Movement

Subsequently, developmental agencies took a lesson from the Naam movement and turned their attention to indigenous soil and water conservation techniques.[7] These techniques included the laying of stone lines across the surface of fields to slow down the flow of rainwater and trap nutrients and soils behind the line. They were not as effective as they might have been, however, because villagers lacked a cheap, reliable means to lay the lines along the contour, and when labor was short, they left too wide a gap between the stones.

Improving the Stone Lines and Planting Pits

Governmental and nongovernmental agencies began working with the Naam groups to improve the stone line technique. They introduced water levels (using water and short lengths of cheap clear plastic tubing) to lay out the contour line and provided help such as making donkey carts available on credit for carting the stones.

They also worked with farmers to develop the traditional shallow planting pits used to break up crusted, barren land and concentrate water and nutrients. Together they found that slightly larger pits, some 30 by 20 centimeters, the addition of manure or vegetative matter at the bottom of the pit, and the placing of the excavated soil downslope of the pit to trap surface runoff could raise yields from 300 kg to 1000 kg a hectare in average rainfall years. Even when rainfall was poor, the improved pits gave some harvest.

In the process, the agencies' scientists have had to throw out some of their prejudices. Termites, for example, often are viewed as destructive agricultural pests, yet in the context of the planting pits, termite activity has proved beneficial. As the termites carry away the manure or dry matter through the bottom of the pit, soil fertility and infiltration are improved.

In 1985, the agencies helped men and women farmers cultivate 1000 hectares of degraded land using these methods. By 1992, at least 10,000 hectares a year were being rehabilitated by farmers, mostly without any special support, as the improvements spread spontaneously among the Naam groups and other village organizations. Farmers particularly appreciate that these improved practices are things they can do on their own, without buying significant additional inputs.

One important outcome, which had not been anticipated by the agencies, is that the improved soil and water conservation methods are being applied, for the most part, to the most degraded and barren lands, the bush fields. Villagers expand their resource base through rehabilitation of useless land as their populations grow.

The agencies are continuing to develop new ideas with the farmers. Recent initiatives include trying out a range of composting methods, testing the effectiveness of level, permeable rock dams to rehabilitate eroded gullies, establishing the cost-effectiveness of correcting soil nutrient deficiencies with purchased inputs, and the interpretation of aerial photographs for village land-use planning.

Women Express Reservation

Many of the women are not entirely satisfied with these initiatives. The improved soil and water conservation practices have increased their workload considerably. They already are overburdened by the additional tasks falling on their shoulders as the men seek paid work elsewhere. Much of the additional labor is heavy work: digging pits and collecting and loading stones onto trucks or carts and laying them on the fields. Yet most of the credit and skills training involved in the provision of the donkey carts, for example, has been made available to men.

Women certainly receive positive returns for their additional labor. Yields on their own fields have increased, increasing their disposable income. They have been able to acquire access to formerly degraded land for women's group fields, to generate capital for investment in other economic enterprises. As yields have risen on the family fields, household food supplies have become more secure. More and more, women also earn income by hiring out their labor to other farmers who want their fields treated.

Nonetheless, women are asking for greater access to skills training in order to increase further the returns to their labor and better recognition of their contribution. Their labor is at least as productive as men's, and they perform the new conservation tasks as well as or better than men, yet they do not receive a proportionate return.

Women are also asking for more assistance to increase their access to multipurpose tree saplings to plant near their compounds and close to their villages along field boundaries. In this way they hope to increase the supply of fuel wood and other produce such as leaves for feeding small stock kept stabled around the compound and more leaf matter for composting, while decreasing the distance they have to go in search of fuel.

The Naam movement is working closely with the Ministry of the Environment to establish village nurseries and engage the help of school-aged children in maintaining them. Individuals also are encouraged to start their own nurseries. Many women, however, feel that not enough attention is paid yet to their preferences and needs in the selection of what types of trees to establish. They also are uncertain as to their rights of tree ownership or rights over the use of tree products. When they invest their time and labor in planting and caring for trees, they would like this to be recognized, but because most of the land is controlled by men, women's tree rights often are rather ambiguous and can lead to disputes.

Further Expansion Hangs on Women's Labor

In essence, women say that the environment cannot be saved if their labor is not fairly counted, valued, and remunerated. The continued expansion of conservation and rehabilitation practices hangs on this. As Seraphine Kabore, a government animal husbandry officer, concludes:

> We women are and remain the pillar of household production and reproduction. Our well-being is decisive for the future of agriculture and the environment. But we must be sure that new practices recognize and reward the pivotal role we play. We are finding our own voice but still there are dangers that the traditional dominance of men will continue to marginalize us.[8]

The Women's Extension Program, Zambia

Women around the world recognize that ways must be found for existing agricultural field services to reach rural women: special services for women only are too expensive, too easily marginalized, and have little influence on the way the dominant structures and systems operate.[9] Changing the attitudes, behaviors, and routines of bureaucracies, however, is not easy. Strategic interventions are needed, based in the first instance on working with and through the male-dominated structures.

The case of the Department of Agriculture in the Western Province of Zambia illustrates the wider problem and opportunities. Most of the department's 200 field staff, called agricultural assistants, are men. There is a much smaller home economics unit at the provincial headquarters, but it has no staff in the field. The unit has relied always on the agricultural assistants to contact women in the village, but the assistants are in any case too few to visit all farmers, and priority is given to visiting male farmers. A survey of five areas in the early 1980s showed that whereas 40 percent of all male heads of households had never received a visit, 80 percent of women household heads had never been visited. As the Provincial Home Economics Officer puts it, "Really, it has always been a struggle. The men feel that anything to do with women farmers and home economics is not their concern."[10]

The Women's Extension Program was set up in 1986, in the words of the first coordinator, Mary Masona, as a "strategic booster" of limited duration.

Apart from the coordinator, it had no staff; its influence was to be based on persuasion and cooperation rather than formal powers over the activities of others. The principal mechanisms identified to bring about change within the existing programs and projects of the department were advocacy, training, information, statistics, and liaison.

Putting Women on the Departmental Agenda

An important first step was to help provincial, district, and field staff to become aware of the importance of women's involvement in agriculture. A series of presentations were made at in-service training courses, by using statistical data from previous surveys. If the men were not convinced by the argument, they could at least not dispute the figures.

The Departmental Coordinating Committee, composed of section heads and project coordinators, also proved a significant forum for gentle training on women's roles in agriculture and the environment. Meanwhile, the coordinator contacted the few senior female staff and began to develop a network among all the women in the department. They met quietly together to share ideas about how to help promote the Women's Extension Program's aims throughout the bureaucracy.

Another step toward putting women on the agenda was to encourage the agricultural assistants to keep records of how many women were attending residential and mobile training courses, field days, and demonstrations. The records soon showed the low level of female participation. Discussion workshops revealed that the agricultural assistants felt shy about encouraging individual women to attend, lest their motives be questioned by husbands and boyfriends while the women themselves felt shy about pushing themselves forward into activities they assumed dealt only with matters of concern to male farmers. In order to break down the barriers, the Women's Extension Program initially emphasized women-only courses and field activities, but as Masona realized: "If women are separated they will always be on their own." Women were gradually encouraged to participate in all courses freely with the men until, by the 1989–1990 season, women's participation in all courses had reached nearly 40 percent.

The mobile training courses, that is, short courses of two or three days on specific topics, held in the village, proved to be particularly popular, and their success brought about a reallocation of training resources, away from the more expensive and formal residential courses. Women can attend without leaving their home duties, while the field-based agricultural assistants realize that their knowledge is relevant and useful also to women farmers. Practical instruction, question-and-answer sessions, and on-the-spot trial and group discussions give rise to highly interactive learning.

Changing Attitudes and Aspirations

One of the most persuasive strategies for changing the attitudes of men and the aspirations of women has been the acquisition of women farmers of the difficult "male" skill of ox-plowing. The use of oxen for plowing is critical to the timeliness of planting and thus essential for increasing crop yields significantly in the difficult rain-fed farming conditions of the Western Province. Women traditionally have had poor access to men's plowing teams, even the relatively few women who owned oxen, and were forbidden by custom to plow themselves. In the early 1980s, the introduction of rice cultivation in the floodplain of the Zambezi river increased the amount of labor women were expected to put into hand-weeding and other manual tasks. It became clear that unless women had access to low-cost ox-drawn implements, the spread of the otherwise profitable new crop would be checked.

While the department pondered how to resolve this dilemma, Masona, then working as an animal husbandry officer, quietly encouraged the women in the rice project area to form groups. She then helped to train the women to handle oxen and the plow. At first the men who heard about it thought it a joke, but when at last they saw the women plowing at an agricultural show, they realized that women could, indeed, "do the job that was taboo." Today, ox-plow training is routinely offered to other groups of women. Women's ox-plow teams have proved to be conscientious and effective, and increasingly women's teams are being hired to plow for others.

Building Women's Self-Image and Organizational Capacity

A colleague in the agricultural department, Lydia Ndulu, became convinced that the best way for women to gain access to the services and support structures of the department was through the mechanism of group development. In 1984, before the Women's Extension Program had started, she began a project to develop a team of women group promoters who could work in a participatory way with village women. The aims were to build farm women's self-image and confidence and develop their organizational capacity so that they could reach out to the existing male-dominated services and articulate their own priorities.

At first, the village headmen were suspicious of the promoters and accused them of wanting to separate women from their families. The promoters themselves were often shy and uncertain of their roles. As they began to talk with women in the villages, however, their own confidence and sense of purpose strengthened. They realized that woman-to-woman contact was a journey of mutual discovery that lessened the isolation and sense of helplessness of everyone. Village women could ask questions of the women promoters on a range of personal and agricultural topics without being made to feel stupid or ignorant.

Village women now value the groups for their own sake. It is one of the few opportunities they have to do their own planning, make their own economic decisions, and build a capital base and financial safety net through group saving. Although the economic benefits in most cases so far have been modest, the group mechanism has enabled the members to link to other programs and activities of the department and thereby learn new skills such as ox-plowing and making dried cassava flakes to sell.

Men in the villages where there are groups also have been impressed and have come to value the benefits to the family. In a number of cases, the groups have admitted male members, seeing a number of advantages to doing so. Supportive men have more leverage to obtain opportunities for the women members when public authorities have to be dealt with; they can mobilize help with the heavier tasks; they can more easily be liaisons with the male-dominated village decision-making structures. Nonetheless, women members agree that no man should become a group officer. They have seen on previous occasions how easily men transform collaborative relationships into power over others.

Rosemary Ntoka, a group leader, sums it up: "To survive, we women have to learn new ideas and methods. I am interested in the group because this way we share our problems, we share ideas and we learn together."[11]

The department as a whole initially was somewhat indifferent to the project. Under the influence of the Women's Extension Program, however, both the provincial and field staff have come to see the groups as a mechanism for improving the efficiency of their own work. They can reach more farmers through the groups than by individual visits. In recognition of this, many of the male agricultural assistants are now forming women's groups, without any special assistance from the project. Further, given the leanness of the department's budget, the senior staff now recognize that the group mechanism gives women a sustainable vehicle for self-reliant development that men lack, at a time when the department itself can do little to promote agricultural growth.

It is accepted that, in the face of inertia and skepticism, women's energy has been essential to bringing about the change of attitude and practice. As the promoter for the Limulunga area clearly recognizes, "If men had been running this project, we wouldn't have progressed so far."[12]

Getting Women's Crop Priorities on the Research Agenda

The Women's Extension Program has facilitated another important link between women farmers and the agricultural department. Scientists working under the field research program of the research section collaborate closely with trial assistants (all of whom are men) and the agricultural assistants. Although the policy of the research section is to include women farmers in its work, until about 1987 the Western Province scientists did not take the policy seriously, and by default, they ended up working only with male farmers.

The coordinator began to challenge the field research team to interview during their surveys women heads of households and wives who farmed. The data helped convince her male colleagues that there were differences in the way men and women farmed and in their priorities, which should be reflected in the research agenda.

One team member who had been sensitized during his postgraduate studies abroad to many of the conceptual issues at stake drafted a position paper for the section head, drawing on his colleagues' survey data, the data provided by the women's extension program, and the information from the women's groups' project. The paper was formally discussed, and as a result, the team began to pay more attention to women's roles in agriculture, principally in three ways.

First, such crops as bambara nuts and cowpeas, which are cultivated mainly by women and which have high potential both as income-earners in local markets and as protein sources in the family diet, were included in the experiment schedule. Second, women are now routinely included in farm surveys. Finally, the agricultural assistants and trial assistants have begun to lay out trials together with the women's groups. As in Botswana, the scientists are learning about the mutual benefits that spring from such collaboration.

Changing the Dynamics of the System as a Whole

Although the women's extension program no longer exists in its old form, its impact has been lasting. An important lesson has been learned along the way. Initially, the way that people explained the challenge was in terms of joining two separate realities together, of forging a link between where women were in their lives and where the department was in its work. The metaphors have changed as a result of the learning process catalyzed by the women's extension program.

As mechanisms are created to bring women in and let their voices be heard, the dynamics of the whole system begin to change. Neither the women activists themselves nor the department as a male-dominated bureaucracy nor the male staff nor men and women in the villages have remained the same. The quality as well as the nature of relationships have changed. The effect has been, however modestly, to raise the efficiency, productivity, fairness, and sustainability of the system as a whole.

Farming for the Future

The cases discussed in this chapter illustrate how women's voices influence the way that agricultural systems and natural resource management are evolving. Women's influence changes the agenda. Their initiatives and collaboration make developmental activity more relevant and effective.

The cases provide in sharp detail further insight into the reasons why keeping women out cannot lead to more sustainable biological, physical, and socioeconomic systems. They do not prove that bringing women in necessarily leads to more sustainable outcomes. No one can be sure what will achieve this, neither men nor women, nor experts nor ordinary people going about their lives. The cases simply show that women also must be at the table when decisions are made about what constitutes improvement.

12

Conclusions

Crisis-driven advocacy of population control policies is both exaggerated and misdirected. Those who formulate population control and environmental policy increasingly are alert to an emerging international consensus that reflects accommodation to the developmental needs of poorer nations and to the concerns of the women's movement. Policy language is being reshaped in the wider dialogue. Simplistic calls for population control are giving way to a four-point program encompassing reproductive health, the education of girls and women, maternal and child health services, and increased access by women to productive resources and income. The concept of family planning is broadening to address the sexuality and fertility concerns of men, adolescents of both sexes, and unmarried as well as married women. The sensitive issue of abortion increasingly is recognized as a compelling public health matter.

The broadening and deepening of the agenda reflect the accumulated experience of numerous different approaches to the challenge of profound, human-led change in the environment. The move toward a holistic approach—which is nonetheless tightly focused—recognizes the multiple ways in which initiatives in one area may reinforce and amplify effects in another.

The material benefits to women are potentially great, and through women's roles in reproduction and environmental management, these benefits cascade into larger benefits for families, communities, and the world as a whole. In other words, response to women's micro needs and priorities leads to achievement of macro policy goals.

The interplay between public policy formulation and the women's movement, through multiple channels and at numerous levels, has done more than add items to the population control and environmental agenda. As the examples of the Mahila Samakhya program, the Bangladesh Women's Health Coalition, and numerous agricultural research programs show, women-centered approaches change the values, the design, and the operation of programs. Norms and standards framed by men's experience of the world are reshaped to reflect a more encompassing perspective that builds on the capacities of both women and men.

Don't Waste Energy on Fear of the Future: Summary of Implications

It is true that there is a population problem in relation to the environment and human well-being, but the pretense that population growth forecloses all futures is simply wrong. It is not even the case that population growth inevitably forecloses all futures plausibly considered desirable. The problem is more exactly specified in terms of how the world might accommodate environmental change and population change, at what cost, and for whom.

Moreover, it is demotivating to create an atmosphere in which people become afraid of a future dominated by such slogans as the "demographic juggernaut" and "ecodisasters." Fear saps the energy that individuals and societies need to make difficult adjustments. If people are presented with unpalatable choices made by others more fortunately placed, about which they have not been consulted and which in any case appear to compromise their own immediate livelihood, the counterproductive response is likely to be indifference or confrontation. Furthermore, fear lends itself to an authoritarian political dynamic in which the powerful dare to impose on others policies that they never would accept for themselves.

Any thoughtful study of the options must deal not only with experimental evidence but with complicated amalgams of information, experience, and suppositions for which various plausible interpretations exist. Moreover, the interpretations are embedded in values, conditions, and histories that are both rooted and dynamic. This does not imply that there is no way of sorting the useful from the dangerous hypotheses or interpretations. It does strongly imply that, more than ever, learning to survive must be as open, as speedy, and as widely shared a process as possible.

Survival is always and necessarily contextual and active. Herein lies both the fear and the hope for the future. The fear is that apparently simple solutions will be applied forcefully to circumstances that they do not fit and in the mistaken belief that people are passive rather than active in shaping their own lives. The grounds for hope lie in the fact that people do respond to circumstance and already are making the choices that render population control and environmental problems more manageable.

More specifically, the fear is that women's rights as women and as human beings with the capacity to shape their own future will be made subordinate to the will of others in the name of common survival. The reproductive life of a woman in Nigeria or India is not the cause of the world's environmental problems, though it may be a source of much ill health and sorrow for the woman herself and a factor in the complex dimensions of poverty within which she lives.

The hope is that economic, population control, and environmental policy-makers are waking up to the fact that healthy, educated, and economically secure women are essential to any conceivably sustainable future and that profligate consumption, pollution, and waste generation by the better off must be controlled and reduced.

Healthy, Educated, Economically Secure Women Are the Key: Findings

Population variables and their effects are extremely sensitive to history and context. The relationship among demographic variables can change rapidly and unpredictably, without recourse to widespread contraceptive use or health interventions. The effects of size, location, density, and rates of change in population on the environment are not uniform, stable over time, or necessarily negative in conditions of either wealth or poverty.

In environmental terms, earth systems are robust. It is the components of earth systems, such as air, soil, water, and plant and animal life that are vulnerable to change, in the short term by way of quality, composition, and distribution, and ultimately in terms of their availability as resources supportive of human existence. The way in which societies and individuals consume, produce, pollute, generate, and recycle waste is critical to the present and future status of the air we breathe, the soil, water, and biological resources. Population dynamics affect but do not in any simple way determine their status.

At present, agriculture makes an important negative, but reducible, contribution to local and global environmental change. It is possible but not inevitable that the increased demand for food, or for specific types of diet, will intensify or amplify the negative effects. Increasingly, however, farmers and agricultural professionals are learning to view agriculture from an ecological perspective that optimizes the positive services agriculture can make to environmental sustainability, even within the margins of an increasing population.

The more uncertain agricultural scenarios derive from the probable yet inconclusive evidence for a rapid rise in mean global temperatures, the depletion of the ozone layer confirmed by both observation and theory, the loss of biodiversity, and regional and more localized hazards such as acid rain, pollution of waterways, depletion of water sources, and toxic waste. All these changes have more to do with the way humanity organizes production and consumption than population growth or population density in itself, although the scale, rate, and location of population change can amplify the effects.

Population relationships and their effects, however, are neither random nor unmanageable. Both the current concern and the grounds for optimism are founded on deliberate policy choices made over the past fifty years. Economic growth, more secure access to more food, and investments in housing, water sanitation, and general health services and maternal and infant care have led to rapid and substantial declines in mortality in most parts of the world.

As more children survive into their reproductive years, the global population inevitably increases and probably will continue to do so for some time to come. At the same time, however, the spread of contraceptive availability, wider contraceptive choice, safer and more user-responsive reproductive health services, healthier and better-fed mothers and infants, the as yet modest gains in the education of girls and women, and rising incomes in the most populous parts of the world have contributed to sharply falling family size in most parts of the world.

The option of allowing mortality to rise to curb global population is not an acceptable or a useful option. High mortality rates, particularly of women and children, encourage and sustain high fertility. On the contrary, healthy mothers bear and raise healthy infants. Fewer deaths among mothers and infants lead to fewer births.

Moreover, an expanded range of reproductive health services, beyond contraceptive supply, supports responsible management of sexuality and fertility among both women and men and helps reduce the large, costly, but avoidable loss of life through unsafe abortion. Investment in services that respond to women's and men's concern to manage their behavior responsibly in the stressful social and economic conditions of today, to protect their sexuality and fertility from infection, to conceive, bear, and raise healthy children, and to manage unwanted pregnancy safely reconciles private desires and public policy goals. Effective, client-responsive reproductive health services are possible even in conditions of intense poverty.

The education of women and girls reduces both total achieved fertility and the desire for children, broadly in step with the number of years of schooling. The impact of education on fertility and the desire for children is strong at 4 to 6 years of schooling and strongest at 7 years or more. Geographically, the response is weakest in sub-Saharan Africa but, even so, unequivocally positive. Cost-effective, large-scale programs for the education of girls with links to formal schooling systems are possible even in conditions of extreme poverty and discrimination against women.

Women who have had access to schooling have a better earning capacity and are able to use their time and labor more productively. For the one-third of households that are headed and largely maintained by women, access to income is an essential condition for the survival of themselves and their children. Providing continuing education to women who already maintain children without resident male support is one challenge; changing the policies and attitudes that force girls to leave school, college, or vocational training if they become pregnant is another. Further, as the major portion of women's income is spent on the well-being of the household, while a variable portion of male income is lost to private consumption and expenditures outside the household domain, the marginal returns to increasing female income are high, for both families and society.

The health, education, and earning capacity of girls and women are intimately related to better management of natural and agricultural resources. The synergistic effects are substantial if, in addition, women's access to land, trees, and water is more secure and their access to such inputs as improved seed, farm and household equipment, agricultural training, and formal markets is improved.

Unfortunately, on all three fronts there are also grounds for concern. Expenditures on health and education in Africa as a whole, for example, are slipping, maternal and infant mortality rates are climbing again, while the impact of HIV infection and the resurgence of diseases once close to being brought under control, such as malaria, are having a devastating effect. The modest gains in providing quality care in reproductive health are in danger of being swamped by renewed calls for focused contraceptive delivery. Major investment to bring the education of girls and women at least to the level of that of boys and men has not yet been committed. The modernization of land title, with the exception of only a few countries in the world, remains largely insensitive to women's rights of use, access, and ownership. Agricultural bureaucracies and assistance programs have not invested in women farmers and resource managers to a degree that is anywhere nearly commensurate with women's contribution.

Economic development policy is woven into both the hopes and the concerns. Economic theories based on a premise of inexhaustible or infinitely substitutable natural resources and a limitless capacity to absorb waste and pollution are obsolete in the sense that they no longer lead to practices that protect and promote the conditions in which human existence is possible.

A particular test of the harm brought about by inappropriate economics is the degree to which the labor and energy of women are stretched. Beyond a threshold of exhaustion, the lives of neither families nor communities can be sustained. Protecting and strengthening the capacities of girls and women is more than a humanitarian gesture or the simple consideration that any citizen has a right to enjoy: it is the bottom line in the survival of humankind as a species dependent on its environment. It is thus essential for human survival that economic theory, policy, and practice in both rich and poor countries begin to measure, value, and reward the services provided by women and by the environment. Foreign aid has a role to play in relieving the stresses of development and in supporting the emerging population and environment agenda. Unfortunately, official developmental assistance is shrinking rather than expanding. American aid budgets peaked in 1985 at $20 billion and have since fallen by more than a quarter. More than two dozen countries now devote a larger proportion of their GNP to foreign assistance than does the United States, and the U.S. contribution has fallen to around 16 percent of the world total. New demands from the former Soviet Union and eastern and central Europe, as well as for emergency relief, are squeezing allocations to the world's poorest countries at a time when industrial economies continue to experience recessionary pressure. In 1992–1993, eight bilateral donors cut their aid spending in real terms, including Japan, the second largest donor. Only four countries, Denmark, Norway, Holland, and Sweden, meet the United Nations target contribution of 0.7 percent of their gross domestic product.

The investment costs of getting population control and environmental policy on track are small, both absolutely and relatively. The World Bank estimated in its *1992 World Development Report* the amount needed to bring the primary education of girls to the level of boys, that is, for 25 million girls a year, at $950 million. This figure represents only 2 percent of total educational expenditures by developing countries. In its *1993 World Development Report*, the World Bank estimated the cost of an "essential health care package," including maternal and child health care, to be $8 per person per year for the world's poorest countries. The Population Crisis Committee, based in Washington, D.C., estimates an average cost of $16 per couple per year to support a family planning program in a developing country, inclusive of such ancillary costs as information provision and public education and biomedical and demographic research.

The Grounds for Hope: Conclusions

The challenge for all of us, wherever we live, is to learn our way into a process of development that secures people's well-being without overtaxing the environment, depleting renewable natural resources, or exhausting the energy and labor of women. Population policy formulated in terms of providing reproductive health care (including maternal and child health services), information and counseling to women, men, and adolescents has an important, essential, but not overriding role to play in the process.

Environmentalists, the women's movement, population control lobbyists, and developing countries have at times been at odds with each other in the learning process. Aggressive advocacy of contraceptive-led fertility control, coercive programming targeted at women, and insensitive or exploitative technological fixes on the one hand, and neglect of people's roles in managing agricultural and natural resources sustainably, and in managing their own sexuality and fertility responsibly on the other, have set one interest group against another. An agenda built on reproductive health, the education of girls and women, and economically secure women and families is truly a common agenda, in everyone's interest.

Both men and women, the young and the old, face unprecedented stress in the conduct of family life and in creating and maintaining stable relationships. It is in everyone's interest that decisions and behaviors governing sexuality and fertility are managed responsibly and safely. Responding to the demands, needs, and preferences of individuals and couples is both necessary to and effective in achieving this goal. At the same time, stronger advocacy of primary education for girls could tip the balance in ensuring that, even where national economies are faltering, expenditures to secure universal primary education of girls are protected.

Environmental policy for its part needs to balance concern for the natural systems on which human life depends with concern for strengthening people's capacities to manage natural systems. An important part of the agenda, that which deals with energy, needs to give more attention to the ways in which women as end users manage energy consumption and, as energy suppliers, develop and sustain energy supply.

The management of energy availability has gone seriously wrong in one particular respect. Women's time, labor, and energy are not infinite; to an increasing degree, women's energy is reaching its limits under misguided economic policies. Women's energy is essential for the maintenance of community relations and the household and for bearing and nurturing children. In many parts of the world, women are the essential energy source for the production of food and other agricultural products. Women's income derived from a multitude of livelihood sources, for an increasing proportion of the world's people, is essential to survival. Neither in richer nor poorer countries can women's energy be infinitely spread over these competing demands.

The pressures on women's energy are in part a reflection of a widespread failure to support and strengthen adequately men's household, parental, and economic roles. From this perspective, increasing men's access to sustainable livelihoods is a necessary part of the environmental agenda. Other initiatives, however, more directly relieve the pressures on women. These are primarily reproductive health care, education, the provision of appropriate technologies to women, and more secure access for women to economic and financial assets, property, and services.

This book has documented a number of cases showing both what can be done and how to do it. There are many more examples, far more than the gloomy doomsayers are willing to acknowledge. Successful programs share a number of fundamental characteristics:

□ Women are fully involved in defining the problem, designing and trying out solutions, evaluating and sharing the results.

□ Involvement goes beyond consultation and collaboration; women play roles as managers, owners, leaders, partners, and allies.

□ The details of the programs are respectful of and respond to local context and priorities.

□ The programs stay on course because they are founded on principles that incorporate values and ethical concerns, which are negotiated rather than imposed, and which serve as the touchstone for decision making.

□ The programs are designed as frameworks for learning; the details can be adapted over time and space as competencies grow, the environment changes, and new opportunities emerge.

The Action Agenda: What To Do

The evidence produced in this book shows the main lines of the action agenda. There is sufficient knowledge, competence, and capacity to do what needs to be done. The action agenda outlined is one around which women's health advocates, environmentalists, agricultural and population specialists, and educationists could forge a strong alliance. The chief items in the agenda are policies that:

1. Balance efforts to stabilize population with efforts to change the consumption and production patterns of rich people and rich countries

2. Guarantee all women over the age of puberty access to reproductive health care, including wide contraceptive choices, pregnancy and delivery care, safe abortion, and prevention and treatment of sexually transmitted diseases

3. Develop technology that women can control that protects against sexual infection as well as unwanted pregnancy

4. Help men take responsibility for their own sexual behavior and fertility, as well as their partners' health and well-being

5. Ensure that reproductive health services and population policies are accountable to women, for as long as women remain their primary clients

6. Invest in universal primary education for girls and the education of women, to bring the schooling of women and girls at least to the levels enjoyed today by boys and men

7. Ensure that women have rights of access, ownership, and use of natural resources and agricultural land

8. Ensure that women receive production inputs such as improved seeds, financial services, agricultural training, appropriate technologies, and producer markets to a degree commensurate with their contribution to agricultural output and their roles in production, processing, preparation, and preservation of foodstuffs and other farm products

9. Respect women's distinctive knowledge and experience

10. Ensure that women are at the table where decisions are made and that their voices, too, are heard in the debate about the world's future

Notes

Chapter 1

1. Westoff, C.F., and L.H. Ochoa (1991). *Unmet Need and the Demand for Family Planning.* Columbia, Md.: Institute for Resource Development/Macro International, Inc.
2. Based on studies conducted by researchers on behalf of the World Bank in Kenya, Ivory Coast, and Burkima Faso. See Bindlish, V., and R. Evenson (1993). "Evaluation of the Performance of T & V Extension in Kenya." Africa Region, Technical Department, Technical Paper No. 208, The World Bank, Washington, D.C.; and Bindlish, V., and R. Evenson (1993). "Evaluation of the Performance of T & V Extension in Burkina Faso." Africa Region, Technical Department, Technical Paper, The World Bank, Washington, D.C. (in press).
3. Zeng, Yi, Tu Ping, Gu Baochang, Xu Yi, Li Bohua, and Li Yongping (1993). "Causes and Implications of the Recent Increase in the Reported Sex Ratio at Birth in China," *Population and Development Review*, Vol. 19, No. 2, June 1993, pp. 283–302.
4. An Interview with Jean Shinoda Bolen, *Women of Power*, Fall 1991, pp. 21–25.
5. In Jiggins, J., ed. (1989). *Women and Land.* Programme on Rural Women, Rural Employment Policies Branch, Geneva, ILO, p. 42.
6. Adams, J. (1990). Population Growth and Conservation, *World Wildlife Fund and Conservation Newsletter*, No. 2. Washington D.C.
7. Seshu, D.V., and M. Dadlani (1989). *Role of Women in Seed Management with Special Reference to Rice.* IRTP Technical Bulletin 5. IRRI, Manila, 1989.
8. Khasiani, S.A., ed. (1992). *Groundwork: African Women as Environmental Managers.* African Centre for Technology Studies, Nairobi. Useful compendiums of methodologies for overcoming gender bias in agricultural development are Feldstein, H., and J. Jiggins, eds. (1994), *Tools for the Field*, Kumarian Press, West Hartford; and Kiriro, A., and C. Juma, eds. (1991), *Gaining Ground: Institutional Innovations in Land-use Management in Kenya*, African Centre for Technology Studies, Nairobi.
9. Erlich, P.R., and A.H. Erlich (1990). *The Population Explosion.* Simon and Schuster, New York.
10. Robin Cole, Chairman of the Condor Conservation Trust, a charity aiming to protect the planet by stabilizing world population, to the 1992 British Association for the Advancement of Science meeting, reported in *New Scientist*, August 29, 1992, p. 11.
11. "Progress Report Highlights," Population/Environment Initiative. Population Communications International, New York, January 10, 1991.
12. Brouwers, J.H.A.M., "Rural People's Response to Soil Fertility Decline: The Adja Case" (Benin, Ph.D. Thesis, Agriculture University, Wageningen, October 1993); Tiffen, M., M. Mortimore, and F.N. Gichuki (1993). *More People, Less Erosion.* Wiley, Chichester.

13. "Understanding How Resources Are Allocated Within Households." International Food Policy Research Institute, Policy Briefs, Washington, D.C., November 8, 1992.

Chapter 2

1. Quoted in N. Cohn (1970). *The Pursuit of the Millennium*, revised and expanded edition. Oxford University Press, Oxford, pp. 201–202, from a translation by G.R. Owst (1933), *Literature and Pulpit in Medieval England*. Cambridge University Press, Cambridge.
2. Sen, G., and C. Grown (1985). *Development, Crises, and Alternative Visions: Third World Women's Perspectives*. DAWN, Stavangar, Norway.
3. Sen and Grown (1985). *Development, Crises, and Alternative Visions: Third World Women's Perspectives*.
4. Srinivasan, Viji (1986). "Women of Chotanagpur: Beginning of Dissent." Paper presented to Workshop on Operational Strategies for Reaching Women in Agriculture, Kijkduin, Netherlands, September 22–26, 1986. Ministry of Agriculture/Ministry of Development Cooperation, p. 9.
5. "State of the World's Children" (1992). UNICEF, New York.
6. Shiva, Vandana (1989). "Development: The New Colonialism," in *Development, Journal of the Society for International Development*. Rome, p. 86.
7. Erlich, P.R., and A.H. Erlich (1990). *The Population Explosion*. Simon and Schuster, New York.
8. Quoted in an article reporting the conference, "A Plague of Humans," *New Scientist*, October 12, 1991.
9. Maurice King, "Health Is a Sustainable State," *The Lancet*, September 15, 1990, and during a debate with Richard Jolly, Deputy Executive Director of UNICEF, at the Free University, Amsterdam, November 20, 1991, reported in *Onze Wereld*, No. 12, December 1991, p. 6.
10. See *Joint Statement* issued by the World Academies Conference on Population, November 1993, New Delhi. The Statement calls for "zero population growth within the lifetime of our children." The African Academy of Sciences, an umbrella group for the continent, criticized the statement (while agreeing with the critics, Uganda and Kenya, were among AAS members that did sign the *Joint Statement*), mainly for focusing on population growth in developing countries, ignoring the problem of infertility, underemphasizing poverty's impact on population variables, and for setting one global target for all countries in one time frame.
11. *The World Bank and the Environment*, Fiscal 1992. The World Bank, Washington, D.C.
12. Sadik, N. (1990). *Investing in Women: The Focus of the '90s*. UNFPA, New York.
13. Reported by *The Washington Post*, "Inquirer's Birth Control Bomb," Style, December 18, 1990.
14. The *Inquirer's* editor, Maxwell King, apologized in print for the December 18 editorial, a move subsequently condemned as suppressing legitimate debate. See also *The Washington Post*, Letters to the Editor, December 29, 1990.
15. Segal, *The Washington Post*, Letters to the Editor, December 29, 1990; and Booth, W., "Judge Orders Birth Control Implant in Defendant," *The Washington Post*, January 5, 1991.
16. Segal, *The Washington Post*, Letters to the Editor, December 29, 1990.

17. Segal, *The Washington Post,* Letters to the Editor, December 29, 1990. Further abuses are documented in Mintzer, B., A. Hardon, and J. Hauhart, eds. (1993). *Norplant: Under Her Skin.* Women's Health Action Foundation, Amsterdam.

Chapter 3

1. The legal Latin can be rendered literally in a number of ways, such as "Words lead to nothing," or "To nothing of account through words" or "To no one in talk."
2. World Development Report 1991. The World Bank, Washington, D.C.
3. Schneider, S. (1990). Cooling It: The Global Warming Debate. *World Monitor,* July, pp. 33–34.
4. Bergström, S. (1993). Family Planning and Maternal Health: Myths and Realities. Paper presented to seminar on Population and Development. Ministry of Foreign Affairs, Copenhagen, September 29, 1993.
5. Dixon-Mueller, R., and J. Wasserheit (1991). *The Culture of Silence: Reproductive Tract Infections Among Women in the Third World.* International Women's Health Coalition, New York, p. 1.
6. *The Culture of Silence,* p. 7.
7. *Reproductive Tract Infections in Women in the Third World.* International Women's Health Coalition, New York, 1991, p. 10.
8. Over, M., and P. Piot (1992). "HIV Infection and Other Sexually Transmitted Diseases." In D.T. Jamison and W.H. Mosley, eds. *Disease Control Priorities in Developing Countries.* Oxford University Press for the World Bank, New York.
9. Schulz, K.F., J. Schulte, and S. Berman (1992). "Maternal Health and Child Survival: Opportunities to Protect Both Women and Children from the Adverse Consequences of Reproductive Tract Infections." In A. Germain, K.K. Holmes, P. Piot, and J.N. Wasserheit, eds., *Reproductive Tract Infections: Global Impact and Priorities for Women's Reproductive Health.* Plenum Press, New York, pp. 145–184.
10. As the authors note, however, the scientific basis for these estimates is not fully established, and some doubt must remain as to the totals, causation, and trends identified. See Oldeman, L.R., R.T.A. Hakkeling, and W.G. Sombroek (1990). *World Map of the Status of Human-Induced Soil Degradation: An Explanatory Note.* Revised 2nd ed. International Soil Reference and Information Centre, Wageningen.
11. Kates, R.W., and V. Haarmann (1991). "Poor People and Threatened Environments: Global Overviews, Country Comparisons, and Local Studies." 1991 World Hunger Program Research Report RR-91-2, Alan Shawn Feinstein World Hunger Program, Rhode Island, Brown University; and Kates, R.W., and V. Haarmann (1992). Where the Poor Live: Are the Assumptions Correct? *Environment,* Vol. 34, No. 4, May, pp. 4–27 *passim.*
12. Monimart, M. (1989). "Women in the Fight Against Desertification." Paper no. 12, London, IIED, December.
13. Box A31, 207, in Reintjes, C., B. Haverkort, and A. Waters-Bayer (1992). *Farming for the Future,* Leusden, ILEIA and Macmillan, London.
14. *Ecclesiastes,* chapter 1, verse 4.
15. See Gould, S.J. (1987), *Time's Arrow, Time's Cycle* (Harvard University Press, Cambridge, Mass. and London) for a fascinating expansion of this theme.

16. World Commission on Environment and Development (1987). *Our Common Future*. Oxford University Press, Oxford. Also known as *The Brundtland Report*.

17. Mathews, J.T. (1989). "Redefining Security." *Foreign Affairs*, Spring, pp. 163–177, p. 173; Germain, A., K. Holmes, P. Piot, and J. Wasserheit, eds. (1992). *Reproductive Tract Infections: Global Impact and Priorities for Women's Reproductive Health*. Plenum Press, New York.

18. First used by Diane Rocheleau during a presentation at the Association of Women in Development Conference, Washington, D.C., September 1989.

Chapter 4

1. A useful initial guide to the literature is to be found in Scoones, I., M. Melnyk, and J.N. Pretty (1992). *The Hidden Harvest: Wild Foods and Agricultural Systems, A Literature Review and Annotated Bibliography*. IIED/SIDA/WWF, London.

2. Table 23 in Horton, D. (1988). *Underground Crops: Long-term Trends in Production of Roots and Tubers*. Winrock International, Morrilton, Arkansas.

3. Parry, M. (1990). *Climate Change and World Agriculture*. Earthscan Publications Ltd., London, in association with The International Institute for Applied Systems Analysis and the United Nations Environment Programme, p. 7.

4. Poleman, T.T. (1989). "Hunger or Plenty? The Food/Population Prospect Two Centuries After Malthus." Staff paper 89-30, Department of Agricultural Economics, Cornell University, Ithaca.

5. Pralhad Rao, N. (1989). "Diet and Nutrition During Drought—An Indian Experience." *Disasters*, Vol. 13, pp. 58–72.

6. For example, see Chen, L. C., E. Huq, and S. d'Souza (1981). "Sex Bias in the Family Allocation of Food and Health Care in Rural Bangladesh." *Population and Development Review*, Vol. 7, No. 1 (March), pp. 55–70.

7. Jiggins, J., ed. (1982). *A Report on the Regional Workshop on Seasonal Variations in the Provisioning, Nutrition and Health of Rural Families, 31 March–2 April*. African Medical and Research Foundation, Nairobi.

8. Jiggins, J. (1986). "Women and Seasonality: Coping with Crisis and Calamity." *IDS Bulletin*, Vol 17, No. 3, July, pp. 9–18.

9. Fowler, A. (1982). "The Seasonal Aspect of Education in East and Southern Africa." In Jiggins, J., *Regional Workshop on Seasonal Variations*, pp. 58–74.

10. Otaala, B. (1980). *Daycare in Eastern Africa: A Survey of Botswana, Kenya, Seychelles, Tanzania, Addis Ababa*. ECA/ATRCW, November.

11. Pittock, A.B. (1991). "Developing Regional Climate Change Scenarios: Their Reliability and Seriousness." CSIRO Division of Atmospheric Research, Mordialloc.

12. *World Economic Survey 1993*. United Nations, New York.

13. Bolin, B., B. Doos, J. Jager, and R. Warrick (1989). *The Greenhouse Effect: Climate Change and Ecosystems*. Wiley, Chichester. Also Hoffman, J. S., M. C. Gibbs, and L. Lewis (1989). "Prospects for Reducing Methane Emissions." Environmental Protection Agency, Washington, D.C.

14. Wilson, E.O., ed. (1989). *Biodiversity*. National Academy Press, Washington, D.C.

15. The Pesticide Action Network based in New York, with more than 300 member organizations worldwide, maintains an extensive bibliography documenting the sale of banned toxic agricultural pesticides in developing countries, the health consequences of handling by farmers, the contamination of mothers' breast milk as pesticides enter the human food chain, the effects of residues on consumers, and the consequences of pesticide use for plants, insects, amphibians, and wild animals.

16. Postel, S. (1992). *Last Oasis: Facing Water Scarcity*. Worldwatch Institute/ Norton, Washington, D.C.

17. Jiggins, J. (1993). "From Technology Transfer to Resource Management." Invited paper to XVII International Grassland Congress, February 8–21, Palmerston North, New Zealand.

18. Dudal, R., and H. Gulinck (1989). Bodemgebruik op weg naar de 21ste eeuw, *Landbouwkundig Tijdschrift*, 101,1, 14–17, Dutch original.

19. Malthus, T.R. *An Essay on the Principle of Population, As It Affects the Future Improvement of Society*, Penguin, Harmondsworth, reprint edition 1978, pp. 6–8.

Chapter 5

1. Eckholm, E. (1975). *The Other Energy Crisis: Firewood*. Worldwatch paper 1, Worldwatch Institute, Washington, D.C.; Parikh, J.K. (1978). "Energy Use for Subsistence and Prospects for Development." *Energy*, Vol. 3, pp. 613–637.

2. Flavin, C. (1990). "Slowing Global Warming," chapter 2 in L. Brown et al., *State of the World 1990*. A Worldwatch Institute Report, W.W. Norton & Co., New York and London.

3. Agarwal, A., and S. Narain (1991). *Global Warming in an Unequal World: A Case of Environmental Colonialism*. Centre for Science and Environment, New Delhi, January.

4. Levine, J.S. (1992). *Global Biomass Burning: Atmospheric, Climatic and Biospheric Implications*. MIT Press, Cambridge, Mass.

5. *Newsweek*, January 21, 1991, p. 25.

6. Schaeffer, R. (1990). "Car Sick, Automobiles Ad Nauseam," *Greenpeace*, May/June, pp. 13–17; MacKenzie, J.J., R.C. Dower, and D.D.T. Chen (1992). *The Going Rate: What It Really Costs to Drive*. World Resources Institute, Washington, D.C., June.

7. Arcia, G. (1990). *Population Growth and the Urban Environment*. Research Triangle Institute, Research Triangle Park, North Carolina, November.

8. *Population Growth and the Urban Environment*, p. 7.

9. Box 2.1., p. 29 in *Sustainable Energy Economy*, sectoral policy document 4, Directorate General of Development Cooperation, Ministry of Foreign Affairs, The Hague, 1992.

10. Johansson, T.B., H. Kelly, A.K.N. Reddy, and R.H. Williams (1993). *Renewable Energy: Sources for Fuels and Electricity*. The Island Press/Earthscan, Washington, D.C.

11. Among the influential proponents of this point of view were Eckholm, E.

(1976), *Losing Ground: Environmental Stress and World Food Prospects*, World-watch Institute, W.W. Norton, New York; and Brown, L., et al. (1978), *The State of the World 1978*, Worldwatch Institute, W.W. Norton, New York.

12. Hamilton, L.S. (1987). "What Are the Impacts of Himalayan Deforestation on the Ganges-Brahmaputra Lowlands and Delta? Assumptions and Facts." *Mountain Research and Development*, Vol.7, No.3, pp. 256–263; Thompson, M., and M. Warburton (1985). "Decision Making under Contradictory Certainties," *Journal of Applied Systems Analysis*, Vol. 12, pp. 3–34; Ives, J., and B. Messerli (1989). *The Himalayan Dilemma: Reconciling Development and Conservation*, Routledge and United Nations University, London and New York.

13. Gill, G.J. (1993). "OK, the Data's Lousy, But It's All We've Got (Being a Critique of Conventional Methods)." Gatekeeper Series No. 38. IIED, London. Gill presents a penetrating if brief summary of the ways in which data can be misread to produce inaccurate interpretations of land use trends in Nepal.

14. Ives, J. (1991). "Floods in Bangladesh: Who Is to Blame?" *New Scientist*, April 13, pp. 34–37; Hossain, M., A.T.M. Aminul Islam, and A.K. Saha (1987). *Floods in Bangladesh, Recurrent Disaster and People's Survival.* University Research Centre, Dhaka.

15. Jodha, N.S., M. Banskota, and T. Partap (1992). *Sustainable Mountain Agriculture*, Kathmandu, ICIMOD/New Delhi, IBH Publishing Co. Pvt. Ltd., 2 vols.; Sharma, P., and M. Bankskota (1992). "Population Dynamics and Sustainable Agricultural Development in Mountain Areas." Chapter 7 in *Sustainable Mountain Agriculture*, pp. 165–184.

16. Bhagavan, M.R., and S. Giriappa (1987). "Class Character of Rural Energy Crisis, Case of Karnataka," *Economic and Political Weekly*, XXII, p. 26, Review of Agriculture, June 27, A-57–A-69.

17. Vidyarthi, V. (1984). "Energy and the Poor in an Indian Village," *World Development*, Vol. 12, No. 8, pp. 821–836.

18. Huss-Ashmore, R. (1982). "Seasonality in Rural Highland Lesotho: Method and Policy." In J. Jiggins, ed., *A Report on a Regional Workshop on Seasonal Variations in the Provisioning, Nutrition and Health of Rural Families*, March 31–April 2, Nairobi, AMREF, pp. 147–160.

19. World Health Organization (1984). *Biomass Fuel Combustion and Health*, Geneva.

20. *Energie et Survie: Guide sur L'Energie, l'Environnement et le Travail des Femmes Rurales*, French original. International Labor Organization, Geneva, 1987.

21. Srinivasan, Viji (1986). "Women of Chotanagpur: Beginning of Dissent." Paper to Workshop on Operational Strategies for Reaching Women in Agriculture, Kijkduin, Netherlands, September 22–26 1986, Ministry of Agriculture/ Ministry of Development Cooperation, pp. 4–5.

22. Agarwal, A. (1985). "Women, Male Migration and Environment," *EcoForum*, Vol. 10, No. 2, pp. 4–5.

23. Kumar, S.K., and D. Hotchkiss (1988). "Consequences of Deforestation for Women's Time Allocation, Agricultural Production, and Nutrition in Hill Areas of Nepal." Report 69, IFPRI, Washington, D.C.

24. Paula Williams, Forest and Society Fellow, Institute of Current World Affairs,

New Hampshire, in a letter to P. Bird, Director, ICWA, dated May 1, 1984, Ouaga-dougou, Haute-Volta (subsequently Burkina Faso).

25. Harrison, P. (1987). "A Tale of Two Stoves," *New Scientist*, May 28, pp. 39–43; *Development Forum*, October 1986, p. 6. For those interested in following the news and views on cookstove improvement and promotion, ITDG (London) publishes *Boiling Point* three times a year.

26. Agarwal, B. (1986). *Cold Hearths and Barren Slopes: The Woodfuel Crisis in the Third World*. Allied Publishers, New Delhi; Leach, G., and R. Mearns (1989). *Beyond the Woodfuel Crisis*. Earthscan, London; Foley, G., P. Moss, and L. Timberlake (1984). *Stoves and Trees*. IIED, London and Washington.

27. Rocheleau, D. (1989). "Gender Complementarity and Conflict in Sustainable Forestry Development, A Multiple User Approach." *Proceedings*, ICRAF, Nairobi; Rocheleau, D. (1991). "Gender, Ecology and the Science of Survival: Stories and Lessons from Kenya." *Agriculture and Human Values*, Vol. 10, No. 1; Fortmann, L., and J. Bruce (1988). *Whose Trees? Proprietary Dimensions of Forestry*. Westview Press, Boulder; Chavangi, N. A. (1984). "Cultural Aspects of Fuelwood Procurement in Kakamega District." KWDP Working Paper No. 4, Kenya Woodfuel Development Project, Nairobi; Owusu-Bempah, K. (1987). "The Role of Women Farmers in Choosing Species for Agroforestry Farming Systems in Rural Areas in Ghana." In S.V. Poats, A. Schmink, and A. Spring, eds., *Gender Issues in Farming Systems Research and Extension*. Westview Press, Boulder, pp. 427–441; Wachira, K.K. (1987). "Women's Use of Off-farm and Boundary Lands: Agroforestry Potentials." 137-page mimeo Project Report to Ford Foundation, ICRAF, Nairobi.

28. Traore, A., and N. F. Kouakou (1985). "Femmes et Environnement: Des Foyers Améliorés Pour L'Economie de Bois de Feu en Côte D'Ivoire." Ministère de la Condition Feminine, Abidjan (French original).

29. From an interview with Dr. Mathai reported in *Development Forum*, October 1986, p. 15.

30. Reported in *WorldWide News*, Sept.–Oct. 1989, p. 1.

31. Philipose, P. (1989). "Women Act: Women and Environmental Protection in India." Chapter 7 in Plant, J. (1989). *Healing the Wounds: The Promise of EcoFeminism*. New Society Publishers, Philadelphia, p. 69.

32. ILO (1988). *The Bankura Story: Rural Women Organise for Change*. Technical Cooperation Report, Rural Employment Policy Branch, World Employment Programme, Geneva.

33. *The Bankura Story*, p. 11.

34. *The Bankura Story*, p. 20.

Chapter 6

1. Safilios-Rothschild, C. (1985). "Socioeconomic Development and the Status of Women in the Third World." Working papers No. 112. Center for Policy Studies, The Population Council, New York.

2. Woman workshop participant, Mahila Samakhya program, Tehri Garwhal, U.P., India, February 15, 1989, MS program records.

3. Vaidyanathan, K. E. (1988). "Status of Women and Family Planning: The

Indian Case." Paper presented at the Conference on Women's Position and Demographic Change in the Course of Development. Oslo, Norway, June 15–18, 1988.

4. Comments from male District Adult Education officers, Baroda District, Karnataka, India, September 20, 1988; author's field notes, Joint Indo-Dutch Appraisal Mission.

5. Lucknow, U.P., India, September 22, 1988, author's field notes, Joint Indo-Dutch Appraisal Mission.

6. Nila, at a meeting of women's group facilitators, Mahila Samakhya program, Bidar District, Karanataka, India, February 12, 1990, author's field notes, First Indo-Dutch Review Mission.

7. Rahman, R.I., and M. Hossain, eds. (1992). Rethinking Rural Poverty. Bangladesh Institute of Development Studies, Dhaka.

8. From a Memo written by BRAC Field Staff, Sulla, 1970s, quoted in Dhaka, BRAC, p. 6.

9. Jharna, Program Officer, Non-Formal Primary Education, Rangpur Training and Resource Center, February 23, 1992, author's field notes, BRAC Mid-Term Evaluation.

10. Sattar, Aleeza, and S. Jahan (1991). The Paralegal Program: A Study of Knowledge Retention. Research and Evaluation Division, Dhaka, BRAC, June.

11. Shamima, Women's Health Development Program Officer, Rangpur Training and Resource Center, February 23, 1992, author's field notes, BRAC Mid-Term Evaluation.

12. Zarina, Rural Development Program Officer, Rangpur TARC, February 23, 1992, author's field notes, BRAC Mid-Term Evaluation.

13. The Net, Vol. 20. BRAC Printers, Dhaka, 1980.

14. For further vivid examples of women's views, see Chen, Marty (1986), *The Quiet Revolution*. The University Press, Dhaka; and Jahan, Rounaq (1988), "Hidden Women, Visible Scars: Violence Against Women in Bangladesh." In Bina Agarwal, ed., *Structures of Patriarchy: State, Community and Household in Modernizing Asia*. KALI for Women, Delhi.

15. Niaz, BRAC NFPE teacher, Nandini village, Jamalpur, February 12, 1992, author's field notes, BRAC Mid-Term Evaluation.

16. Zarina, Junior Consultant, WHDP, Bogra Area Office, February 22, 1992, author's field notes, BRAC Mid-Term Evaluation.

17. "Bangladesh: Strategies for Enhancing the Role of Women in Economic Development." World Bank, Annex 5, Dhaka and Washington, D.C., 1990, p. 147.

Chapter 7

1. Author's field notes, First Indo-Dutch Review Mission, February 1990.

2. Chapter 4, National Policy on Education, 1986. Department of Education, Ministry of Human Resource Development, Government of India, New Delhi.

3. Group leader, Manikpur Banda, U.P., February 8, 1990; author's field notes, First Indo-Dutch Review Mission, February 1990.

4. Group leader, Manikpur Banda, U.P., addressing the Assistant District Magis-

trate, February 8, 1990; author's field notes, First Indo-Dutch Review Mission, February 1990.

5. Spoken respectively by a nongovernmental organization activist, Lucknow, U.P., February 10, 1990; a government officer, Ahmedabad, Gujarat, February 1, 1990; and a female Mahila Samakhya program functionary, New Delhi, February 2, 1990; author's field notes, First Indo-Dutch Review Mission, February 1990.

6. Department of Education, New Delhi, September 5, 1988; author's field notes, Indo-Dutch Appraisal Mission, September 1988.

7. Jagori, New Delhi, January 30, 1990; author's field notes, First Indo-Dutch Review Mission, February 1990.

8. Department of Education (1988). *Mahila Samakhya*, Program for Education for Women's Equality, Ministry of Human Resource Development, New Delhi, October.

9. Department of Education (1991). *Mahila Samakhya*, Education for Women's Equality, Ministry of Human Resource Development, New Delhi, April.

10. Respectively, Nalithi, group leader, Lucknow, U.P. February 10, 1990, and Bina, group facilitator, Bidar, Karnataka, February 12, 1990; author's field notes, First Indo-Dutch Review Mission, February 1990.

11. Padma, participant in the first all-Karnataka assembly, March 2–7, 1990, Kowlagi village, Bijapur; reported in *From Paddy to Rice*, Report on the First All-Karnataka Mahila Samakhya Sammelan, State Program Office, 1990, Bangalore, Karnataka.

12. *From Paddy to Rice*.

13. *From Paddy to Rice*.

14. Veershetty, Bidar District, March 1990; quoted in Bidar District Implementation Unit (1991). Bidar District Progress Report, December–March, Karnataka.

15. Respectively, Kamla, women's group leader, Manikpur Banda, U.P., February 8, 1990; Nalini, women's group leader, at a meeting in Bidar, Karnataka, February 12, 1990; author's field notes, First Indo-Dutch Review Mission, February 1990; and Pushpa, group member, Sabarkantha, Gujarat, September 20, 1988; Malithi, group member, Sabarkantha, Gujarat, September 20, 1988; author's field notes, Indo-Dutch Appraisal Mission, September 1988.

16. Reported in *Mahila Samakhya Karnataka, A Progress Report, January to June 1990*, State Program Office, 1990. Bangalore, Karnataka.

17. *From Paddy to Rice*, Report on the First All-Karnataka Mahila Samakhya Sammelan, State Program Office, 1990, Bangalore, Karnataka.

Chapter 8

1. Sinding, S.W. (1992). "Getting to Replacement: Bridging the Gap between Individual Rights and Demographic Goals." Paper presented at the International Planned Parenthood Foundation Family Planning Congress, October 23–25, New Delhi. The Rockefeller Foundation, New York.

2. Cates, William, and Katherine M. Stone (1992). "Family Planning: The Responsibility to Prevent Both Pregnancy and Reproductive Tract Infections." In Adrienne Germain, King K. Holmes, Peter Piot, and Judith N. Wasserheit, eds.

(1992). *Reproductive Tract Infections: Global Impact and Priorities for Women's Reproductive Health.* Plenum Press, New York and London, pp. 93–130.

3. Germain, A., and Jane Ordway (1989). *Population Control and Women's Health: Balancing the Scales.* International Women's Health Coalition, New York, June.

4. Holck, Susan (1990). "Contraceptive Safety." In *Special Challenges in Third World Women's Health.* Presentations at the 1989 Annual Meeting of the American Public Health Association, International Women's Health Coalition, New York, pp. 23–30.

5. Faundes, Anibal (1991), quoted in "Creating Common Ground, Women's Perspectives on the Selection and Introduction of Fertility Regulation Technologies." Report of a meeting between women's health advocates and scientists, Geneva, February 20–22, 1991, organized by the Special Program of Research, Development and Research Training in Human Reproduction, World Health Organization and International Women's Health Coalition, p. 34.

6. Dixon-Mueller, R., and A. Germain (1992). "Stalking the Elusive 'Unmet Need' for Family Planning." *Studies in Family Planning,* Vol. 23, No. 5, September/October, pp. 330–335.

7. Rosenfield, A., M.F. Fathalla, A. Germain, and C.L. Indriso, eds. (1989). "Women's Health in the Third World: The Impact of Unwanted Pregnancy." *International Journal of Gynecology and Obstetrics,* Supplement 3.

8. Rooney, C. (1992). "Antenatal Care and Maternal Health: How Effective Is It? A Review of the Evidence." Maternal Health and Safe Motherhood Program, World Health Organization, Geneva, p. 36.

9. Brunham, Robert C., and Joanne E. Embree (1992). "Sexually Transmitted Diseases: Current and Future Dimensions of the Problem in the Third World." In A. Germain et al., eds. (1992). *Reproductive Tract Infections,* pp. 35–60; p. 38.

10. Wasserheit, Judith (1989). "Reproductive Tract Infections." Paper presented at 117th Annual meeting of the American Public Health Association, Chicago, October 17.

11. *World Development Report 1993,* Box 1.2, pp. 30 and 33. The World Bank, Washington, D.C.; Cross, S., and A. Whiteside (1993). *Facing Up to AIDS: The Socio-Economic Impact in Southern Africa.* Macmillan, London and Basingstoke.

12. "Creating Common Ground, Women's Perspectives on the Selection and Introduction of Fertility Regulation Technologies." Report of a meeting between women's health advocates and scientists, Geneva, February 20–22, 1991, organized by the Special Program of Research, Development and Research Training in Human Reproduction. World Health Organization and International Women's Health Coalition, 1991.

13. *The World's Women 1970–1990, Trends and Statistics.* United Nations, New York, 1991.

14. Bruce, Judith (1992). The Population Council, in a presentation to Synergos, New York, January 21, 1992, based on an ongoing study of Family Structure, Female Headship and the Implications for Poverty. The Population Council, New York, and the International Center for Research on Women, Washington, D.C.; Bruce, J., (1989). "Homes Divided." *World Development,* Vol. 17,

No. 7), pp. 979–991; Bruce, J., and C.B. Lloyd (1992). "Family Research and Policy Issues for the 1990s." In *Understanding How Resources are Allocated within Households*, Policy Briefs 8, Washington, D.C., FPRI, November 1992, pp. 3–4.

15. Cain, Mead (1988). "The Material Consequences of Reproductive Failure in Rural South Asia." In D. Dwyer and J. Bruce, eds. (1988). *A Home Divided: Women and Income in the Third World*, pp. 20–38. Stanford University Press, Stanford.

16. Bruce, J. (1992). The Population Council, in a presentation to Synergos, New York, January 21, 1992, based on an ongoing study of Family Structure, Female Headship, and the Implications for Poverty, The Population Council, New York, and the International Center for Research on Women, Washington, D.C.

17. Division for the Advancement of Women, U.N. Office at Vienna (1991). "Women and Households in a Changing World." In E. Masini and S. Stratigos, eds. (1991). pp. 30–54; p. 40.

18. Walkowitz, Judith R. (1980). *Prostitution and Victorian Society: Women, Class and the State.* Cambridge University Press, Cambridge.

19. Spoken by a woman arrested under the Acts to Josephine Butler, feminist repeal leader. Reported in the *Shield*, London, May, 9, 1870, quoted in Walkowitz, J.R. (1980), *Prostitution and Victorian Society: Women, Class and the State.* Cambridge University Press, Cambridge, p. 128.

20. This section draws on the author's field notes, personal interviews with a number of those involved in the events described here, and the following publications: Akhter, Farida (1986), "Depopulating Bangladesh: A Brief History of the External Intervention into the Reproductive Behavior of a Society," Occasional Paper, Dhaka, UBINIG; ESCAP (1981), *Bangladesh*, ESCAP Country Monograph Series No. 8, Population Division, Bangkok, ESCAP; Hartmann, Betsy (1987), *Reproductive Rights and Wrongs*, The Global Politics of Population Control and Contraceptive Choice, Harper and Row Publishers, New York; RED (1991), "Divorce and Breakup of Joint Family: An Analysis of Reasons and Familial Dislocations," Dhaka, BRAC, August; Simmons, Ruth, Michael A. Koenig, and A.A. Zahidul Huque (1990), "Maternal-Child Health and Family Planning: User Perspectives and Service Constraints in Rural Bangladesh," *Studies in Family Planning*, Vol. 21, No. 4, July/August, 187–196.

21. Creating Common Ground (1991), p. 25, based on a presentation by Sandra Kabir.

22. Creating Common Ground, p. 25.

Chapter 9

1. Kay, Bonnie J., Adrienne Germain, Maggie Bangser (1991). *The Bangladesh Women's Health Coalition.* Qualité series. The Population Council, New York, and BWHC, 1990–1991, Dhaka.

2. Dr. J.A.M. Otubu, Department of Ob-Gyn, Jos Teaching Hospital, November 30, 1990, based on a prevalence survey of reproductive tract infections among clients of Teaching Hospital Ob-Gyn departments.

3. Quoted in Andrea Irvin, Trip Report, International Women's Health Coalition, January 1990, and author's field notes.
4. Personal communication, Dr. Eka Williams, immunologist, University of Calabar Teaching Hospital, December 1990, author's field notes.
5. Personal communication, Haiya Zahra S. Nanono, Kano, November 27, 1992, author's field notes.
6. Her Excellency, Mrs. Maryam Babangida, Address to the Women's Rally, World AIDs Day, Lagos City Hall, November 29, 1989, official copy.
7. Personal communication, Dr. Dora Chizea, Lagos, December 7, 1989, author's field notes.
8. Personal communication, Mrs. Hannah Omole, Zaria, November 28, 1989, author's field notes.

Chapter 10

1. "Women in Agricultural Production," *Women in Agriculture*, No. 1 ESHW. FAO, Rome, 1984; "Women in Agricultural Production." *Women in Agriculture*, No. 4 ESHW. FAO, Rome, 1985. Aggregate data show that women contribute some 40 percent of agricultural labor in Latin America and between 60 and 80 percent in both Asia and Africa.
2. Shiva, V. (1991). *Most Farmers in India Are Women*. FAO, New Delhi.
3. 1989 FAO survey data show that about 5 percent of all agricultural extension resources worldwide are directed to female farmers and only 15 percent of the world's extension personnel are female. FAO, 1993. "Agricultural Extension and Farm Women in the 1980s." FAO, Rome, 1989. See also Potash, B. (1985), "Female Farmers, Mothers-in-Law and Extension Agents: Development Planning and a rural Luo community in Kenya." In R. Gallin and A. Spring, eds., *Women Creating Wealth: Transforming Economic Development*, Association of Women in Development, Washington, D.C.
4. Fones-Sundell, M. (1984). "The Assistance Gap: Aid to Female Agricultural Producers in Botswana." International Rural Development Center, Swedish University of Agricultural Sciences, Uppsala, April, mimeo.
5. Shiva, V. (1988). *Staying Alive: Women, Ecology and Development*. Zed Books, London.
6. Mies, M., and V. Shiva, 1993. *Ecofeminism*. ZED Books, London.
7. Reported in *New Scientist*, November 21, 1992, pp. 38–31.
8. Chamala, S., and C. Holsinger Hicks (1990). "The Role of Women in Agricultural Development and Landcare." Discussion paper presented to QPDI Workshop, Extension Strategies Involving Rural Women, Queensland Department of Primary Industry, Gympie.
9. Chen, M., M. Mitra, G. Athreya, A. Dholakia, P. Law, and A. Rao (1986). *Indian Women: A Study of Their Role in the Dairy Movement*. Vikas Publishing House Pvt. Ltd., New Delhi.
10. Quoted in Harold, Jane L. (1991). "Empowerment: A Feminist Approach to Understanding and Action." Unpublished M.Sc. thesis presented to the Faculty of Graduate Studies, University of Guelph, Ontario, April, p. 74.
11. Prasad, C., R.P. Singh, and K.S. Krishnan (1988). *Review of Research Studies on*

Women in Agriculture in India, Implications for Research and Extension. Indian Council of Agricultural Research, New Delhi.

12. Quoted in Vukasin, H., and J. Chimbadzwa (1991). "Training to Suit Rural Women's Needs." *ILEIA Newsletter*, Vol. 3, pp. 8–9.

13. Feldstein, H., and J. Jiggins, eds. (1994). *Tools for the Field.* Kumarian Press, West Hartford, Conn.; Jiggins, J. (1986). "Gender-Related Impacts and the Work of the International Agricultural Research Centers." Study Paper 17, The World Bank, Washington, D.C.

14. Quoted in Seur, H. (1992). *Sowing the Good Seed: The Interweaving of Agricultural Change, Gender Relations and Religion in Serenje District, Zambia.* Published Ph.D. dissertation, Agricultural University, Wageningen, 1992, p. 237.

15. Mazumdar, V., K. Samar, and L. Sarkar (1988). "Legislative Measures and Policy Directions for Improving the Lot of Farm Women." Paper presented to International Conference on Appropriate Agricultural Technologies for Farm Women, New Delhi, November 30 to December 6, 1988. Indian Council of Agricultural Research, New Delhi, and International Rice Research Institute, Manila, p. 9.

16. Boserup, E. (1965). *The Conditions of Agricultural Growth, The Economics of Agrarian Change Under Population Pressure.* Allen and Unwin, London.

17. Geertz, C. (1963). *Agricultural Involution.* University of California Press, Berkeley.

18. Lele, U., and S.W. Stone (1989). "Population Pressure: The Environment and Agricultural Intensification, Variations on the Boserup Hypothesis." MADIA Discussion Paper 4, The World Bank, Washington, D.C.

19. Parts 1–4 of the figure were presented in Jiggins, J. (1993). "Questioning the Population-Environment Crisis." Seminar on Sustainable Development for DANIDA, September 29, 1993. Copenhagen, Centre for Development Research (forthcoming, 1994), based on an earlier presentation at a meeting in 1993 in Nigeria, supported by The Rockefeller Foundation. Empirical data in support of part 4 of the figure are to be found in numerous publications, for example, van Liere, M.J. (1993). "Coping with Household Food Insecurity: A Longitudinal and Seasonal Study among the Otammari in North-Western Benin." Ph.D. Thesis, Agriculture University, Wageningen, November 1993.

Chapter 11

1. This section is based on discussions with Thecla Meesters, who was employed by the project to work with the women, and Meesters, T. (1992). "At Your Service." *ILEIA Newsletter*, January 1992, p. 24.

2. This section is based on the author's field notes and Bangladesh Agricultural Research Council (1991). "Homestead Vegetable Gardening, A Brief Progress Report." BARC, Dhaka, August, mimeo; Gupta, M., and M. Aktheruzzaman (1991). "Women Integrate Fish and Farming." *ILEIA Newsletter*, April 1991, p. 14.

3. Gupta, M., and M. Aktheruzzaman (1991). "Women Integrate Fish and Farming." *ILEIA Newsletter*, April 1991, p. 14.

4. This section is based on discussions with members of the ATIP team and

researchers from Botswana during the 1990 and 1992 International Symposia of the Association for Farming Systems Research and Extension, Michigan State University; and Baker, D. (1993). "Women and Trials Management in Botswana: Experiences with Farmer Groups." In H. Feldstein and J. Jiggins, eds., *Tools for the Field*. Kumarian Press, West Hartford, Conn.; and Box 5.2. p. 53, in D. Norman and C. Lightfoot (1992). *Formative Evaluation of the FAO/SIDA Farming Systems Programme*. FAO/SIDA, Gaborone, November.

5. This section is based on "Soil and Water Conservation in Sub-Saharan Africa." Report prepared for IFAD by the Center for Development Cooperation Services, Amsterdam, Free University, Rome, International Fund for Agricultural Development, 1992; and Yoon, Soon Young (1983). "The Women's Dam (The Mossi of Upper Volta)." Consultant report, Water and Sanitation Unit, UNICEF, New York, September, mimeo.

6. Quoted in "The Women's Dam," p. 19.

7. "Soil and Water Conservation in sub-Saharan Africa." International Fund for Agricultural Development, 1992.

8. Translated from the French during an African regional workshop on women's access to land, reported by J. Jiggins (1989), in *Women and Land*, Regional African Workshop on Women's Access to Land as a Strategy for Employment Promotion, Poverty Alleviation and Household Food Security, organized by the International Labor Office in collaboration with the University of Harare, in Harare, Zimbabwe, October 17–21, 1988; Rural Employment Policies Branch, International Labor Office, Geneva,

9. This section is based on the author's field notes and Jiggins, J., with Paul Maimbo and Mary Masona (1992). "Breaking New Ground: Reaching Out to Women Farmers in Western Zambia." *Seeds*. The Population Council, New York.

10. "Breaking New Ground," p. 6.

11. From Lilu village, Limulunga, Mongu District, quoted in "Breaking New Ground," p. 12.

12. "Breaking New Ground," p. 12.

Bibliography

Chapter 1. Why Women's Perspectives Matter

Recommended Reading

Agarwal, B., "Engendering the Environment Debate: Lessons from the Indian Sub-continent," CASID Distinguished Speaker Series No. 8, Center for Advanced Study of International Development (Michigan: Michigan State University, January 1991). A distinguished economist examines primary and intermediary causes of environmental degradation, and class and gender effects, from an ecofeminist perspective.

Conscience, Vol. XIV, No. 3, Autumn 1993. A news journal of prochoice Catholic opinion, this issue contains articles by leading feminists, environmentalists, population and family planning experts, which set out the current lines of controversy in the population-environment debate.

Germain, A., K.K. Holmes, P. Piot, and J. N. Wasserheit, eds. *Reproductive Tract Infections: Global Impact and Priorities for Women's Reproductive Health* (New York and London: Plenum Press, 1992). An up-to-date review of the evidence and experience, based on papers presented at a meeting co-sponsored by the International Women's Health Coalition and The Rockefeller Foundation in 1991.

Gilligan, C., *In a Different Voice* (Cambridge: Harvard University Press, 1982). A restatement of human psychology, refocusing on the female personality.

Green, C.P., "The Environment and Population Growth: Decade for Action," *Population Reports* (Series M, No. 10, May 1992). Strong advocacy for population control, based on scenarios of further environmental degradation, famine, deforestation, water shortages, urban breakdown, and increased carbon dioxide emissions as consequences of population growth, with useful bibliography of key references to the population control literature.

Silver, C.S., with R.S. DeFries, *One Earth, One Future: Our Changing Global Environment* (Washington D.C.: National Academy of Sciences, 1990). An easy-to-read survey of global environmental problems and the science behind them, and the impact of human activities on the earth as a unified system.

World Bank, *The World Bank and the Environment* (Washington D.C.: The World Bank, Fiscal 1993). Chapter 3, pp. 81–100, summarizes the current Bank view of the synergy among investments to improve women's status, promote population stabilization, safeguard the environment, and alleviate poverty.

World Bank, *World Development Report 1993* (Washington D.C.: The World Bank, 1993). Chapter 2, pp. 37–51, on "Households and Health," summarizes current Bank thinking on the links between investments in human resources (i.e., people), especially women, and the social and environmental returns to healthy households.

Additional Reading and References

Adams, J., "Population Growth and Conservation, Washington D.C.," *World Wildlife Fund and Conservation Newsletter*, No. 2. 1989.

Anker, R., M. Buvinic, and N. Youssef, *Women's Roles and Population Trends in the Third World* (London: Croom Helm, 1982).

Diamond, I., and G.F. Orenstein, eds., *Reweaving the World: The Emergence of Ecofeminism* (San Fransisco: Sierra Club Books, 1990).

Erlich, P.R., and A. H. Erlich, *The Amicus Journal* (Winter 1990), p. 25.

Erlich, P.R., and A. H. Erlich, *The Population Explosion* (New York: Simon and Schuster, 1990).

Feldstein, H., and J. Jiggins, eds., *Tools for the Field* (West Hartford: Kumarian Press, 1994).

Hallen, P., "Making Peace with the Environment: Why Ecology Needs Feminism," *Canadian Women's Studies* (Vol. 9, No. 1, 1988), pp. 9–18.

Hodge, R.W., and N. Ogawa, *Fertility Change in Contemporary Japan* (Chicago: Chicago University Press, 1992).

Jackson, C., "Questioning Synergism: Win-Win with Women in Population and Environment Policies?" Paper presented at British Society of Population Studies Conference on Population and the Environment, Oxford, September 9–11, 1992.

Jiggins, J., ed., *Women and Land*, Programme on Rural Women, Rural Employment Policies Branch (Geneva: ILO, 1989).

Khasiani, S.A., ed., *Groundwork: African Women as Environmental Managers* (Nairobi: African Center for Technology Studies, 1992).

Kiriro, A., and C. Juma, eds., *Gaining Ground: Institutional Innovations in Land-use Management in Kenya* (Nairobi: African Center for Technology Studies, 1991).

Naess, A., "The Deep Ecology Movement: Some Philosophical Aspects," *Philosophical Inquiry* (Vol. 8, Nos. 1 & 2, 1986), pp. 10–31.

Naess, A., *Ecology, Community, Lifestyles* (Cambridge: Cambridge University Press, 1989).

Pimentel, D., L.M. Fredrickson, D.B. Johnson, J.H. McShane, and Hsiao-Wei Yuan, "Environment and Population: Crises and Policies." Chapter 14 in D. Pimentel and C.W. Hall, eds., *Food and Natural Resources* (San Diego: Academic Press, 1989), pp. 363–389.

Population/Environment Initiative, "Progress Report Highlights," (New York: Population Communications International, January 10, 1991).

Repetto, R., "Population, Resources, Environment: An Uncertain Future," (Washington D.C.: Population Reference Bureau, 1987).

Seshu, D.V., and M. Dadlani, "Role of Women in Seed Management with Special Reference to Rice," IRTP Technical Bulletin #5 (Manila: IRRI, August 1989).

Stone, C.D., *The Gnat Is Older Than Man: Global Environment and the Human Agenda* (Princeton: Princeton University Press, 1993).

UNFPA, *Investing in Women: The Focus of the '90s* (New York: UNFPA, 1990).

UNFPA, *Women, Population and the Environment* (New York: UNFPA, March 1992).

UNFPA, *The State of the World Population 1993* (New York: UNFPA, 1993).

UN Population Division, "Population Growth and Changes in the Demographic

Structure: Trends and Diversity." Paper prepared for the UN Expert Group Meeting on Population Growth and Demographic structure (Paris: UN Population Division, November 1992).

Women of Power, "An Interview with Jean Shinoda Bolen" (Vol. 21, Fall 1991), pp. 21–25.

Chapter 2. The Game Is Not Fairly Divided

Recommended Reading

Agarwal, B., "Neither Sustenance nor Sustainability: Agricultural Strategies, Ecological Degradation and Indian Women in Poverty," in B. Agarwal, ed., *Structures of Patriarchy, State, Community and Household in Modernizing Asia* (London: Zed Books, 1988), pp. 83–120.

Commonwealth Secretariat, "Engendering Adjustment for the 1990s," Report of a Commonwealth Expert Group on Women and Structural Adjustment (London: Commonwealth Secretariat, 1989). Examines how short-term stabilization measures have too often been in conflict with long-term development goals, causing hardships, especially for women, sufficiently severe to undermine economic adjustment efforts.

Daly, H.E., and J.B. Cobb, Jr., *For the Common Good: Redirecting the Economy Toward Community, the Environment and a Sustainable Future* (Boston: Beacon Press, 1989). Critiques growth-oriented industrial economies and neoclassical economic theory as leading to environmental disaster and offers alternatives based on social ethics and ecological rationality.

George, S., *The Debt Boomerang: How Third World Debt Harms Us All* (Geneva: Pluto Press with the Transnational Institute, 1992). A careful analysis of the way in which debt and its multiple consequences produce negative environmental, economic, social, financial, and other feedbacks. Concludes with salutary reminders that Third World debt has been largely repaid; those who borrowed were rarely elected by the people who suffered the consequences; those who gave loans were irresponsible in that they were unaccountable for the consequences and made debtors subservient to their own interests; and the international funding agencies are largely beyond accountability to the public.

Mintzes, B., A. Hardon, and J. Hanhart, *Norplant: Under Her Skin* (Netherlands: Women's Health Action Foundation, 1993). Reports on an investigation of the views of users of the long-acting hormonal implant, in Finland, the United States, Brazil, Indonesia, Egypt, and Thailand. The researchers document evidence of neglect and disregard of women's experience of side effects and other anxieties, the impact of using Norplant on their social and personal lives, provider abuse, and poor counseling and follow-up, with suggestions for improvements.

Tavris, C., *The Mismeasure of Woman: Why Women Are Not the Better Sex, The Inferior Sex, or The Opposite Sex* (New York: Touchstone/Simon & Schuster, 1993). Examines the tendency for male standards and performance to be accepted as the norm across a range of socioeconomic indices, with well-researched examples of the implications of sexual and gender stereotyping for individuals and society.

Vickers, J., *Women and the World Economic Crisis* (London: Zed Books, March

1991). Examines the impact of economic adjustment policies on women, with case studies from Ghana, Jamaica, Mexico, the Philippines, and Zambia.

Waring, M., *If Women Counted: A New Feminist Economics* (San Fransisco: Harper & Row, 1988). Classic text critiquing mainstream economic practice and theory, with detailed analysis and examples of the difference it makes if women's work is counted and valued appropriately.

Additional Reading and References

Benda, P., "Dr. Maurice King op de rand van de demografische valkuil die hij zelf gegraven heeft" (The Hague: *onzeWereld*, January 1992), pp. 85–87.

Cairncross, F., *Costing the Earth* (London: The Economist Books/Business Books, 1991).

Cohn, N., *The Pursuit of the Millennium*, revised and expanded edition (Oxford: Oxford University Press, 1970).

Elson, D., "How Is Structural Adjustment Affecting Women?" *Development* (Vol. 1, 1989), pp. 67–74.

Erlich, P.R., and A.H. Erlich, *The Population Explosion* (New York: Simon and Schuster, 1990).

Han, Suyin, "Family Planning: The Chinese Experience," *The Unesco Courier* (July 27, 1974), pp. 52–55.

van Hulst, W., "Medische ethiek 'Kindersterfte houdt groei bevolking in de hand" (The Hague: *onzeWereld*, December 1991), p. 6 (Dutch original).

IDRC, "The Global Cash Crunch: An Examination of Debt and Development" (Ottawa: IDRC, 1992).

Jacobsen, J., "Population Dynamics and Poverty in Developing Countries in a Relatively Advanced State of Urbanization." Paper prepared for the UN Expert Group Meeting on Population Growth and Demographic Structure (Paris: November 1992).

Kakwani, N., E. Makonnen, and J. van der Gaag, "Structural Adjustment and Living Conditions in Developing Countries," Working Papers PRE #467 (Washington D.C.: The World Bank, 1990).

McAfee, K., *Storm Signals: Structural Adjustment and Development Alternatives in the Caribbean* (London: Zed Books, 1990).

Moser, C., "The Impact of Recession and Structural Adjustment on Women," *Development* (Vol. 1, 1989), pp. 75–83.

Palmer, I., "Gender and Population in the Adjustment of African Economies: Planning for Change," *Women, Work and Development* 19 (Geneva: International Labour Office, 1991).

Pearce, D., E. Barbier, and A. Markandya, *Sustainable Development: Economics and Environment in the Third World* (Aldershot: Gower Publishing Co., 1990).

Plant, J., ed., *Healing the Wounds: The Promise of Ecofeminism* (Philadelphia: New Society, 1989).

Reimers, F., "Economic Adjustment and Choices in Education," *The Forum for Advancing Basic Education and Literacy* (Vol. 2, No. 4, August 1993), pp. 10–11.

Repetto, R., and W. B. Magrath, *Wasting Assets: Natural Resources in the National Income Accounts* (Washington D.C.: World Resources Institute, 1989).

Shaw, C., and N. Saravanamuttoo, "Can We Swap Debt for Education?" *Donors to*

African Education Newsletter (Vol. 5, No. 2, September-November 1993), pp. 1–3.

Shiva, V., "Development: The New Colonialism," *Development* (journal of the Society for International Development) (Rome: 1989), pp. 84–87.

Snyder, M., "WOMEN: The Key to Ending Hunger" (New York: The Hunger Project, 1991).

Srinivasan, V., "Women of Chotanagpur: Beginning of Dissent." Paper to Workshop on Operational Strategies for Reaching Women in Agriculture, Ministry of Agriculture/Ministry of Development Cooperation (Kijkduin, Netherlands: September 22–26, 1986).

UNFPA, *Investing in Women: The Focus of the '90s* (New York: UNFPA, 1990).

World Bank, *The World Bank and the Environment* (Washington D.C.: The World Bank, Fiscal 1992).

World Bank, *Annual Report 1993* (Washington D.C.: The World Bank, 1993).

Wu, Cangping, "The Status of Women in Relation to Population Issues in China" in *Women on the Move* (Paris: The UNESCO Press, 1984), pp. 297–304.

Chapter 3. Do We Know What's Going On?

Recommended Reading

Barker, A., and B. Guy Peters, *The Politics of Expert Advice: Creating, Using and Manipulating Scientific Knowledge for Public Policy* (Edinburgh: Edinburgh University Press, 1993). Examines the conduct of public policy in an environment of uncertainty, with reference to examples in industrialized countries, concluding that complex decisions require sophisticated analysis and dialogue with a range of advisers, including those holding minority points of view and those drawn from the public at large.

Bhatia, J.C., "A Study of Maternal Mortality in Anantapur District, Andhra Pradesh, India" (Bangalore: Indian Institute of Management, 1988). Commissioned by the World Health Organization, this pioneering study of maternal death at the community level documented, among other important findings, the underreporting of deaths among women of fertile age, by more than 50 percent, and the underreporting of maternal mortality by more than a third.

Bourriau, J., ed., *Understanding Catastrophe* (Cambridge: Cambridge University Press, 1992). Among other important contributions to cross-disciplinary understanding, the book shows how the mathematics of catastrophe theory can be used to discover how gradual change may lead to discontinuous phenomena.

Krimsky. S., and D. Golding, *Social Theories of Risk* (New York: Praeger/Eurospan, 1993). Examines, among other topics, the differences of view among those who hold nature to be vulnerable rather than resilient, the implications of the uncertain and indeterminate nature of risk, and the relation between risk assessments and social and personal values.

Additional Reading and References

Bergstrom, S., "Family Planning and Maternal Health—Myths and Realities." Paper presented to seminar on Population and Development (Copenhagen: Ministry of Foreign Affairs, September 29, 1992).

Brown, P., and E.J. Mikkelson, *No Safe Place: Toxic Waste, Leukaemia and Community Action* (Berkeley: University of California Press, 1990).

Chow, W.H., et al., "IUD Use and Subsequent Tubal Ectopic Pregnancy," *American Journal of Public Health* (Vol. 76, p. 536, 1986).

Dixon-Mueller, R., and J. Wasserheit, "The Culture of Silence: Reproductive Tract Infections Among Women in the Third World" (New York: International Women's Health Coalition, 1991).

Germain, A., K. Holmes, P. Piot, and J. Wasserheit, eds., *Reproductive Tract Infections: Global Impact and Priorities for Women's Reproductive Health* (New York: Plenum Press, 1989).

Gould, S.J., *Time's Arrow, Time's Cycle* (Cambridge, Mass. and London: Harvard University Press, 1987).

IWHC, "Reproductive Tract Infections in Women in the Third World" (New York: International Women's Health Coalition, 1991).

Kates, R.W., and V. Haarmann, "Poor People and Threatened Environments: Global Overviews, Country Comparisons, and Local Studies," Alan Shawn Feinstein World Hunger Program, World Hunger Program Research Report RR-91-2 (Providence, R.I.: Brown University, 1991).

Kates, R.W., and V. Haarmann, "Where the Poor Live: Are the Assumptions Correct?" *Environment* (Vol. 34, No. 4, May 1992), pp. 4–27.

Lee, N.C., G.L. Rubin, H.W. Ory, and R.T. Burkman, "Type of Intruterine Device and the Risk of Pelvic Inflammatory Disease," *Obstetrics and Gynecology* (Vol. 62, No. 1, 1983).

Liljestand, J., and W.G. Povey, eds., *Maternal Health Care in an International Perspective*. Proceedings of the XXII Berzelius Symposium, Stockholm, May 27–29, 1991 (Uppsala: Department of Obstetrics and Gynecology, Uppsala University/Geneva: WHO, 1992).

Mathews, J.T., "Redefining Security," *Foreign Affairs* (Spring 1989), pp. 163–177.

McNicoll, G., "The United Nations' Long-Range Population Projections," *Population and Development Review* (Vol. 18, No. 2, June 1992), pp. 333–340.

McNicoll, G., "The Agenda of Population Studies: A Commentary and a Complaint," *Population and Development Review* (Vol. 18, No. 2, September 1992), pp. 399–420.

Monimart, M., "Women in the Fight Against Desertification," Paper No. 12 (London: IIED, December 1989).

Mortimore, M., *Adapting to Drought* (Cambridge: Cambridge University Press, 1989).

Nelson, R., *Dryland Management: The "Desertification" Problem* (Washington D.C.: The World Bank, 1990)

Odum, H.T., "Energy, Environment and Public Policy: A Guide to the Analysis of Systems," Regional Seas Reports and Studies No. 95 (Nairobi: UNEP, 1988).

Reintjes, C., B. Haverkort, and A. Waters-Bayer, *Farming for the Future* (Leusden: ILEIA and London: Macmillan, 1992).

Roughgarden, J., R. M. May, and S. A. Levin, eds., *Perspectives in Ecological Theory* (Princeton: Princeton University Press, 1989).

Schneider, S., "Cooling It: The Global Warming Debate," *World Monitor* (July 1990), pp. 30–38.

Simon, J.L., "On Aggregate Empirical Studies Relating Population Variables to Economic Development," *Population and Development Review* (Vol. 15, No. 2, June 1989), pp. 323–332.

World Commission on Environment and Development, *Our Common Future* (Oxford: Oxford University Press, 1987).

Chapter 4. Food and Agriculture: Is There Room to Maneuver?

Recommended Reading

Brouwers, J.H.A.M., *Rural People's Response to Soil Fertility Decline: The Adja Case (Benin)*, Ph.D. Thesis, Wageningen Agricultural University Papers 93–4 (Wageningen: Agricultural University, 1993).

ICCO/DGIS, "Matching Poverty Alleviation with Sustainable Land Use," Programme Evaluation No. 44 (The Hague: ICCO/DGIS, 1993). Careful analysis based on field studies of the programs of four nongovernmental agencies in India, with special reference to the relationship between concepts of sustainability and gender.

Lipton, M., with R. Longhurst, *New Seeds and Poor People* (London: Unwin Hyman, 1989). Analyzes both the technical features of modern varieties and their contribution to increasing food output, and their impact when introduced into agricultural settings deeply marked by social and economic inequities, to show how additional output does not necessarily lead to eradication of poverty or hunger.

Additional Reading and References

Achebe, C., C. Magadza, A. Palo Okeyo, and G. Hyden, *Beyond Hunger in Africa* (London: James Currey/Nairobi: Heineman, 1990).

Armstrong, A., ed., *Women and Law in Southern Africa* (Harare: Zimbabwe Publishing House).

Cleveland, D.A., and D. Soleri, *Food from Dryland Gardens: An Ecological, Nutritional and Social Approach to Smallscale Household Food Production* (Tucson: Center for Food, People and Environment, 1991).

Diaz, H.F., and V. Markgraf, *El Niño: Historical and Paleoclimatic Aspects of the Southern Oscillation* (Cambridge: Cambridge University Press, 1993).

Downing, T.E., "Climatic Variability, Food Security and Smallholder Agriculturalists in 6 Districts of Central and Eastern Kenya." Unpublished Ph.D. Thesis (Worcester: Clark University, 1988).

Dudal, R., and H. Gulinck, "Bodemgebruik op weg naar de 21ste eeuw," *Landbouwkundig Tijdschrift* (Vol. 101, No. 1, 1989) pp. 14–17 (Dutch original).

Fowler, A., "The Seasonal Aspect of Education in East and Southern Africa," in J. Jiggins, ed., "A Report on the Regional Workshop on Seasonal Variations in the Provisioning, Nutrition and Health of Rural Families" (Nairobi: African Medical and Research Foundation, March 31 to April 2, 1982), pp. 58–74.

Horton, D., *Underground Crops: Long-term Trends in Production of Roots and Tubers* (Morrilton, Arkansas: Winrock International, 1988).

Jiggins, J., ed., "A Report on the Regional Workshop on Seasonal Variations in the

Provisioning, Nutrition and Health of Rural Families" (Nairobi: African Medical and Research Foundation, March 31 to April 2, 1982).

Jiggins, J., "Women and Seasonality: Coping with Crisis and Calamity," *IDS Bulletin* (Vol. 17, No. 3, July 1986), pp. 9–18.

Jiggins, J., "Agricultural Technology: Impact, Issues and Action," Review article 1 in R. S. Gallin, M. Aronoff, and A. Ferguson, eds., *The Women and International Development Annual*, Vol. I (Boulder: Westview Press, 1989), pp. 25–56.

Jiggins, J., "From Technology Transfer to Resource Management," invited paper to XVII International Grassland Congress, Palmerston North, New Zealand, February 8–21, 1993.

Leuning, R., Y.P. Wang, D. Depury, T. Denmead, F. Dunin, T. Condon, S. Nonhebel, and J. Goudriaan, "Water Use Efficiency of Wheat under Present and Future Levels of Carbon Dioxide," *Environmental Mechanics* (Vol. 17, No. 9, October 29, 1992), pp. 2–5.

Malthus, T.R., *An Essay on the Principle of Population as it Affects the Future Improvement of Society* (Harmondsworth: Penguin, reprint edition, 1970; London: J. Johnson, second edition, 1803).

Merchant, C., "The Theoretical Structure of Ecological Revolutions," *Environmental Review* (Winter 1987), pp. 265–274.

National Research Council, *Alternative Agriculture*, Board on Agriculture, Committee on the Role of Alternative Farming Methods in Modern Production Agriculture (Washington D.C.: National Academy Press, 1989).

Otaala, B., "Daycare in Eastern Africa: A Survey of Botswana, Kenya, Seychelles, Tanzania, Addis Ababa" (Addis Ababa: ECA/ATRCW, November 1980).

Parry, M., *Climate Change and World Agriculture* (London: Earthscan Publications Ltd., in association with The International Institute for Applied Systems Analysis and the United Nations Environment Programme, 1990).

Pittock, A.B., "Developing Regional Climate Change Scenarios: Their Reliability and Seriousness." Paper presented by CSIRO Climate Impact Group to Hawkesbury Centenary Conference, University of Western Sydney, November 25–27, 1991.

Poleman, T.T., "Hunger or Plenty? The Food/Population Prospect Two Centuries After Malthus," Staff paper 89–30, Department of Agricultural Economics (Ithaca: Cornell University, 1989).

Postel, S., *Last Oasis: Facing Water Scarcity* (Washington D.C.: Worldwatch Institute/Norton, 1992).

Pralhad, Rao N., "Diet and Nutrition During Drought—an Indian Experience," *Disasters* (Vol. 13) pp. 58–72.

Wilson, K., and G.E.B. Morren, Jr., *Systems Approaches for Improvements in Agriculture and Resource Management* (New York: Macmillan, 1990).

Chapter 5. Energy and Trees: Where Do Women Really Fit In?

Recommended Reading

Bruggink, J.J.C., and F.D.J. Nieuwenhout, eds., "Energy Cooperation for Development: Options and Obstacles," Poverty, Self-Reliance and Development:

Analysis and Policy No. 6 (The Hague: Ministry of Foreign Affairs, 1993). An overview based on the latest available data of renewable and nonrenewable energy consumption and production and carbon dioxide emissions, and a review of issues and options, drawing on material from Asia, Europe, the Americas, and other developing countries.

Environment Liaison Centre International, "Women's Participation in Forestry Activities in Africa: Project Summary and Policy Recommendations" (Nairobi: Environment Liaison Centre International, 1993). Summarizes from women's perspectives recent nongovernmental organization experience, through case studies from six countries and a regional workshop.

Johansson, T.B., H. Kelly, A.K N.Reddy, and R.H. Williams, eds., *Renewable Energy: Sources for Fuels and Electricity* (Washington D.C.: Island Press/London: Earthscan, 1993). Twenty-three chapters of up-to-date, detailed information concerning renewable energy developments around the world, covering technologies, economics, applications, environmental impacts, socioeconomic concerns, and policy recommendations.

Schipper, L., and S. Meyers, with R. Howarth and R. Steiner, *Energy Efficiency and Human Activity* (Cambridge and Stockholm: Cambridge University Press/Stockholm Environment Institute, 1993). Surveys world energy use since 1970, debates future prospects under varying structures of resource allocation and patterns of activity, and reviews energy policies that would encourage energy efficiency. Extensive references at the end of each chapter.

Additional Reading and References

Agarwal, A., "Women, Male Migration and Environment," *EcoForum* (Vol. 10, No. 2, 1985), pp. 4–5.

Agarwal, A., and S. Narain, *Global Warming in an Unequal World: A Case of Environmental Colonialism* (New Delhi: Centre for Science and Environment, January 1991).

Agarwal, B., *Cold Hearths and Barren Slopes: The Woodfuel Crisis in the Third World* (New Delhi: Allied Publishers, 1986).

Arcia, G., "Population Growth and the Urban Environment" (North Carolina: Research Triangle Institute, November 1990).

Bhagavan, M.R., and S. Giriappa, "Class Character of Rural Energy Crisis, Case of Karnataka," *Economic and Political Weekly*, Review of Agriculture (Vol. XXII, No. 26, June 27, 1987), pp. A-57–A-69.

Brown, L., et al., *The State of the World 1978* (New York: Worldwatch Institute/W.W. Norton & Co., 1978).

Chavangi, N.A., "Cultural Aspects of Fuelwood Procurement in Kakamega District," KWDP Working Paper No. 4 (Nairobi: Kenya Woodfuel Development Project, 1984).

Clark, R.N., and G.H. Stankey, "New Forestry or New Perspectives? The Importance of Asking the Right Questions," *Forest Perspectives* (Vol. 1, No. 1, March 1991), pp. 9–13.

DGIS, "Sustainable Energy Economy," Sectoral Policy Document 4 (The Hague: Directorate General of Development Cooperation, Ministry of Foreign Affairs, 1992).

Eckholm, E., *The Other Energy Crisis: Firewood*, Worldwatch Paper 1 (Washington D.C.: Worldwatch Institute, 1975).

Eckholm, E., *Losing Ground: Environmental Stress and World Food Prospects* (New York: Worldwatch Institute/ W. W. Norton & Co., 1976).

Flavin, C., "Slowing Global Warming," Chapter 2 in L. Brown et al., *State of the World 1990: A Worldwatch Institute Report* (New York and London: W. W. Norton & Co., 1990).

Foley, G., P. Moss, and L. Timberlake, *Stoves and Trees* (London and Washington D.C.: IIED, 1984).

Fortmann, L., and J. Bruce, *Whose Trees? Proprietary Dimensions of Forestry* (Boulder: Westview Press, 1988).

Hamilton, L.S., "What Are the Impacts of Himalayan Deforestation on the Ganges-Brahmaputra Lowlands and Delta? Assumptions and Facts," *Mountain Research and Development* (Vol. 7, No. 3, 1987), pp. 256–263.

Harrison, P., "A Tale of Two Stoves," *New Scientist*, May 28, 1987, pp. 39–43.

Hossain, M., A.T.M. Aminul Islam, and A. K. Saha, *Floods in Bangladesh, Recurrent Disaster and People's Survival* (Dhaka: University Research Centre, Dhaka University, 1987).

Huss-Ashmore, R., "Seasonality in Rural Highland Lesotho: Method and Policy," in J. Jiggins, ed., "A Report on a Regional Workshop on Seasonal Variations in the Provisioning, Nutrition and Health of Rural Families" (Nairobi: African Medical and Research Foundation, March 31 to April 2, 1982), pp. 147–160.

ILO, "Energie et Survie: Guide sur L'Energie, l'Environnement et le Travail des Femmes Rurales"(Geneva: International Labour Organisation, 1987), French original.

ILO, *The Bankura Story, Rural Women Organise for Change,* Technical Cooperation Report, Rural Employment Policy Branch, World Employment Programme (Geneva: International Labour Organisation, 1988).

Ives, J., "Floods in Bangladesh: Who Is to Blame?" *New Scientist* (April, 13 1991), pp. 34-37.

Ives, J., and B. Messerli, *The Himalayan Dilemma: Reconciling Development and Conservation* (London and New York: Routledge/United Nations University, 1989).

Jodha, N.S., M. Banskota, and T. Partap, eds., *Sustainable Mountain Agriculture*, 2 vols. (Kathmandu: ICIMOD/New Delhi: IBH Publishing Co. Pvt. Ltd., 1992).

Ki-zerbo, J., "Women and the Energy Crisis in the Sahel," *Unasylva* (Vol. 33, No. 133, 1981), pp. 5–10.

Kumar, S.K., and D. Hotchkiss, "Consequences of Deforestation for Women's Time Allocation, Agricultural Production, and Nutrition in Hill Areas of Nepal." Report 69 (Washington D.C.: IFPRI, 1988).

Leach, G., and R. Mearns, *Beyond the Woodfuel Crisis* (London: Earthscan, 1989).

Levine, J.S., *Global Biomass Burning: Atmospheric, Climatic and Biospheric Implications* (Cambridge, Mass.: MIT Press, 1992).

MacKenzie, J.J., R.C. Dower, and D.D.T. Chen, *The Going Rate: What it Really Costs to Drive* (Washington D.C.: World Resources Institute, June 1992).

Owusu-Bempah, K., "The Role of Women Farmers in Choosing Species for Agroforestry Farming Systems in Rural Areas in Ghana," in S. V. Poats, A. Schmink, and A. Spring, eds., *Gender Issues in Farming Systems Research and Extension* (Boulder: Westview Press, 1987), pp. 427–441.

Parikh, J.K., "Energy Use for Subsistence and Prospects for Development," *Energy* (Vol. 3, 1978), pp. 613–637.

Philipose, P., "Women Act: Women and Environmental Protection in India," Chapter 7 in J. Plant, ed., *Healing the Wounds: The Promise of EcoFeminism* (Philadelphia: New Society Publishers, 1989), pp. 67–75.

Rocheleau, D., "Gender Complementarity and Conflict in Sustainable Forestry Development, A Multiple User Approach," *Proceedings* (Nairobi: ICRAF, 1989).

Rocheleau, D., "Gender, Ecology and the Science of Survival: Stories and Lessons from Kenya," *Agriculture and Human Values*, (Vol. 10, No. 1, 1991).

Schaeffer, R., "Car Sick, Automobiles Ad Nauseam," *Greenpeace* (May/June 1990), pp. 13-17.

Sharma, P., and M. Bankskota, "Population Dynamics and Sustainable Agricultural Development in Mountain Areas," Chapter 7 in N. S.Jodha, M. Banskota, and T. Partap, eds., *Sustainable Mountain Agriculture*, (Kathmandu: ICIMOD/New Delhi: IBH Publishing Co. Pvt. Ltd., 1992), pp. 165–184.

Srinivasan, V., "Women of Chotanagpur: Beginning of Dissent." Paper presented to Workshop on Operational Strategies for Reaching Women in Agriculture (Kijkduin, Netherlands: Ministry of Agriculture/Ministry of Development Cooperation, September 22–26, 1986).

Thompson, M., and M. Warburton, "Decision Making Under Contradictory Certainties," *Journal of Applied Systems Analysis* (Vol. 12, 1985), pp. 3–34.

Traore, A., and N.F. Kouakou, "Femmes et Environnement: Des Foyers Ameliores Pour L'Economie de Bois de Feu en Cote D'Ivoire," (Abidjan: Ministere de la Condition Feminine, 1985), French original.

Vidyarthi, V., "Energy and the Poor in an Indian Village," *World Development* (Vol. 12, No. 8, 1984), pp. 821–836.

Wachira, K.K., "Women's Use of Off-farm and Boundary Lands: Agroforestry Potentials," mimeo Project Report (Nairobi: Ford Foundation/ICRAF, 1987).

Weber, T., *Hugging the Trees: The Story of the Chipko Movement* (New Delhi: Penguin, 1989).

WHO, *Biomass Fuel Combustion and Health* (Geneva: World Health Organization, 1984).

WWF, *Forests in Trouble* (Gland: World Wildlife Fund, 1992).

Chapter 6. A Price Worth Paying

Recommended Reading and References

Bellew, R., and E.M. King, eds., *Women's Education in Developing Countries: Barriers, Benefits and Policy* (Washington D.C.: The World Bank, 1991). Analysis of the social and economic returns to female education and the policy adjustments required to overcome some of the key barriers to girls' access, performance, and attainments.

Prather, C., ed., *Primary Education for All: Learning from the BRAC Experience*

(Washington D.C.: ABEL, 1993). A balanced, detailed and insightful case study with clearly presented data, conclusions, and discussion of the implications.

Subharao, K., and L. Raney, "Social Gains from Female Education: A Cross-National Study," Working Paper No. 1045 (Washington D.C.: The World Bank, 1992). Statistical demonstration of the robustness of gains to female education in many different settings.

Summers, L.H., "Investing in All the People," Quad-i-Azam lecture, 8th Annual General Meeting, Pakistan Society of Development Economists, Islamabad, January 1992/Working Paper No. 905 (Washington D.C.: The World Bank, 1992). Powerful advocacy of the economic and social returns to female education from the former Vice-President and Chief Economist of The World Bank.

UNICEF, "Strategies to Promote Girls' Education—Policies and Programmes that Work" (New York: UNICEF, 1992). Review of the lessons of UNICEF experience in strengthening and supporting investment in female education.

Additional Reading and References

BRAC, *BRAC at 20* (Dhaka: BRAC, 1992).

BRAC, *The Net* (Dhaka: BRAC Printers, 1980).

Chen, M., *The Quiet Revolution* (Dhaka: The University Press, 1986).

Donor Liaison Office, "BRAC Mid-Term Evaluation, Draft Summary," (Dhaka: Donor Liaison Office, March 2, 1992).

Jahan, R., "Hidden Women, Visible Scars: Violence Against Women in Bangladesh," in B. Agarwal, ed., *Structures of Patriarchy: State, Community and Household in Modernising Asia* (Delhi: KALI for Women, 1988).

Jiggins, J., A. Dighe, S. Jain, and H. op het Veld, "Mahila Samakhya: Report of an Indo-Dutch Review Mission," Vols. I and II (New Delhi: Ministry of Human Resource Development/The Hague: Ministry of Foreign Affairs, March 1990).

Schultz, T.P., "Returns to Women's Education," PHRWD Working Paper No. 001 (Washington D.C.: The World Bank, 1989).

World Bank, "Bangladesh: Strategies for Enhancing the Role of Women in Economic Development" (Dhaka and Washington D.C.: The World Bank, 1990).

Chapter 7. The Mahila Samakhya Program, India

Recommended Reading

Department of Education, *Mahila Samakhya* (New Delhi: Ministry of Human Resource Development, October 1988).

Department of Education, *Mahila Samakhya, Education for Women's Equality* (New Delhi: Ministry of Human Resource Development, September 1991).

Additional Reading and References

Department of Education, "Bihar Education Project," (Patna: Department of Education/New Delhi: Ministry of Human Resource Development, February 1990).

Department of Education, "National Overview Report," National Project Office (New Delhi: Ministry of Human Resource Development, September 1991).

Department of Education, "The Unfolding . . . 1991 Mahila Samakhya Gujerat State,"

National Project Office (New Delhi: Ministry of Human Resource Development, 1991).

Department of Education, "Mahila Samakhya Uttar Pradesh: An Overview 1989–1991," National Project Office (New Delhi: Ministry of Human Resource Development, September 1991).

Helleman, C., I. Capoor, C. Diepeveen, K. Sharma, P. Mahale, and H. H. Soree, "Alternative Avenues to Women's Empowerment and Education for Women's Equality," Report of the Second Indo-Dutch Review Mission, Vols. I, II, and III (New Delhi: Ministry of Human Resource Development/The Hague: Ministry of Foreign Affairs, January 1992).

Jiggins, J., A. Jain, J. Roy, and K. de Wilde, "Mahila Samakhya, Education for Women's Equality, India: Report of a Programme Appraisal Mission" (New Delhi: Ministry of Human Resource Development/The Hague: Ministry of Foreign Affairs, March 1989).

Jiggins, J., A. Dighe, S. Jain, and H. op het Veld, "Mahila Samakhya: Report of an Indo-Dutch Review Mission," Vols. I and II (New Delhi: Ministry of Human Resource Development/The Hague: Ministry of Foreign Affairs, March 1990).

National Project Office, "Mahila Samakhya, Uttar Pradesh, April 1989–January 1990" (New Delhi: National Project Office, 1990).

National Project Office, "An Overview of the Mahila Samakhya Programme in Karnataka, from July 1990 to June 1991" (New Delhi: National Project Office, August 1991).

State Programme Office, "Mahila Samakhya Karnataka, A Progress Report, January to June 1990" (New Delhi: National Project Office, 1990).

State Programme Office, "From Paddy to Rice," Report of the First All-Karnataka Mahila Samakhya Sammelan, held in Kowlagi Village, Bijapur, March 2–7, 1990 (New Delhi: National Project Office, 1990).

Chapter 8. The Shrieking Sisterhood

Recommended Reading

Chester, E., *Woman of Valor: Margaret Sanger and the Birth Control Movement* (New York: Simon and Schuster, 1992). A sensitive biography of one of the founders of the birth control movement, detailing the social background and Sanger's skirmishing with religious and political authorities as she fought to ensure that women need not die worn out by childbearing, nor from unwanted preganancy, sexual infection, or ignorance.

IFPRI, "Understanding How Resources Are Allocated Within Households," Policy Briefs 8 (Washington D.C.: IFPRI, November 1992). Overviews and summaries of the latest available evidence identifying the policy costs of ignoring how resources are allocated and decisions are made within households.

Koblonsky, M., J. Timyan, and G. Gay, eds., *The Health of Women: A Global Perspective* (Boulder: Westview Press, 1993). Based on papers presented at the National Council for International Health Conference held in Arlington, Virginia, in 1991, each chapter provides a comprehensive and up-to-date overview of the evidence on key topics such as sexually transmitted disease, women's health and poverty, abortion, quality of care, and methods for eliciting women's views of their own health needs and services.

Additional Reading and References

Akhter, F., "Depopulating Bangladesh: A Brief History of the External Intervention into the Reproductive Behaviour of a Society," Occasional Paper (Dhaka: UBINIG, 1986).

Alauddin, M., "Maternal Mortality in Rural Bangladesh: The Tangail District," *Studies in Family Planning* (Vol. 17, No. 13, 1986).

Birke, L., S. Himmelweit, and G. Vines, *Tomorrow's Child: Reproduction Technology in the 90s* (London: Virago, 1990).

Bruce, J., "Homes Divided," *World Development* (Vol. 17, No. 7, 1989), pp. 979–991.

Bruce, J., "Family Structure, Female Headship and the Implications for Poverty," lecture given at Synergos, New York, January 21, 1992 (New York: The Population Council/Washington D.C.: International Centre for Research on Women, 1992).

Bruce, J., and C.B. Lloyd, "Family Research and Policy Issues for the 1990s," in IFPRI, "Understanding How Resources Are Allocated Within Households" (Washington, D.C.: IFPRI, November 1992), pp. 3–4.

Brunham, R.C., and J.E. Embree, "Sexually Transmitted Diseases: Current and Future Dimensions of the Problem in the Third World," in A. Germain et al., eds., *Reproductive Tract Infections: Global Impact and Priorities for Women's Reproductive Health* (New York and London: Plenum Press, 1992), pp. 35–60.

Cain, M., "The Material Consequences of Reproductive Failure in Rural South Asia," in D. Dwyer and J. Bruce, eds., *A Home Divided* (Stanford: Stanford University Press, 1988), pp. 20–38.

Cates, William, and Katherine M. Stone, "Family Planning: The Responsibility to Prevent Both Pregnancy and Reproductive Tract Infections," in A. Germain *et al.*, eds., *Reproductive Tract Infections: Global Impact and Priorities for Women's Reproductive Health* (New York and London: Plenum Press, 1992), pp. 93–130.

Cross, S., and A. Whiteside, eds., *Facing Up to AIDs: The Socio-Economic Impact in Southern Africa* (London: Macmillan, 1993).

Division for the Advancement of Women, UN Office at Vienna, "Women and Households in a Changing World," in E. Masini and S. Stratigos, eds., *Women, Households and Change* (Tokyo: United Nations University Press, 1991), pp. 30–54.

Dwyer, D., and J. Bruce, eds., *A Home Divided: Women and Income in the Third World* (Stanford: Stanford University Press, 1988).

ESCAP, *Bangladesh*, ESCAP Country Monograph Series No. 8, Population Division (Bangkok: ESCAP, 1981).

Folbre, N., "Women on their Own: Global Patterns of Female Headship," review article 3 in R.S. Gallin, and A. Ferguson, eds., *The Women and International Development Annual*, Vol. 2 (Boulder: Westview Press, 1991), pp. 89–128.

Germain, A., and J. Ordway, "Population Control and Women's Health: Balancing the Scales" (New York: International Women's Health Coalition, June 1989).

Hartmann, B., *Reproductive Rights and Wrongs: The Global Politics of Population Control and Contraceptive Choice* (New York: Harper and Row, 1987).

Holck, S., "Contraceptive Safety," in "Special Challenges in Third World Women's Health," Presentations at the 1989 Annual Meeting of the American Public Health Association (New York: International Women's Health Coalition, 1990), pp. 23–30.

Khan, A.R., F.A. Jahan, and S.F. Begum, "Maternal Mortality in Rural Bangladesh: The Jamalpur District," *Studies in Family Planning* (Vol. 17, No. 7, 1986).

Masini, E., and S. Stratigos, eds., *Women, Households and Change* (Tokyo: United Nations University Press, 1991).

ODI, "Confronting the Socio-economic Impact of AIDs," *Development Research Insights* (London: ODI, Spring 1992).

Ranger, T., and P. Slack, eds., *Epidemics and Ideas: Essays on the Historical Perception of Pestilence* (Cambridge: Cambridge University Press, 1992).

RED/BRAC, "Divorce and Breakup of Joint Family: An Analysis of Reasons and Familial Dislocations" (Dhaka: BRAC, August 1991).

Riddle, J.M., *Contraception and Abortion from the Ancient World to the Renaissance* (Cambridge, Mass.: Harvard University Press, 1992).

The Rockefeller Foundation, "Mobilizing Resources to Satisfy Unmet Demand for Contraception and Complete the Demographic Transition," Discussion Paper, Population Sciences Division (New York: The Rockefeller Foundation, 1992).

Rooney, C., "Antenatal Care and Maternal Health: How Effective Is It? A Review of the Evidence," Maternal Health and Safe Motherhood Programme (Geneva: World Health Organization, 1992).

Rosenfield, A., M.F. Fathalla, A. Germain, and C.L. Indriso, eds., "Women's Health in the Third World: The Impact of Unwanted Pregnancy," *International Journal of Gynaecology and Obstetrics* (Supplement 3, 1989).

Simmons, R., M.A. Koenig, and A.A. Zahidul Huque, "Maternal-Child Health and Family Planning: User Perspectives and Service Constraints in Rural Bangladesh," *Studies in Family Planning* (Vol. 21, No. 4, July/August 1990), pp. 187–196.

Sinding, S.W., "Getting to Replacement: Bridging the Gap Between Individual Rights and Demographic Goals." Paper presented to IPPF Family Planning Congress, October 23–25, Delhi (New York: The Rockefeller Foundation, 1992).

United Nations, *The World's Women 1970–1990, Trends and Statistics* (New York: United Nations, 1991).

Walkowitz, J.R., *Prostitution and Victorian Society: Women, Class and the State* (Cambridge: Cambridge University Press, 1980).

Wasserheit, J., "Reproductive Tract Infections." Paper presented at 117th Annual Meeting of the American Public Health Association, Chicago, October 17, 1989.

WHO/IWHC, "Creating Common Ground, Women's Perspectives on the Selection and Introduction of Fertility Regulation Technologies." Report of a meeting between women's health advocates and scientists, February 20–22, Special Programme of Research, Development and Research Training in Human Reproduction (Geneva: WHO, 1991).

Winikoff, B., and M. Sullivan, "Assessing the Role of Family Planning in Reducing Maternal Mortality," *Studies in Family Planning* (Vol. 18, No. 3, May/June 1987), pp. 128–143.

Chapter 9. Reproductive Health Initiatives in Bangladesh and Nigeria

Recommended Reading

Guyer, J.I., "Household and Community in African Studies," *African Studies Review* (Vol. XXIV, Nos. 2 & 3, 1981), pp. 87–137. Reviews models, definitions, and measurement of the "household" and community, arguing persuasively with examples of the need for empirical studies rather than statistical data if the distinctiveness of African household formation is to be understood and respected in developmental interventions.

Rosenfield, A., M.F. Fathalla, A. Germain, and C. L. Indriso, eds., "Women's Health in the Third World: The Impact of Unwanted Pregnancy," *International Journal of Gynaecology and Obstetrics* (Supplement 3, 1989). A key resource for data on abortion, its incidence, management, impact and consequences, the legal and policy context, and the prevention of avoidable abortion-related mortality and morbidity.

Additional Reading and References

BWHC, *Annual Report*, 1990–91 (Dhaka: Bangladesh Women's Health Coalition, 1991).

Caldwell, J.C., and P. Caldwell, "The Cultural Context of High Fertility in Sub-Saharan Africa," *Population and Development Review* (Vol. 13, No. 3), pp. 409–437.

Fapohunda, E.R., and M.P. Todaro, "Family Structure, Implicit Contracts, and the Demand for Children in Southern Nigeria," *Population and Development Review* (Vol. 14, No. 4, December 1988), pp. 571–594.

Kay, B.J., A. Germain, and M. Bangser, *The Bangladesh Women's Health Coalition*, Qualite series No. 3 (New York: The Population Council, 1991).

Chapter 10. Green and Just

Recommended Reading

Martin-Brown, J., and W. Ofosu-Amaah, *Proceedings*, Volumes I and II, Global Assembly of Women and the Environment, "Partners in Life" (Washington D.C.: United Nations Environment Program, 1992). Presents 218 stories of women's successful actions to safeguard the environment, which meet the criteria of being affordable, visible, sustainable, and repeatable, from all regions of the world.

Merchant, C., *The Death of Nature: Women, Ecology and the Scientific Revolution* (New York: Harper & Row, 1980). Argues for a science based on a feminist epistemology generated by the distinctive experience associated with women's lives in a gendered society, while attacking the detachment from nature and objectification of the natural world characteristic of Cartesian method and linked to the power over and control of women and nature by patriarchal society.

Additional Reading and References

Bleier, R., ed., *Feminist Approaches to Science* (New York: Pergamon Press, 1986).

Boserup, E., *The Conditions of Agricultural Growth: The Economics of Agrarian Change Under Population Pressure* (London: Allen and Unwin, 1965).

Brown, V., and M. Switzer, "Women and Ecologically Sustainable Development: Engendering the Debate," Office of the Status of Women (Canberra: Department of the Prime Minister and Cabinet, 1991).

Chamala, S., and C. Holsinger Hicks, "The Role of Women in Agricultural Development and Landcare." Discussion paper presented at Workshop on Extension Strategies Involving Rural Women, Forest Training Centre (Gympie: Queensland Department of Primary Industry, 1990).

Chen, M., M. Mitra, G. Athreya, A. Dholakia, P. Law, and A. Rao, *Indian Women: A Study of Their Role in the Dairy Movement* (New Delhi: Vikas Publishing House Pvt. Ltd., 1986).

Crouch, M.L., "Biotechnology and Sustainable Agriculture: Philosophical Musings by an Ex-Genetic Engineer," *Journal of New World Agriculture* (Vol. 8, No. 2, Fall 1986), pp. 5, 13.

Feldstein, H., and J. Jiggins, eds., *Tools for the Field* (West Hartford: Kumarian Press, 1994).

Fones-Sundell, M., "The Assistance Gap: Aid to Female Agricultural Producers in Botswana," International Rural Development Centre (Uppsala: Swedish University of Agricultural Sciences, April 1984).

Geertz, C., *Agricultural Involution* (Berkeley: University of California Press, 1963).

Harding, S., *The Science Question in Feminism* (Ithaca: Cornell University Press, 1986).

Harold, J.L., "Empowerment: A Feminist Approach to Understanding and Action," unpublished M.Sc. Thesis presented to the Faculty of Graduate Studies (Guelph: University of Guelph, April 1991).

Indian Farming Special Issue: "Women in Agriculture," *Indian Farming* (Vol. XXXVIII: November 8, 1988).

Keller, E.F., "Feminist Perspectives on Science Studies," *Science, Technology and Human Values* (Vol. 13, Nos. 3 & 4, Summer and Autumn, 1988), pp. 235–249.

Kloppenburg, J., "Social Theory and the De/Reconstruction of Agricultural Science: Local Knowledge for an Alternative Agriculture," *Rural Sociology* (Vol. 56, No. 4, 1991), pp. 519–548.

Lele, U., and S.W. Stone, "Population Pressure, The Environment and Agricultural Intensification, Variations on the Boserup Hypothesis," MADIA Discussion Paper 4 (Washington D.C.: The World Bank, 1989).

van liere, M.J., "Coping with Household Food Insecurity: A Longitudinal Study

Among the Otammari in North-Western Benin," Ph.D. Thesis (Wageningen: Agriculture University, November 1993).

Mazumdar, V., K. Samar, and L. Sarkar, "Legislative Measures and Policy Directions for Improving the Lot of Farm Women." Paper presented to International Conference on Appropriate Agricultural Technologies for Farm Women, New Delhi, November 30 to December 6 (New Delhi: Indian Council of Agricultural Research/Manila: International Rice Research Institute, 1988).

National Women's Consultative Council, "A Question of Balance: Australian Women's Priorities for Environmental Action" (Canberra: National Women's Consultative Council, 1992).

Paolisso, M., and S.W. Yudelman, "Women, Poverty and the Environment in Latin America" (Washington D.C.: International Center for Research on Women, September 1991).

Prasad, C., R.P. Singh, and K.S. Krishnan, *Review of Research Studies on Women in Agriculture in India: Implications for Research and Extension* (New Delhi: Indian Council of Agricultural Research, 1988).

Seur, H., "Sowing the Good Seed: The Interweaving of Agricultural Change, Gender Relations and Religion in Serenje District, Zambia," published Ph.D. Dissertation (Wageningen: Agricultural University, 1992).

Shiva, V., *Staying Alive: Women, Ecology and Development* (London: Zed Books, 1988).

Shiva, V., *The Violence of the Green Revolution: Ecological Degradation and Political Conflict* (London: Zed Books, May 1991).

Shiva, V., *Most Farmers in India Are Women* (New Delhi: FAO, 1991).

Vukasin, H., and J. Chimbadzwa, "Training to Suit Rural Women's Needs," *ILEIA Newsletter* (Vol. 3, 1991), pp. 8–9.

Chapter 11. Five Cases

Additional Reading and References

Baker, D., "Women and Trials Management in Botswana: Experiences with Farmer Groups," in H. Feldstein and J. Jiggins, eds., *Tools for the Field* (West Hartford: Kumarian Press 1994).

Bangladesh Agricultural Research Council, "Homestead Vegetable Gardening, A Brief Progress Report," (Dhaka: BARC, August 1991).

Gupta, M., and M. Aktheruzzaman, "Women Integrate Fish and Farming," *Ileia Newsletter* (No. 4/91, 1991), p. 14.

IFAD, "Soil and Water Conservation in Sub-Saharan Africa," (Amsterdam: Centre for Development Cooperation Services, Free University/Rome: International Fund for Agricultural Development, 1992).

Jiggins, J., ed., *Women and Land*, Regional African Workshop on Women's Access to Land as a Strategy for Employment Promotion, Poverty Alleviation and Household Food Security, organized by the Rural Employment Policies Branch, ILO, in collaboration with the University of Harare, in Harare, Zimbabwe, October 17–21 (Geneva: International Labour Organisation, 1989).

Jiggins, J., with Paul Maimbo and Mary Masona, "Breaking New Ground: Reaching

Out to Women Farmers in Western Zambia," *Seeds* (New York: The Population Council, 1992).

Meesters, T., "At Your Service," *ILEIA Newsletter* (No. 1/92, 1992), p. 24.

Norman, D., and C. Lightfoot, "Formative Evaluation of the FAO/SIDA Farming Systems Programme" (Gaborone: FAO/SIDA, November 1992).

Yoon, Soon Y., "The Women's Dam (The Mossi of Upper Volta)," consultant report, Water and Sanitation Unit (New York: UNICEF, September 1983).

Index

Abortion, 155–56
Action agenda, 246–47
Action Health Incorporated (AHI) in Nigeria, 191–93
Activist energy, 9–10
Adaptive nature of human behavior, 3–4, 17–18
Adolescent sexuality and fertility, 191–93
Africa:
  agricultural resources for women in, 5, 213
  charcoal/fuel wood consumption in, 87, 89
  climate change and agriculture, 76
  debt crisis in, 30
  desertification in, 55, 56
  educating women/girls in, 108
  food aid to, 69
  marital instability in, 160
  root crops and tubers in, 66
  tree planting in, 97–98
  see also specific countries
Agarwal, A., 85
Agricultural resources for women, 4, 5, 197–98, 238
  Chotanagpur women (India), 29
  collaboration between scientists and women farmers (Botswana & Bangladesh), 224–28, 236–37
  decision-making capabilities, 206–9
  fish ponds integrated with gardens (Bangladesh), 220–24
  gender relations and, 14–15
  income and expenditure, 199–200
  men and women working together, 217–18
  Naam movement (Burkina Faso), 228–33
  population-environment debate scenarios, 213–15
  production/consumption/surplus at household level, 71–72
  services to agricultural sector, 200–202, 207, 233–36
  surpluses, technical capacity to maintain, 70–75
  technology development, 209–11
  water supply development (Kenya), 218–20
  women-centered principles, 202–6
  Women's Extension Program (Zambia), 233–36

World Bank proposals and, 21
Agricultural Technology Improvement Project (ATIP), 226–27
Agriculture:
  agriculturalists, xv
  biodiversity in, 13–14
  devaluation of women's work in, 199, 211–12, 215–16, 233
  global problems and, 77–78
  natural resources in relation to, 78–80
  ox-plowing, 235
  productivity and, xvi, 94
  see also Food and agriculture
AIDS (acquired immune deficiency syndrome), 189–91
Aid to foreign countries, 31, 68–69, 244
Antrobus, Peggy, 209
Application of Science and Technology to Rural Areas (ASTRA), 143–44
Asia, 19, 76, 82, 108
Assessment, risk, 51–54
Association of Women in Development, 10
Assumptions about best interests of women, 5–6
Attitudinal barriers against women, xvii, 109, 235
Australia, xvii, 27, 83, 205–6

Baby boom in Western Europe, 19
BAIF (Indian agency), 143
Bangladesh:
  Bangladesh Rural Advancement Committee (BRAC), 112–16
  educating women/girls in, 109–12
  fish ponds integrated with gardens in, 220–24
  HIV in, 82
  marital instability in, 159–60
  population-driven policies of, 164–72
  schools program in, BRAC, 116–24
Bangladesh Agricultural Council (BARC), 221–22
Bangladesh Women's Health Coalition (BWHC):
  background of, 176–77
  lessons for Bangladesh, 183
  openness to clients, 178–79
  quality of reproductive care, 179–83
El-Baz, Farouk, 56

About the Author

After finishing a history degree in England, Jiggins pursued doctoral studies at the Universities of Vidyodaya and Peradeniya in Sri Lanka, which sparked her interest in discontinuity as a phenomenon in historical time, with the example of the rise and decline of the great irrigation-based civilizations of Anuradhapura and Peradeniya as a stimulus. While working at the Overseas Development Institute in London, Jiggins discovered networking as a means of sharing information widely and rapidly around the world among different domains of knowledge. Subsequent experience in the more remote agricultural districts of Zambia provoked reflection on the nature of farming systems and farm development in areas where 30 to 40 percent of all rural households are headed by women without resident male support. A spell with the Ford Foundation in Kenya provided Jiggins with rich opportunities for appreciating the quality of numerous successful endeavors, rarely captured in the statistics, which are building a new future among African communities.

For the past 14 years Jiggins has been living in the Netherlands while working as an international consultant. Her professional life combines research and writing, consultancy (most often in sub-Saharan Africa and South Asia), and university teaching, primarily at the University of Guelph, Ontario, where she holds an Associate Professorship. Her work as a program adviser to the International Women's Health Coalition during these years has been especially rewarding.

The experience of living in a country that lies mostly below sea level and that is considerably more densely populated than Indonesia, Pakistan, or India has sharpened Jiggins's appreciation of the need for rich countries to make adjustments in lifestyle, consumption, and production to safeguard their own sustainability, of the ecological limits to high-input intensive farming, and of nature as a man-made phenomenon.